Highly Tweetable

5000+ Awesome Quotes to Use

on Twitter and Social Media

By Devin Metzger

Highly Tweetable: 5000+ Awesome Quotes to Use on Twitter and Social Media

EPIGRAPH

"If you're on Twitter, what you're saying is, 'I'm important enough for you to care what I think.'" -- Donald Glover

Quotes

1. Being deeply loved by someone gives you strength, while loving someone deeply gives you courage. -Lao Tzu

2. The person who knows 'how' will always have a job. The person who knows 'why' will always be his boss. -Diane Ravitch

3. Originality is the fine art of remembering what you hear but forgetting where you heard it. -Laurence J. Peter

4. Lying increases the creative faculties, expands the ego, and lessens the frictions of social contacts.-Clare Booth Luce

5. I love drugs, but I hate hangovers, and the hatred of the hangover wins by a landslide every time. -Margaret Cho

6. The whole world steps aside for the man who knows where he is going. - Anon.

7. There is no victory at bargain basement prices. - Dwight D. Eisenhower

8. Public speaking is very easy. -Dan Quayle

9. The only good luck many great men ever had was being born with the ability and determination to overcome bad luck. -Channing Pollock

10. Language is a city to the building of which every human being brought a stone. - Mark Twain

11. It isn't kind to cultivate a friendship just so one will have an audience. - Lawana Blackwell

12. You have to have your heart in the business and the business in your heart. -Thomas J. Watson

13. He wins every hand who mingles profit with pleasure. -Horace

14. An incompetent attorney can delay a trial for months or years. A competent attorney can delay one even longer. -Evelle J. Younger

15. When I sit down at my writing desk, time seems to vanish. I think it's a wonderful way to spend one's life. -Erica Jong

16. Beautiful hands are those that do.....deeds that are noble, good, and true. - Anon.

17. You can't lead anyone else further than you have gone yourself. -Gene Mauch

18. I have this theory - that if we're told we're bad, then that's the only ideal we'll ever have. - Jewel

19. What we do for ourselves dies with us. What we do for others and the world remains and is immortal. -Albert Pine

20. It is only prudent never to place complete confidence in that by which we have even once been deceived. - Rene Descartes

21. Let me tell you quite bluntly that this king business has given me personally nothing but headaches. - Mohammed Reza Pahlavi

22. As we grow old the beauty steals inward. - Ralph Waldo Emerson

23. You know it was only a generation ago that actors couldn't be buried in the churchyard. - Ronald Reagan

24. Push on, friend. You're just one exciting step from the banquet hall of life. - Zig Ziglar

25. The memories of men are too frail a thread to hang history from. - John Still

26. Whatever is begun in anger ends in shame. - George Eliot

27. There is never a right way to do the wrong thing. - Anon.

28. Courageous risks are life-giving, they help you grow, make you brave, and better than you think you are. -Joan L. Curcio

29. Where is human nature so weak as in a bookstore? -Henry Ward Beecher

30. Silence is the ultimate weapon of power. - Charles De Gaulle

31. I love those who yearn for the impossible. - Johann von Goethe

32. There lives more faith in honest doubt, believe me, than in half the creeds. -Alfred Lord Tennyson

33. I may climb perhaps to no great heights but I will climb alone. – Cyrano de Bergerac

34. Meetings are indispensable when you don't want to do anything.- John Kenneth Galbraith

35. The gates of hell are open night and day; Smooth the descent and easy the way.- Virgil

36. Learning without thought is labor lost; thought without learning is perilous.- Confucius

37. He who fails to prepare, prepares to fail.

38. Some people see more in a walk around the block than others see in a trip around the world. -Unknown

39. What broke in a man when he could bring himself to kill another? - Alan Stewart Paton

40. He has great tranquility of heart who cares neither for the praises nor the fault-finding of men. - Honore de Balzac

41. Experience is that marvelous thing that enables you to recognize a mistake when you make it again.- Franklin P. Jones

42. There are no secrets to success. It is the result of preparation, hard work, and learning from failure. -Colin Powell

43. The soul would have no rainbow if the eyes had no tears. -Unknown

44. Oh, how fine it is to know a thing or two. - Jean Baptiste Poquelin Molière

45. It is as Queen of Canada that I am here, Queen of Canada and all Canadians not just one or two ancestral strains.- Elizabeth II

46. The danger is not that a particular class is unfit to govern. Every class is unfit to govern.- Emerich Edward Dalberg Acton

47. Violence is the last refuge of the incompetent.- Isaac Asimov

48. Make friends, not enemies, and you will always have eyes in the back of your head. - Eric Pio

49. Nothing is impossible, the word itself says 'I'm possible!'–Audrey Hepburn

50. Life isn't long enough for love and art.- W. Somerset Maugham

51. You are... the lens in the beam. You can only receive give and possess the light as the lens does.- Dag Hammarskjöld

52. Judge of your natural character by what you do in your dreams. - Ralph Waldo Emerson

53. Weakness of attitude becomes weakness of character.- Albert Einstein

54. Generosity is giving more than you can, and pride is taking less than you need. -Kahlil Gibran

55. Reading well is one of the great pleasures that solitude can afford you.- Harold Bloom

56. What is written without effort is in general read without pleasure. - Samuel Johnson

57. When a man is no longer anxious to do better than well, he is done for. -Benjamin Haydon

58. Without courage, wisdom bears no fruit.- Baltasar Gracian

59. A wise man will make more opportunities than he finds. -Francis Bacon

60. A good friend of my son's is a son to me.- Lois McMaster Bujold

61. It is those we live with and love and should know who elude us. - Norman Maclean

62. What great delight it is to see the ones we love and then to have speech with them. - Vincent McNabb

63. Life is a succession of moments. To live each one is to succeed. - Coretta Scott King

64. We must conquer war or war will conquer us.- Ely Culbertson

65. Boys will be boys... and so will most men. - Jean R. Langley

66. Then indecision brings its own delays and days are lost lamenting o'er lost days. -Johann Wolfgang von Goethe

67. They should rule who are able to rule best. -Aristotle

68. Words are a heavy thing...they weigh you down. If birds talked they couldn't fly. - Christian Williams

69. Mankind must put an end to war or war will put an end to mankind. -John F. Kennedy

70. Music is a medicine for many... Silence is a poison for some... -Jacqui Webb

71. Truth, confront us at every turn, in every guise. -Denise Levertov

72. The winds and waves are always on the side of the ablest navigators. - Edward Gibbon

73. The course of true love never did run smooth.- William Shakespeare

74. Observe your enemies for they first find out your faults.- Antisthenes

75. Nursing her wrath to keep it warm. - Robert Burns

76. If it seems a childish thing to do, do it in remembrance that you are a child.- Frederick Buechner

77. Happy laughter and family voices in the home will keep more kids off the streets at night than the strictest curfew.

78. The biggest liar in the world is "They Say."- Douglas Malloch

79. I always win. Except when I lose, but then I just don't count it.

80. The easiest thing of all is to deceive one's self for what a man wishes he generally believes to be true.- Demosthenes

81. Washington D.C. is a city of Southern efficiency and Northern charm.- John F. Kennedy

82. To make oneself an object to make oneself passive is a very different thing from being a passive object.- Simone de Beauvoir

83. It is not the oath that makes us believe the man, but the man the oath.-Aeschylus

84. Knowing is not enough; we must apply. Willing is not enough; we must do.- Johann von Goethe

85. If indeed you must be candid, be candid beautifully.- Kahlil Gibran

86. There are victories of the soul and spirit. Sometimes, even if you lose, you win.- Elie Wiesel

87. This is the first test of a gentleman: his respect for those who can be of no possible value to him. William Lyon Phelps

88. By outward show let's not be cheated; an ass should like an ass be treated. - John Gay

89. God never built a Christian strong enough to carry today's duties and tomorrow's anxieties piled on top of them. - Theodore Ledyard Cuyler

90. Fear clouds your mind it distracts your thoughts, to survive in dangerous times you must learn to suppress it and think. - Unknown

91. Enthusiasm is a volcano on whose top never grows the grass of hesitation. -Kahlil Gibran

92. Let us not be content to wait and see what will happen, but give us the determination to make the right things happen. -Peter Marshall

93. Never invoke the gods unless you really want them to appear. It annoys them very much. -Gilbert Keith Chesterton

94. No one gossips about other people's secret virtues. -Bertrand Russell

95. Lust is pure passion. Love tempers passion with reason. -John W. Kennedy

96. Beautiful faces are those that wear whole-souled honesty printed there. -Ellen Palmer Allerton

97. Take hope from the heart of man and you make him a beast of prey. - Ouida

98. The doctor is to be feared more than the disease. -Latin Proverb

99. A man may well bring a horse to the water but he cannot make him drink. -John Heywood

100. All your dreams come true, if you have the courage to pursue them. - Walt Disney

101. Love builds bridges where there are none. - R. H. Delaney

102. Our dignity is not in what we do but what we understand. - George Santayana

103. Relativity keeps anything from happening at once. Quantum mechanics keeps everything from really happening at all. - Lou A. Riley

104. Vital papers will demonstrate their vitality by spontaneously moving from where you left them to where you can't find them.

105. Take your life in your own hands and what happens? A terrible thing: no one to blame. -Erica Jong

106. Travelers from afar can lie with impunity. -French Proverb

107. Like as the waves make towards the pebbled shore / So do our minutes hasten to their end. -William Shakespeare

108. To have one's individuality completely ignored is like being pushed quite out of life - like being blown out as one blows out a light.

109. The majority of husbands remind me of an orangutan trying to play the violin. -Honore de Balzac

110. I love such mirth as does not make friends ashamed to look upon one another next morning. -Nelson Boswell

111. It is not these well-fed long-haired men that I fear, but the pale and the hungry-looking. -Julius Caesar

112. The quickest way to reach the point of success is to follow a straight line that carves through failure. -Josh Traeger

113. If all my friends were to jump off a bridge, I wouldn't jump with them. I'd be at the bottom to catch them. -Unknown

114. Nothing whatever pertaining to godliness and real holiness can be accomplished without grace. -Saint Augustine

115. A will finds a way. -Orison Swett Marden

116. Once in a while, you have to take a break and visit yourself. -Audrey Giorgi

117. Success requires no explanations, failure permits no alibis. -Napoleon Hill

118. The beauty of a statue is in its outward form of a man in his conduct. -Demophilus

119. A true friend is somebody who can make us do what we can. -Ralph Waldo Emerson

120. Nothing can come out of nothing any more than a thing can go back to nothing. -Marcus Aurelius

121. Make the best use of what is in your power, and take the rest as it happens. -Epictetus

122. Let him that would move the world first move himself. - Socrates

123. There is no doubt that the first requirement for a composer is to be dead. -Arthur Honegger

124. Freedom is the right to live as we wish. -Epictetus

125. Roses are red / Violets are blue / Most poems rhyme / This one doesn't

126. Accuracy is the twin brother of honesty; inaccuracy, of dishonesty. - Charles Simmons

127. Love and marriage, love and marriage go together like a horse and carriage. Dad was told by mother. You can't have one without the other. - Sammy Cahn

128. Traditionalists are pessimists about the future and optimists about the past. -Lewis Mumford

129. We forfeit three-fourths of ourselves in order to be like other people. -Arthur Schopenhauer

130. The man of understanding finds everything laughable. -Johann Wolfgang von Goethe

131. Live daringly, boldly, fearlessly. Taste the relish to be found in competition - in having put forth the best within you. -Henry J. Kaiser

132. There is that maketh himself rich yet hath nothing there is that maketh himself poor yet hath great riches. -Proverbs Bible

133. Don't document the program; program the document.

134. Only so far as a man believes strongly, mightily, can he act cheerfully, or do anything that is worth doing. -Frederick W. Robertson

135. What do we live for if not to make life less difficult for each other? - Roger Bannister

136. Never trust a computer you can't throw out a window. -Steve Wozniak

137. Every man has a right to life. That means that he also has a right to make a comfortable living. -Franklin Delano Roosevelt

138. Love means never having to say you're sorry. -Erich Segal

139. All power corrupts but we need the electricity. -Unknown

140. I've learned that when you plan to get even with someone, you are only letting that person continue to hurt you. - Andy Rooney

141. If you don't like something, change it. If you can't change it, change your attitude. Don't complain. -Maya Angelou

142. Killing time murders opportunities.

143. Critics search for ages for the wrong word, which, to give them credit, they eventually find. -Peter Ustinov

144. Love is like a violin. The music may stop now and then but the strings remain forever. -June Masters Bacher

145. Perfection is attained by slow degrees; it requires the hand of time. -François Voltaire

146. You ought not to practice childish ways since you are no longer that age. -Homer

147. The most important of my discoveries have been suggested to me by my failures. -Humphrey Davy

148. Great Spirit, help me never to judge another until I have walked in his moccasins for two weeks. -Sioux Indian Prayer

149. Let us so live that when we die, even the undertaker will be sorry. -Mark Twain

150. There is no real excellence in all this world which can be separated from right living. -David Starr Jordan

151. Until the day of his death, no man can be sure of his courage. -Jean Anouilh

152. The better work men do is always done under stress and at great personal cost. -William Carlos Williams

153. Give what you have. To someone it may be better than you dare to think. -Henry Wadsworth Longfellow

154. Love is but the discovery of ourselves in others, and the delight in the recognition. -Alexander Smith

155. Never trust a man who speaks well of everybody. -John Collins

156. The capacity of human beings to bore one another seems to be vastly greater than that of any other animal. -H.L. Mencken

157. My one regret in life is that I am not someone else. -Woody Allen

158. If a relationship, or a person does not bring you peace...that's all you need to get out.

159. An expert is someone who knows some of the worst mistakes that can be made in his subject and how to avoid them. -Werner Karl Heisenberg

160. Trust in Allah, but tie your camel. -Muslim Proverb

161. Assume a virtue if you have it not. -William Shakespeare

162. Why did I want to win? Because I didn't want to lose! -Max Schmeling

163. We have all the light we need, we just need to put it in practice. - Pilgrims

164. Now we sit through Shakespeare in order to recognize the quotations. -Orson Welles

165. Doubt is the father of invention. -Galileo

166. I leave this rule for others when I'm dead. Be always sure you're right - then go ahead. - Davy Crockett

167. When dealing with the insane, the best method is to pretend to be sane. -Hermann Hesse

168. Greed is a lasting slavery. -Ali bin Abi Talib

169. When you are content to be simply yourself and don't compare or compete, everybody will respect you. -Lao Tzu

170. Get the facts first. You can distort them later. -Mark Twain

171. Create your future from your future, not your past. -Werner Erhard

172. Don't let the mistakes and disappointments of the past control and direct your future. -Zig Ziglar

173. As is a tale, so is life: not how long it is, but how good it is, is what matters. -Seneca

174. Be honorable yourself if you wish to associate with honorable people. -Welsh Proverb

175. A happy home is one in which each spouse grants the possibility that the other may be right though neither believes it. -Don Fraser

176. I have not yet begun to fight. -John Paul Jones

177. No longer forward nor behind look in hope or fear, but grateful take the good I find the best of now and here. -John Greenleaf Whittier

178. Rough diamonds may sometimes be mistaken for worthless pebbles. - Sir Thomas Browne

179. Nothing is wrong with California that a rise in the ocean level wouldn't cure. -Ross MacDonald

180. Yet do I fear thy nature, it is too full o' the milk of human kindness. -William Shakespeare

181. When ideas fail, words come in very handy. -Johann Wolfgang von Goethe

182. Opera is when a guy gets stabbed in the back and instead of bleeding he sings. -Ed Gardner

183. Many individuals have, like uncut diamonds, shining qualities beneath a rough exterior. -Juvenal

184. As soon as any man says of the affairs of the state, "What does it matter to me?" The state may be given up for lost. -Jean Jacques Rousseau

185. Careful. We don't want to learn from this. -Bill Watterson

186. It is the darkest hour before dawn. -Unknown

187. The judge is condemned when the criminal is absolved. -Publilius Syrus

188. The art of life lies in a constant readjustment to our surroundings. -Okakura Kakuzo

189. To love and win is the best thing; to love and lose, the next best.

190. I think that maybe if women and children were in charge we would get somewhere. -James Grover Thurber

191. I have read your book and much like it. -Moses Hadas

192. Happiness is a choice that requires effort at times. - Anon.

193. If things get any worse, I'll have to ask you to stop helping me.

194. Being an optimist after you've got very thing you want doesn't count. -Ken Hubbard

195. The least of learning is done in the classrooms. -Thomas Merton

196. All men make mistakes but married men find out about them sooner.

197. All of us could take a lesson from the weather. It pays no attention to criticism.

198. Live together like brothers, and do business like strangers. - Anonymous

199. Success of today resulted from the failure of yesterday.

200. Style is not neutral; it gives moral directions. - Martin Amis

201. Education is what remains after one has forgotten everything one learned in school. -Albert Einstein

202. I do not confer praise or blame, I accept. I am the measure of all things. I am the center of the world. -W. Somerset Maugham

203. Walking is also an ambulation of mind. -Gretel Ehrlich

204. Every disappointment gives you opportunity to make another appointment. -B. A. Fajimi

205. We all live in a televised goldfish bowl. -Kingman Brewster Jr.

206. The descent to Hades is the same from every place. -Anaxagoras

207. Fortitude is the guard and support of the other virtues. -John Locke

208. The greatest motivational act one person can do for another is to listen. -Roy E. Moody

209. You can tell the ideals of a nation by its advertisements. -Norman Douglas

210. Parents like the idea of kids; they just don't like their kids. -Morley Safer

211. No one is without knowledge except him who asks no questions. - West African Saying

212. The intelligent man is one who has successfully fulfilled many accomplishments and is yet willing to learn more. -Ed Parker

213. If we don't succeed we run the risk of failure. -Dan Quayle

214. Don't follow the crowd, let the crowd follow you.

215. Never before have we had so little time in which to do so much. - Franklin Delano Roosevelt

216. I would rather fail in a cause that will ultimately triumph than to triumph in a cause that will ultimately fail. -Woodrow Wilson

217. Discretion is the perfection of reason and a guide to us in all the duties of life. -La Bruyere

218. You're in a much better position to talk with people when they approach you than when you approach them. -Pilgrims

219. A woman in love can't be reasonable - or she probably wouldn't be in love. - Mae West

220. The soul of this man is in his clothes. -William Shakespeare

221. And when it rains on your parade, look up rather than down. Without the rain, there would be no rainbow. - Jerry Chin

222. He will live ill who does not know how to die well. -Seneca

223. Error always addresses the passions and prejudices; truth scorns such mean intrigue, and only addresses the understanding and the conscience.

224. He not busy being born is busy dying. -Bob Dylan

225. Faith without works is dead. -Bible

226. Those who bring sunshine to the lives of others cannot keep it from themselves. -Sir James M. Barrie

227. Try not to become a man of success but rather try to become a man of value. -Albert Einstein

228. The Future is something which everyone reaches at the rate of sixty minutes an hour whatever he does, whoever he is. -Clive Staples Lewis

229. It isn't the people you fire who make your life miserable; it's the people you don't. -Harvey Mackay

230. God bears with the wicked but not forever. -Miguel de Cervantes

231. Faith is a continuation of reason. -William Adams

232. Too many parents make life hard for their children by trying, too zealously, to make it easy for them. -Goethe

233. Success is always temporary. When all is said and done, the only thing you'll have left is your character. -Vince Gill

234. A man has one hundred dollars and you leave him with two dollars that's subtraction. -Mae West

235. No one has a finer command of language than the person who keeps his mouth shut. -Sam Rayburn

236. Ambition is the germ from which all growth of nobleness proceeds. -Thomas Dunn English

237. Happiness comes when we test our skills towards some meaningful purpose. -John Stossel

238. Never forget what a man says to you when he is angry. -Henry Ward Beecher

239. He's the kind of a guy who lights up a room just by flicking a switch. -Unknown

240. The secret of eternal youth is arrested development. -Alice Roosevelt Longworth

241. You can change anything you want. You just can't change everything you want. -Peter McWilliams

242. Thorough preparation makes its own luck. -Joe Poyer

243. Fear is the tax that conscience pays to guilt. -George Sewell

244. Man never made any material as resilient as the human spirit. -Bern Williams

245. Money doesn't talk, it swears. -Paul Aubuchon

246. It is through the cracks in our brains that ecstasy creeps in. -Logan Pearsall Smith

247. Nothing is said that has not been said before. -Terence

248. No change of circumstances can repair a defect of character. -Ralph Waldo Emerson

249. Our determination to imitate Christ should be such that we have no time for other matters. -Desiderius Erasmus

250. Give a man a fish, he'll eat for a day. Teach a man how to fish, he'll eat for a lifetime. -Ancient Proverb

251. Pleasure of love lasts but a moment / Pain of love lasts a lifetime. -Jean Pierre Claris De Florian

252. At a certain age some people's minds close up; they live on their intellectual fat. -Irish Blessing

253. I've learned that everyone wants to live on top of the mountain, but that all the happiness and growth occurs while you're climbing it. -Andy Rooney

254. I shall be as secret as the grave. -Miguel de Cervantes

255. Turn on, tune in, and drop out. -Timothy Leary

256. Our greatest glory is not in never falling, but in rising every time we fall. -Confucius

257. Every man has his own destiny: the only imperative is to follow it, to accept it, no matter where it leads him. -Henry Miller

258. Nothing is so good as it seems beforehand. -George Eliot

259. Every problem has a gift for you in its hands. -Richard Bach

260. If you are losing your leisure, look out, you are losing your soul. -Logan Pearsall Smith

261. One's religion is whatever one is most interested in. -James Barrie

262. We cannot really love anybody with whom we never laugh. -Agnes Repplier

263. The past is the tomorrow that got away. -Leonard L. Levinson

264. Never mistake knowledge for wisdom. One helps you make a living; the other helps you make a life. - Sandra Carey

265. God must become an activity in our consciousness. -Joel S. Goldsmith

266. Golf is like a love affair; if you don't take it seriously, it's no fun. If you do take it seriously, it breaks your heart. -Arnold Daly

267. Fools rush in - and get all the best seats. -Unknown

268. The mind of a poet begins with an H and ends with a T, listening with an EAR in between. - Lori Herber

269. The aim of life is to live and to live means to be aware - joyously, drunkenly, serenely, divinely aware.-Henry Miller

270. Never feel self-pity, the most destructive emotion there is. How awful to be caught up in the terrible squirrel cage of self. - Millicent Fenwick

271. No one does anything from a single motive. -Samuel Taylor Coleridge

272. What seems impossible one minute becomes, through faith, possible the next. -Norman Vincent Peale

273. I know for sure that what we dwell on is who we become. -Oprah Winfrey

274. Nothing is so powerful as gentleness; nothing is so gentle as true strength. –St. Francis de Sales

275. The best way to keep children home is to make the home atmosphere pleasant - and let the air out of the tires. -Dorothy Parker

276. The greatest test of courage on earth is to bear defeat without losing heart. -Robert Green Ingersoll

277. Boxing is just show business with blood. -Frank Bruno

278. Do not think that what your thoughts dwell on does not matter. Your thoughts are making you. –Edward Steere

279. A deadline is negative inspiration. Still, it's better than no inspiration at all. -Rita Mae Brown

280. Every parting is a form of death as every reunion is a type of heaven. - Tryon Edwards

281. Since thou art not sure of a minute, throw not away an hour. - Benjamin Franklin

282. If a man is not there for you at your worst, he does not deserve to see you at your best.

283. It is hard to stumble when you're on your knees.

284. Why do some displays of "I love you only" Valentine cards sell them in multi-packs?

285. The world cannot continue to wage war like physical giants and to seek peace like intellectual pygmies. -Basil O'Connor

286. We must combine the toughness of the serpent and the softness of the dove a tough mind and a tender heart. -Martin Luther King Jr.

287. No padlocks, bolts, or bars can secure a maiden better than her own reserve. - Miguel De Cervantes

288. The definition of virtue: Insufficient temptation. -George Bernard Shaw

289. People who do the world's real work don't usually wear neckties.

290. If you tell Congress everything about the world situation, they get hysterical. If you tell them nothing, they go fishing. -Harry S. Truman

291. Early morning cheerfulness can be extremely obnoxious. -William Feather

292. They always win who side with God. -Frederick W. Faber

293. Even I don't wake up looking like Cindy Crawford. - Cindy Crawford

294. In order to conquer, what we need is to dare, still to dare, and always to dare. -Georges Danton

295. There would be no society if living together depended upon understanding each other. -Eric Hoffer

296. There are three sides to any story, my side, his side and the truth.

297. The truth is not always the same as the majority decision. -Pope John Paul II

298. To do nothing is also a good remedy. - Hippocrates

299. The more one judges, the less one loves. -Honore de Balzac

300. The great thing about a computer notebook is that no matter how much you stuff into it, it doesn't get bigger or heavier. -Bill Gates

301. There is a god within us and we have intercourse with heaven. That spirit comes from abodes on high. -Ovid

302. Getting older, everything gets worse; except forgetfulness...That gets better.

303. Human things must be known to be loved: but Divine things must be loved to be known.

304. Pray that your loneliness may spur you into finding something to live for great enough to die for. -Dag Hammarskjöld

305. We spent our whole youth to obtain wealth and our whole wealth to obtain youth.

306. Few friendships would survive if each one knew what his friend says of him behind his back. -Blaise Pascal

307. Creativity involves breaking out of established patterns in order to look at things in a different way. -Edward De Bono

308. In the confrontation between the stream and the rock, the stream always wins, not through strength but by perseverance. -H. Jackson Brown

309. A man spends the first half of his life learning habits that shorten the other half of his life.

310. There is no fate that cannot be surmounted by scorn. -Albert Camus

311. If a brown cow eats green grass, why is its milk white?

312. Opinions founded on prejudice are always sustained with the greatest violence. -Hebrew Proverb

313. The family is changing, not disappearing. We have to broaden our understanding of it, look for the new metaphors. -Mary Catherine Bateson

314. History is philosophy teaching by examples. -Henry St. John Bolingbroke

315. There are many things of which a wise man might wish to be ignorant. -Ralph Waldo Emerson

316. Nurture your mind with great thoughts for you will never go any higher that you think... -Benjamin Disraeli

317. A person who makes no mistakes, generally makes nothing.

318. Times of luxury do not last long but pass away very quickly nothing in this world can be long enjoyed. -Buddha

319. Big egos are big shields for lots of empty space. -Diana Black

320. The feeling remains that God is on the journey too. -Saint Teresa of Avila

321. I take it that what all men are really after is some form or perhaps only some formula of peace. -Joseph Conrad

322. Do you know what a pessimist is a man who thinks everybody is as nasty as himself and hates them for it? -George Bernard Shaw

323. The man who wins may have been counted out several times but he didn't hear the referee. -H. E. Jansen

324. Handsome is that handsome does. - Henry Fielding

325. The hardest thing to explain is the glaringly evident which everybody had decided not to see. -Ayn Rand

326. When you hear a kind word spoken about a friend, tell him so. -H. Jackson Brown Jr.

327. Courage is not the absence of fear, but rather the judgment that something else is more important than fear. -Ambrose Redmoon

328. Efforts and courage are not enough without purpose and direction. - John F Kennedy

329. Good food ends with good talk. -Geoffrey Neigher

330. Truth is incontrovertible, malice may attack it and ignorance may deride it, but, in the end, there it is. -Winston Churchill

331. My concern today is not with the length of a person's hair but with his conduct. (On campus radicals) -Richard Milhous Nixon

332. Gambling undermines the moral fiber of society. - Gordon B. Hinkley

333. Houston has its largest crowd of the night here this evening. -Jerry Coleman

334. Democracy is the recurrent suspicion that more than half of the people are right more than half the time. -E. B. White

335. Days change so many things - yes hours - we see so differently in suns and showers. -George Klingle

336. I'm not running and I'm not walking fast. I'm going where I need to be. -Johnny McEntyre

337. Whenever I hear anyone arguing for slavery, I feel a strong impulse to see it tried on him personally. -A. Lincoln

338. My ambition is to do a good job. I never plan anything. (running for mayor of Bucharest, Romania) -Ilie Nastase

339. In the depth of my soul there is a wordless song. -Kahlil Gibran

340. I am not afraid of storms, for I am learning how to sail my ship. -Louisa May Alcott

341. Men are failures, not because they are stupid, but because they are not sufficiently impassioned. —Maxwell Struthers Burt

342. I don't know why you use a fancy French word like détente when there's a good English phrase for it - cold war. -Golda Meir

343. All you need to know is the user interface.

344. No man is exempt from saying silly things; the mischief is to say them deliberately. -Michel de Montaigne

345. So full of artless jealousy is guilt. It spills itself in fearing to be spilt. -William Shakespeare

346. All of our dreams can come true - if we have the courage to pursue them. -Walt Disney

347. No man loves life like him that's growing old. -Sophocles

348. The public is wonderfully tolerant. It forgives everything except genius. -Oscar Wilde

349. Government never furthered any enterprise but the alacrity with which it got out of the way. -Henry David Thoreau

350. Hindsight is always twenty-twenty. -Billy Wilder

351. A fanatic is one who can't change his mind and won't change the subject. -Sir Winston Churchill

352. Millions of spiritual creatures walk the earth Unseen both when we wake and when we sleep. -John Milton

353. Learning is forging ahead. Thinking is foraging a head.

354. Live always in the best company when you read. Sydney Smith

355. You don't always get what you ask for, but you never get what you don't ask for... unless it's contagious! - Unknown

356. Humans are not proud of their ancestors and rarely invite them round to dinner. Douglas Adams

357. We're always lucky I said, and like a fool, I did not knock on wood. -Ernest Hemingway

358. How many a man has dated a new era in his life from the reading of a book. -Henry David Thoreau

359. Analyzing humor is like dissecting a frog. Few people are interested and the frog dies of it. -E. B. White

360. You teach best what you most need to learn. -Richard Bach

361. Eternal nothingness is fine if you happen to be dressed for it. -Woody Allen

362. Under all that we think, lives all we believe, like the ultimate veil of our spirits. -Antonio Machado

363. Death is a friend of ours and he that is not ready to entertain him is not at home. -Francis Bacon

364. Under every stone lurks a politician. -Aristophanes

365. The truth is rarely pure and never simple. -Oscar Wilde

366. James T. Farrell If you let conditions stop you from working they'll always stop you.

367. A winner never whines. -Paul Brown

368. The men who come on the stage at one period are all found to be related to each other. Certain ideas are in the air. –R. W. Emerson

369. Grace is but glory begun and glory is but grace perfected. -Jonathan Edwards

370. The secret to a rich life is to have more beginnings than endings. -Dave Weinbaum

371. When you are trying to convince yourself something is right, it is usually wrong.

372. To fill the hour - that is happiness. -Ralph Waldo Emerson

373. The nice thing about being a celebrity is that when you bore people, they think it's their fault. -Henry Kissinger

374. Don't play for safety - it's the most dangerous thing in the world. -Hugh Walpole

375. The advertisement is the most truthful part of a newspaper. -Thomas Jefferson

376. My way of joking is to tell the truth. It's the funniest joke in the world. -Sir Walter Besant

377. I think your whole life shows in your face and you should be proud of that. - Lauren Bacall

378. I try to avoid looking forward or backward and try to keep looking upward. -Charlotte Bronte

379. A total commitment is paramount to reaching the ultimate in performance. -Tom Flores

380. One's mind once stretched by a new idea never regains its original dimensions. -Oliver Wendell Holmes

381. The conscience of a people is their power. -John Dryden

382. No amount of artificial reinforcement can offset the natural inequalities of human individuals. -Henry P. Fairchild

383. Be bold. Be confident. Be alive. A gallery of possibilities awaits for you when you make change your friend. -Bob Bone

384. A heart that loves is always young. -Greek Proverb

385. Attend Church weekly NOT weakly.

386. It's not how much we have, but how much we enjoy, that makes happiness. -Charles Haddon Spurgeon

387. How can a guy hit and think at the same time? -Lawrence Peter Berra

388. War is a series of catastrophes that results in a victory. -Georges Clemenceau

389. Never criticize a man until you've walked a mile in his moccasins. - American Indian Proverb

390. Garner up pleasant thoughts in your mind for pleasant thoughts make pleasant lives. -John Wilkins

391. It's very hard to take yourself too seriously when you look at the world from outer space. -Thomas K. II Mattingly

392. Fools learn from experience. Wise men learn from the experience of others. -Otto von Bismarck

393. To err is human to forgive divine. -Alexander Pope

394. Keep your goals away from the trolls. -Peter McWilliams

395. Just as courage imperils life fear protects it. -Jewish Proverb

396. Sweet is the remembrance of troubles when you are in safety. - Euripides

397. The grand essentials of happiness are something to do something to love and something to hope for. -Allan K. Chalmers

398. Often it is the most deserving people who cannot help loving those who destroy them. -Hermann Hesse

399. The Devil finds work for idle hands. -Proverb

400. I came into the world either too early or too late; at present, I am good for nothing. - Klemens von Metternich

401. Friendship is constant in all other things, save in the office and affairs of love. George Santayana

402. The only calendar I need is just outside my window. With eyes to see and ears to hear, nature keeps me posted. -Alfred A. Montapert

403. The end always passes judgement on what has gone before. -Publilius Syrus

404. This bud of love by summer's ripening breath / May prove a beauteous flower when next we meet. -William Shakespeare

405. The love we give away is the only love we keep. - Elbert Hubbard

406. A man who lives in a glass house should change in basement.

407. It takes people a long time to learn the difference between talent and genius, especially ambitious young men and women. -Louisa May Alcott

408. Life does not require us to make good; it asks only that we give our best at each level of experience. -Harold Ruopp

409. There's no reason to be the richest man in the cemetery. You can't do any business from there. -Colonel Sanders

410. Nobody got anywhere in the world by simply being content. -Louis L'Amour

411. When you don't know what to do, walk fast and look worried.

412. Assassination has never changed the history of the world. -Benjamin Disraeli

413. America is a vast conspiracy to make you happy. -John Updike

414. You've got to say, I think that if I keep working at this and want it badly enough I can have it. It's called perseverance. -Lee Iacocca

415. Skier; one who pays an arm and a leg for the opportunity to break them.

416. If the facts don't fit the theory change the facts. - Albert Einstein

417. Forget injuries never forget kindnesses. -Confucius

418. Anything that has been accomplished by any other human being in the physical realm is within the field of possibility. -Wayne Dyer

419. If it is tourist season, why can't we shoot them?

420. Society attacks early when the individual is helpless. - B. F. Skinner

421. We do not need more of the things that are seen, we need more of the things that are unseen. -Calvin Coolidge

422. Reason to rule, but mercy to forgive: The first is the law the last prerogative. -John Dryden

423. The greatest use of life is to spend it for something that will outlast it. -William James

424. Memory feeds imagination. -Amy Tan

425. May you live your life as if the maxim of your actions were to become universal law. -Immanuel Kant

426. Sow an act and you reap a habit. Sow a habit and you reap a character. Sow a character and you reap a destiny. -Charles Reade

427. There is still no cure for the common birthday. -John Glenn

428. The world is composed of givers and takers. The takers may eat better, but the givers sleep better.

429. Lose not yourself in a far off time, seize the moment that is thine. - Johann Friedrich Von Schiller

430. Religion is the idol of the mob it adores everything it does not understand. -Frederick the Great

431. We would often be sorry if our wishes were gratified. -Aesop

432. No one can wear a mask for very long. -Seneca

433. If you can lay your head on your pillow each night knowing you gave hundred per cent to your day, success will find you. -Russell L. Mason

434. If you don't like the way you were born, try being born again.

435. A woman who thinks she is intelligent demands the same rights as man. An intelligent woman gives up. -Colette

436. Nothing strengthens the judgment and quickens the conscience like individual responsibility. -Elizabeth Cady Stanton

437. We will often find compensation if we think more of what life has given us and less about what life has taken away. -William Barclay

438. Remember that nobody will ever get ahead of you as long as he is kicking you in the seat of the pants. -Walter Winchell

439. If a man is destined to drown he will drown even in a spoonful of water. -Yiddish Proverb

440. The advice of their elders to young men is very apt to be as unreal as a list of the hundred best books. -Oliver Wendell Holmes

441. Failure is the opportunity to begin again more intelligently. -Moshe Arens

442. When you make a world tolerable for yourself you make a world tolerable for others. -Anais Nin

443. A man can be happy with any woman as long as he does not love her. -Oscar Wilde

444. But soft what light through yonder window breaks? It is the east and Juliet is the sun. -William Shakespeare

445. If I had my life to live over I would have invited friends over to dinner even if the carpet was stained and the sofa faded. -Erma Bombeck

446. Englishmen hate Liberty and Equality too much to understand them. But every Englishman loves a pedigree. -George Bernard Shaw

447. Responsibility walks hand in hand with capacity and power. - Josiah Gilbert Holland

448. Poor are poor because rich are rich. -B. J. Gupta

449. Anger makes dull men witty, but it keeps them poor. -Elizabeth I

450. Decision and determination are the engineer and fireman of our train to opportunity and success. -Burt Lawlor

451. You must be the change you wish to see in the world. -Gandhi

452. All movements go too far. -Bertrand Russell

453. Never keep up with the Joneses. Drag them down to your level. - Quentin Crisp

454. I think the next best thing to solving a problem is finding some humor in it. -Frank A. Clark

455. What's the use of worrying? It never was worthwhile. -George Asaf

456. One of the things that makes God different from people is that God is always available to listen. -Rabbi David Wolpe

457. Thoughts lead to acts. Acts lead to habits. Habits lead to character. And our character will determine our eternal destiny.

458. It is better to be making the news than taking it to be an actor rather than a critic. -Sir Winston Leonard Spenser Churchill

459. Adversity does teach who your real friends are. -Lois McMaster Bujold

460. But a stranger in a strange land, he is no one: men know him not - and to know not is to care not for. - Jonathan Swift

461. With so much information now online, it is exceptionally easy to simply dive in and drown. - Alfred Glossbrenner

462. When the congregation falls asleep it is time for the minister to wake up.

463. Anyone can stop a man's life but no one his death; a thousand doors open on to it. - Seneca

464. Employees make the best dates. You don't have to pick them up and they're always tax-deductible. - Andy Warhol

465. The limitations are limitless. -Beck

466. Sincere diplomacy is no more possible than dry water or wooden iron. -Josef Stalin

467. The way to get things done is not to mind who gets the credit for doing them. -Benjamin Jowett

468. Judge of a man by his questions rather than by his answers. -Voltaire

469. Idealism increases in direct proportion to one's distance from the problem. -Darcy E. Gibbons

470. The only place where success comes before work is a dictionary. - Vidal Sassoon

471. We are confronted with insurmountable opportunities. -Walt Crawford Kelly

472. It is worthwhile for anyone to have behind him a few generations of honest hard-working ancestry. -John Phillips Marquand

473. If it were done when tis done, then 'twere well it were done quickly. -William Shakespeare

474. Did you hear about the first death from an overdose of Viagra? A man took twelve pills and his wife died.

475. I think the mistake a lot of us make is thinking the state-appointed psychiatrist is our friend. -Jack Handey

476. Colleges don't make fools. They only develop them. -George Horace Lorimer

477. Education is the movement from darkness to light. -Allan Bloom

478. There is one thing stronger than all the armies of the world and that is an idea whose time has come. -Victor Hugo

479. Hope, deceitful as it is, serves at least to lead us to the end of our lives by an agreeable route. -Robert Green Ingersoll

480. The only reason some people get lost in thought is because it's unfamiliar territory. -Paul Fix

481. I am not young enough to know everything. -Oscar Wilde

482. When we have done our best, we should wait the result in peace. -J Lubbock

483. The man is only half himself the other half is his expression. -Ralph Waldo Emerson

484. Hey everybody, we're all gonna get laid. -CaddyShack, Al Czervik

485. Faith is not faith until it's all you're holding on to.

486. The end excuses any evil. -Sophocles

487. I came upstairs into the world for I was born in a cellar. -William Congreve

488. God will be present whether asked or not. -Latin Proverb

489. To encourage literature and the arts is a duty which every good citizen owes to his country. -George Washington

490. Sometimes only a change of viewpoint is needed to convert a tiresome duty into an interesting opportunity. -Alberta Flanders

491. The Lord gets His best soldiers out of the highlands of affliction. -Charles Haddon Spurgeon

492. When it seems that someone has shattered your dreams....pick up even the smallest of pieces and use them to build bigger and better dreams.

493. An American is a man with two arms and four wheels. -A Chinese Child

494. To die for an idea is to place a pretty high price on conjecture. -Anatole France

495. Many an opportunity is lost because a man is out looking for four-leaf clovers. -Anon.

496. The subtlety of nature is greater many times over than the subtlety of the senses and understanding. -Francis Bacon

497. The way to love anything is to realize that it might be lost. - Joan Crawford

498. Broadly speaking, the short words are the best and the old words best of all. -Sir Winston Churchill

499. Happiness is like a sunbeam which the least shadow intercepts while adversity is often as the rain of spring. -Chinese Proverb

500. Outside of the killings, Washington has one of the lowest crime rates in the country. -Marion Barry

501. Every day there's sad news and bad news, but each day itself is glad news.

502. As men we are all equal in the presence of death. -Publilius Syrus

503. You can't win at everything but you can laugh at everything. -Robert Killinger

504. It's a lot better to hope than not to. -Benjamin J. Stein in The American Spectator

505. The people who teach us that it is wrong to be skeptical are themselves the reasons that we should be skeptical. -Donald G. Smith

506. How wonderful it is that nobody need wait a single minute before starting to improve the world. -Anne Frank

507. When you are down and out something always turns up-and it is usually the noses of your friends. -Orson Welles

508. As flies to wanton boys are we to the gods. They kill us for their sport. -William Shakespeare

509. Roam abroad in the world and take thy fill of its enjoyments before the day shall come when thou must quit it for good. -Saadi

510. To the good listener half a word is enough. -Danish proverb

511. Artists who seek perfection in everything are those who cannot attain it in anything. -Eugene Delacroix

512. Art is long, life short, judgment difficult, opportunity transient. -Johann Wolfgang von Goethe

513. If you must speak ill of another do not speak it . . . write it in the sand near the water's edge. -Napoleon Hill

514. Why isn't there mouse-flavored cat food?

515. Tough times never last, but tough people do. -Dr. Robert Schuller

516. When you reach the end of your rope tie a knot in it and hang on. -Thomas Jefferson

517. A real leader faces the music even when he doesn't like the tune. -Anon.

518. Extremism in the defense of liberty is no vice. And moderation in the pursuit of justice is no virtue. -Barry Goldwater

519. Deep Thoughts: In weightlifting I don't think sudden uncontrolled urination should automatically disqualify you. -Jack Handey

520. A reputation for good judgment for fair dealing for truth and for rectitude is itself a fortune. -Henry Ward Beecher

521. He who limps is still walking. -Stanislaw Lec

522. While I take inspiration from the past, like most Americans, I live for the future. -Ronald Reagan

523. Nothing is so admirable in politics as a short memory. -John Kenneth Galbraith

524. The beginning of knowledge is the discovery of something we do not understand. -Frank Herbert

525. What is youth except a man or a woman before it is ready or fit to be seen? -Evelyn Waugh

526. Drama is life with the dull bits cut out. -Sir Alfred Joseph Hitchcock

527. Do not consider painful what is good for you. -Euripides

528. I know nothing except the fact of my ignorance. -Socrates

529. If I had to choose between betraying my country and betraying my friend, I hope I should have the guts to betray my country. -E. M. Forster

530. Nobody understands anyone who's 18, including those who are 18. – Jim Bishop

531. I stopped believing in Santa Claus when my mother took me to see him in a department store and he asked for my autograph. -Shirley Temple

532. To achieve the impossible it is precisely the unthinkable that must be thought. -Tom Robbins

533. True courage is a result of reasoning. A brave mind is always impregnable. -Jeremy Collier

534. Illusions are art for the feeling person and it is by art that you live if you do. -Elizabeth Bowen

535. Distrust any enterprise that requires new clothes. -Henry David Thoreau

536. We can't all and some of us don't. That's all there is to it. -Alan Alexander Milne

537. Charity sees the need, not the cause. -German Proverb

538. Youth wastes away, but immaturity can last a lifetime.

539. The first responsibility of a leader is to define reality. The last is to say thank you. In between the leader is a servant. -Max De Pree

540. The right to be heard does not automatically include the right to be taken seriously. -Hubert Humphrey

541. In love of home, the love of country has its rise. -Charles Dickens

542. Those who say religion has nothing to do with politics do not know what religion is. -Mohandas Gandhi

543. While men talk of killing time, slowly time kills men.

544. If you want a quality act as if you already had it. Try the as if technique. -William James

545. Your ignorance cramps my conversation. -Sir Anthony Hawkins

546. If a man's mind becomes pure his surroundings will also become pure. -Buddha

547. Success is never permanent and failure is never final. -Mike Ditka

548. Behind every successful man is his woman. Behind the fall of a successful man is usually another woman. - Sim York Soo

549. You can't let one bad moment spoil a bunch of good ones. -Dale Earnhardt

550. Now the Name of Jesus is a concrete and powerful means of transforming men and women into their hidden, innermost utmost reality. -Bible

551. I would give all the wealth of the world, and all the deeds of all the heroes, for one true vision. -Henry David Thoreau

552. To me the meanest flower that blows can give / Thoughts that do often lie too deep for tears. -William Wordsworth

553. People used to switch on TV's after getting bored with their routine work. Now they switch to routine work after getting bored with TV.

554. When holy and devout religious men are at their beads, 'tis hard to draw them thence; so sweet is zealous contemplation. -William Shakespeare

555. Always do sober what you said you'd do drunk. That will teach you to keep your mouth shut. -Ernest Hemingway

556. We do not have to visit a madhouse to find disordered minds our planet is the mental institution of the universe. -Johann von Goethe

557. The artist is nothing without gift, but gift is nothing without work. - Émile Zola

558. Do not, for one repulse, forego the purpose that you resolved to effect. -William Shakespeare

559. Love is like war - easy to begin, but very hard to stop. -Henry Louis Mencken

560. You can't say that civilization don't advance however, for in every war, they kill you in a new way. -Will Rogers

561. I myself prefer my New Zealand eggs for breakfast. (After she was pelted with eggs during a walkabout on New Zealand visit) -Elizabeth II

562. Personality is born out of pain. It is the fire shut up in the flint. -J. B. Yeats

563. If you look long enough into the void the void begins to look back through you. -Friedrich Wilhelm Nietzsche

564. Never go to a doctor whose office plants have died. - Jacob Braude

565. I can live without money but I cannot live without love. -Judy Garland

566. Courage is the willingness to accept fear and act anyway. -Author unknown

567. People demand freedom of speech as a compensation for the freedom of thought which they seldom use. -Kierkegaard

568. If you chase two rabbits, both will escape. -Author unknown

569. Laughter is a tranquilizer with no side effects. -Arnold Glasgow

570. A true friend is someone who is there for you when he'd rather be anywhere else. -Len Wein

571. I am not an adventurer by choice but by fate. -Vincent Van Gogh

572. The function of prayer is not to influence God, but rather to change the nature of the one who prays. -Kierkegaard

573. If you wish to live wisely, ignore sayings including this one. -Anonymous

574. Time is the most valuable thing a man can spend. -Theophrastus

575. We may eventually come to realize that chastity is no more a virtue than malnutrition. -Alexander Comfort

576. Toil to make yourself remarkable by some talent or other.- Seneca

577. The gaudy blabbing and remorseful day is crept into the bosom of the sea. -William Shakespeare

578. Eighty percent of life's satisfaction comes from meaningful relationships. -Brian Tracy

579. A person determined never to be wrong won't likely accomplish much. -Ken Wisdom

580. Wise are they who have learned these truths. Trouble is temporary. Time is tonic. Tribulation is a test tube. -William Arthur Ward

581. Jerome K. Jerome It is impossible to enjoy idling thoroughly unless one has plenty of work to do.

582. Those who educate children well are more to be honored than parents, for these only gave life, those the art of living well. -Aristotle

583. Every chance taken is another chance to win. -Unknown Author

584. If you are never scared, embarrassed or hurt, it means you never take chances. -Julia Soul

585. You can't always control the wind, but you can control your sails. -Anthony Robbins

586. You'll never have a quiet world till you knock the patriotism out of the human race. -George Bernard Shaw

587. The more I want to get something done the less I call it work. -Richard Bach

588. If we cannot live so as to be happy let us least live so as to deserve it. -Immanuel Hermann Fichte

   • would some power the giftie give us to see ourselves as others see us. -Robert Burns

589. People who are smart get into Mensa. People who are really smart look around and leave. -James Randi

590. I do not distinguish by the eye but by the mind which is the proper judge. -Seneca

591. If you want to be a winner, hang around with winners. - Christopher D. Furman

592. There is only one success-to be able to spend your life in your own way. -Christopher Morley

593. Real glory springs from the silent conquest of ourselves. -Joseph P. Thompson

594. It matters not whether you win or lose what matters is whether I win or lose. -Darrin Weinberg

595. Memory is not so brilliant as hope but it is more beautiful and a thousand times as true. -George Dennison Prentice

596. As you grow older you'll find the only things you regret are the things you didn't do. -Zachary Scott

597. Everything that deceives may be said to enchant. -Plato

598. It is better to remain silent and be thought a fool than to open your mouth and prove it.

599. Don't believe in miracles - depend on them. -Laurence J. Peter

600. Nobody is hurt. Hurt is in the mind. If you can walk you can run. - Vince Lombardi

601. Geoffrey F. Albert The most important thing about having goals is having one.

602. Be glad today. Tomorrow may bring tears. Be brave today. The darkest night will pass. And golden rays will usher in the dawn. - Sarah Knowles Bolton

603. Judge a man by his questions rather than his answers.- Voltaire

604. Edwin Holt Hughes If we were to be asked suddenly to give a definition of humility we would doubtless be greatly embarrassed.

605. When we blindly adopt a religion a political system a literary dogma we become automatons. We cease to grow.- Anais Nin

606. Chinese Proverb With time and patience the mulberry leaf becomes a silk gown.

607. One's dignity may be assaulted, vandalized and cruelly mocked, but cannot be taken away unless it is surrendered. -Michael J. Fox

608. I've learned that I wish I could have told my mom that I love her one more time before she passed away. - Andy Rooney

609. An individual cannot know what he is till he has made himself real by action. -Unknown

610. The government solution to a problem is usually as bad as the problem. -Milton Friedman

611. Better be ill spoken of by one before all than by all before one. - Scottish Proverb

612. The most important trip you may take in life is meeting people halfway. -Henry Boyle

613. By the time a man notices that he is no longer young his youth has long since left him. -W. Somerset Maugham

614. Keep your love of nature for that is the true way to understand art more and more. -Vincent Van Gogh

615. Nobody can be exactly like me. Sometimes even I have trouble doing it. -Tallulah Bankhead

616. A printer consists of three main parts: the case, the jammed paper tray and the blinking red light.

617. God is the God of truth and every spiritual quality must live with that holy attribute. -Edwin Holt Hughes

618. To change and to change for the better are two different things. -German proverb

619. All poetic inspiration is but dream interpretation. -Hans Sachs

620. Depend not on fortune but on conduct. -Publilius Syrus

621. There is no higher religion than human service. To work for the common good is the greatest creed. -Woodrow Wilson

622. Little deeds of kindness little words of love help to make earth happy like the heaven above.-Julia A. Fletcher Carney

623. I'm not going to buy my kids an encyclopedia. Let them walk to school like I did. -Lawrence Peter Berra

624. You have to kiss a lot of toads before you find a handsome prince. -American Proverb

625. Money won't buy happiness but it will pay the salaries of a large research staff to study the problem. -Bill Vaughan

626. Washing one's hands of the conflict between the powerful and the powerless means to side with the powerful not to be neutral. -Paulo Freire

627. Good plans shape good decisions. That's why good planning helps to make elusive dreams come true. —Lester Bittel

628. How can we expect another to keep our secret if we cannot keep it ourselves? -François de La Rochefoucauld

629. The best performance improvement is the transition from the nonworking state to the working state. -John Ousterhout

630. You can be confident and secure and know that you do a good job at what you do. But you don't know to be arrogant about it. -Ruben Studdard

631. Fire is the test of gold adversity of strong men. -Seneca

632. Only the educated are free. -Epictetus

633. Differences in political opinion are as unavoidable as to a certain point they may perhaps be necessary. -George Washington

634. The love of liberty is the love of others the love of power is the love of ourselves. -William Hazlitt

- what a heaven is love, O what a hell. -Thomas Dekker

635. A conference is a gathering of important people who individually can't do anything but together can decide that nothing can be done.

636. A child miseducated is a child lost. -John Fitzgerald Kennedy

637. I dress for women and I undress for men. - Angie Dickenson

638. The true traveler is he who goes on foot and even then he sits down a lot of the time. -Colette

639. A friend in need is a friend to be avoided. -Lord Samuel

640. Keep your broken arm inside your sleeve. -Chinese Proverb

641. A wise man makes his own decisions an ignorant man follows the public opinion. -Chinese Proverb

642. The most wasted of all days is one without laughter. -e e cummings

643. It is no profit to have learned well if you neglect to do well. -Publilius Syrus

644. The laws of probability so true in general so fallacious in particular. - Edward Gibbon

645. I am a poet and did not know it. I make a rhyme every time.

646. Stranger if you passing meet me and desire to speak to me why should you not speak to me And why should I not speak to you? - Walt Whitman

647. The truth, of course, is that a billion falsehoods told a billion times by a billion people are still false. -Travis Walton

648. Age does not protect you from love. But love to some extent protects you from age. -Anais Nin

649. The father is always a Republican toward his son and his mother's always a Democrat. -Robert Frost

650. Deep Thoughts: Consider the daffodil. And while you're doing that I'll be over here looking through your stuff. -Jack Handey

651. Try to learn something about everything and everything about something. -Thomas Huxley

652. The most onerous slavery is to be a slave to oneself. -Seneca

653. Sometimes it is a great joy just to listen to someone we love talking. - Vincent McNabb

654. The trouble with the rat race is that even if you win you're still a rat. -Jane Wagner

655. Law, without force, is impotent. -Blaise Pascal

656. A hard beginning maketh a good ending. -John Heywood

657. Just to be is a blessing. Just to live is holy. -Abraham Joshua Heschel

658. Paintings have a life of their own that derives from the painter's soul. -Vincent Van Gogh

659. Things do not have meaning. We assign meaning to everything. -Anthony Robbins

660. The difference between our decadence and the Russians is that while theirs is brutal ours is apathetic. -James Grover Thurber

661. Everyone is a genius at least once a year. The real geniuses simply have their bright ideas closer together. -Georg Christoph Lichtenberg

662. Nothing is capable of being well set to music that is not nonsense. -Joseph Addison

663. The irony is that the person not taking risks feels the same amount of fear as the person who regularly takes risks. -Peter McWilliams

    • tyrant love to what do you not drive the hearts of men. -Virgil

664. We are no more than candles burning in the wind. -Japanese Proverb

665. It is not what you gather but what you scatter that tells what kind of life you have lived.

666. If you do not conquer self you will be conquered by self. -Napoleon Hill

667. The censure of those who are opposed to us is the highest commendation that can be given us. -Antoine De Saint-Exupery

668. Oh I have loved him too much to feel no hate for him. -August Strindberg

669. Perfection is achieved, not when there is nothing more to add, but when there is nothing left to take away. -Antoine de Saint-Exupery

670. Look and you will find it - what is unsought will go undetected. -Sophocles

671. People do not attract that which they want, but that which they are. -James Allen

672. We cannot destroy kindred. Our chains stretch a little sometimes, but they never break. -Marie de Rabutin-Chantal

673. Prudence which degenerates into timidity is very seldom the path to safety. -Edgar Algernon Robert Cecil

674. Readiness of speech is often inability to hold the tongue. -Jean Baptiste Rousseau

675. Just to be is a blessing. Just to live is holy. -Rabbi Abraham Heschel

676. What the caterpillar calls the end, the rest of the world calls a butterfly. -Lao Tzu

677. There are only two ways of telling the complete truth - anonymously and posthumously. -Thomas Sowell

678. The only routine with me is no routine at all. -Jackie Kennedy

679. For an idea ever to be fashionable is ominous since it must afterwards be always old-fashioned. -George Santayana

680. If you don't want to do something, one excuse is as good as another. -Yiddish Proverb

681. The best audience is intelligent well-educated and a little drunk. -Alvin Barkley

682. Style is knowing who you are what you want to say and not giving a damn. -Gore Vidal

683. We often see further through a tear, than through a telescope.

684. This time like all times is a very good one if we but know what to do with it. -Ralph Waldo Emerson

685. The price is wrong bitch. -Happy Gilmore, Happy

686. Maybe I'm lucky to be going so slowly, because I may be going in the wrong direction. -Ashleigh Brilliant

687. Problems are only opportunities in work clothes. -Henry J. Kaiser

688. My advice is to look out for engineers. They begin with sewing machines and end up with nuclear bombs. - Marcel Pagnol

689. Success is how high you bounce when you hit bottom. -George S. Patton

690. The deepest experience of the creator is feminine for it is experience of receiving and bearing. -Rainer Maria Rilke

691. It is only when they go wrong that machines remind you how powerful they are. -Clive James

692. There is only one terminal dignity - love. -Helen Hayes

693. Many men know how to flatter; few men know how to praise. -Greek Proverb

694. Few men have the natural strength to honor a friend's success without envy. -Aeschylus

695. The soul's Rialto hath its merchandise, I barter for curl upon that mart. - Elizabeth Barrett Browning

696. Nothing is really work unless you would rather be doing something else. -Sir James Barrie

697. Anything is possible, but only a few things actually happen. -Richard Rosen

698. Better to remain silent and be thought a fool, than to speak and remove all doubt. -Abraham Lincoln

699. You may be deceived if you trust too much, but you will live in torment if you do not trust enough. -Frank Crane

700. Hell's afloat in lover's tears. -Dorothy Rothschild Parker

701. Realize that there are not hopeless situations; there are only people who take hopeless attitudes. -Norman Vincent Peale

702. All these years I've been feeling like I was growing into myself. Finally I feel grown. -Oprah Winfrey

703. Ability can take you to the top, but it takes character to keep you there.

704. The distance between insanity and genius is measured only by success. -James Bond, Tomorrow Never Dies

705. We know accurately only when we know little with knowledge doubt increases. -Johann Wolfgang von Goethe

706. A good beginning makes a good end. -English Proverb

707. It is the province of knowledge to speak, and it is the privilege of wisdom to listen. -Oliver Wendell Holmes

708. The secret of life is honesty and fair dealing. If you can fake that you've got it made. -Julius Henry Marx

709. Where we love is home, home that our feet may leave but not our hearts. -Oliver Wendell Holmes

710. Certain flaws are necessary for the whole. It would seem strange if old friends lacked certain quirks. -Johann von Goethe

711. Freedom is first of all a responsibility before the God from whom we come. -Alan Keyes

712. You may deceive all the people part of the time and part of the people all the time but not all the people all the time. -Abraham Lincoln

713. Keeping score of old scores and scars getting even and one-upping always makes you less than you are. -Malcolm Stevenson, Forbes

714. When we conquer without danger our triumph is without glory. -Pierre Corneille

715. A lot of children know absolutely nothing about guns other than what they see on T.V. and those are the wrong things. -Marion Hammer

716. Talking much about oneself can also be a means to conceal oneself. -Friedrich Wilhelm Nietzsche

717. Great things are done when men and mountains meet. -William Blake

718. Insanity in individuals is something rare - but in groups, parties, nations, and epochs it is the rule. -Friedrich Wilhelm Nietzsche

719. There are moments when everything goes well don't be frightened it won't last. -Jules Renard

720. The way you see people is the way you treat them. And the way you treat them is what they become. -Johann W. Von Goeth

721. The important thing is to learn a lesson every time you lose. -John McEnroe

722. If you haven't the strength to impose your own terms upon life, you must accept the terms it offers you. -T. S. Eliot

723. Our vision is more obstructed by what we think we know than by our lack of knowledge. -Krister Stendahl

724. There was never a good biography of a good novelist. There couldn't be. He is too many people if he's any good. -F. Scott

725. What is not fully understood is not possessed. -Johann Wolfgang von Goethe

726. Excuse me while I kiss the sky. -Jimi Hendrix

727. Delegating work works, provided the one delegating works, too. - Robert Half

728. The act of repeating erroneously the words of another. -Ambrose Bierce

729. The superior man is firm in the right way, and not merely firm. - Confucius

730. The truly important things in life - love, beauty, and one's own uniqueness - are constantly being overlooked. -Pablo Casals

731. Courage doesn't always roar. Sometimes courage is the little voice at the end of the day that says...I'll try again tomorrow.

732. An angry person is seldom reasonable; a reasonable person is seldom angry.

733. History does not long entrust the care of freedom to the weak or the timid. -Dwight D. Eisenhower

734. A failure establishes only this, that our determination to succeed was not strong enough. -John Christian Bovee

735. I said I didn't want to run for president. I didn't ask you to believe me. -Mario M. Cuomo

736. To accept a favor is to forfeit liberty. - Louise H. Leber

737. When you have exhausted all possibilities, remember this - you haven't. - Thomas Edison

738. If our house be on fire without inquiring whether it was fired from within or without, we must try to extinguish it. -Thomas Jefferson

739. Any change, even a change for the better, is always accompanied by drawbacks and discomforts. -Arnold Bennett

740. Rest not Life is sweeping by go and dare before you die. Something mighty and sublime leave behind to conquer time. -Johann von Goethe

741. We must not measure greatness from the mansion down but from the manger up. -Jesse Louis Jackson

742. Reputation is what the world thinks a man is; character is what he really is. -Anonymous

743. To get to heaven we must take it with us. -Henry Drummond

744. We have forty million reasons for failure, but not a single excuse. -Rudyard Kipling

745. The 8 Equities: Physical, Spiritual, Psychological, Intellectual, Emotional, Financial, Social and Family. -Michael Vance

746. I want to live my life so that my nights are not full of regrets. -D. H. Lawrence

747. The head never rules the heart but just becomes its partner in crime. -Mignon McLaughlin

748. The world needs anger. The world often continues to allow evil because it isn't angry enough. -Bede Jarrett

749. Whenever you want to marry someone go have lunch with his ex-wife. -Francis William Bourdillon

750. Every failure is a step to success... -William Whewell

751. History is the version of past events that people have decided to agree upon. -Napoleon Bonaparte

752. All words are pegs to hang ideas on. -Henry Ward Beecher

753. We want to have a testimony, but we don't want the test.

754. Goodbye cruel world. -Gloria Shayne

755. In great attempts it is glorious even to fail. -Vince Lombardi

756. Nothing can add more power to your life than concentrating all your energies on a limited set of targets. -Nido Qubein

757. Think like a queen. A queen is not afraid to fail. Failure is another steppingstone to greatness. -Oprah Winfrey

758. I generally avoid temptation unless I can't resist it. -Mae West

759. Humility is the only true wisdom by which we prepare our minds for all the possible changes of life. - George Arliss

760. Children might or might not be a blessing but to create them and then fail them was surely damnation. -Lois McMaster Bujold

761. There is a wisdom of the head and ... a wisdom of the heart. -Charles Dickens

762. I don't think anyone should write their autobiography until after they're dead. -Samuel Goldwyn

763. In baseball you don't know nothing. -Lawrence Peter Berra

764. Dreams come true. Without that possibility nature would not incite us to have them. -John Updike

765. A ship in port is safe but that's not what ships are built for. -Grace Murray Hopper

766. Most of the problems a President has to face have their roots in the past. -Harry S. Truman

767. Forbes Diversity, the art of thinking independently together. -Malcolm Stevenson

768. All power corrupts, but we need the electricity.

769. Men are apt to offend (tis true) where they find most goodness to forgive. -William Congreve

770. Obviously crime pays or there'd be no crime. -G. Gordon Liddy

771. Get mad, then get over it. - Colin Powell

772. Why don't you write books people can read? -Nora Joyce to her husband, James

773. Never look for birds of this year in the nests of the last. -Miguel de Cervantes

774. So of cheerfulness or a good temper the more it is spent the more it remains. -Ralph Waldo Emerson

775. The law is an ass - an idiot. -Charles Dickens

776. You can outdistance that which is running after you but not what is running inside you. -Rwandan Proverb

777. I conceive the essential task of religion to be to develop the consciences the ideals and the aspirations of mankind. -Robert Millikan

778. Prosperity belongs to those who learn new things the fastest. -Paul Zane Pilzer

779. Knowledge is a process of piling up facts wisdom lies in their simplification. -Martin H. Fischer

780. Active minds that think and study like swift brooks are seldom muddy. -Arthur Guiterman

781. You can't force anyone to love you or lend you money. -Jewish Proverb

782. Charity begins at home. -Terence

783. What a lot we lost when we stopped writing letters. You can't reread a phone call. -Liz Carpenter

784. A computer once beat me at chess, but it was no match for me at kick boxing.

785. It is a small world, but I wouldn't like to have to paint it.

786. You must accept the truth from whatever source it comes. - Maimonides

787. Laughter is like changing a baby's diaper. It doesn't permanently solve any problems, but it makes thing more acceptable for a while.

788. Before everything else, getting ready is the secret of success. -Henry Ford

789. Truth is the summit of being justice is the application of it to affairs. -Ralph Waldo Emerson

790. Chance favors only the prepared mind. -Louis Pasteur

791. A lie gets halfway around the world before the truth has a chance to get its pants on. -Sir Winston Leonard Spenser Churchill

792. First and last what is demanded of genius is love of truth. -Johann von Goethe

793. Hope doesn't come from calculating whether the good news is winning out over the bad. It's simply a choice to take action. -Anna Lappe

794. Of all the properties which belong to honorable men, not one is so highly prized as that of character. - Henry Clay

795. The easiest way to grow up is to surround yourself with people who are smarter than you.

796. All men are frauds. The only difference between them is that some admit it. I myself deny it. -H.L. Mencken

797. One thing at a time, is my motto - and just play that thing for all it is worth, even if it's only two pair and a jack. -Mark Twain

798. Wherever you go, go with all your heart. -Confucius

799. Many things have fallen only to rise higher. -Seneca

800. In every difficult situation is potential value. Believe this, then begin looking for it. -Norman Vincent Peale

801. It only takes years for a liberal to become a conservative without changing a single idea. -Robert Anton Wilson

802. I pray thee cease thy counsel which falls into mine ears as profitless as water in a sieve. -William Shakespeare

803. Lonely people talking to each other can make each other lonelier. -Lillian Hellman

804. Owners of digital watches: Your days are numbered!

805. True friends stab you in the front. -Oscar Wilde

806. The real secret to success is enthusiasm. -Walter Chrysler

807. If you have fear of those that command you, spare those that obey you. -Rabbi Ben Azai

808. ...The task is overwhelming and the chance is slight. We must take the chance or die. -Robert Hutchins

809. Dieting is wishful shrinking.

810. This world is a harsh place, this world. -Zulu Proverb

811. Happiness is not something you experience, it's something you remember. -Oscar Levant

812. Knowledge exists to be imparted. -Ralph Waldo Emerson

813. Poor is the man whose pleasures depend on the permission of another. -Madonna

814. Money glitters, beauty sparkles, and intelligence shines.

815. What the heart has once owned and had it shall never lose. -Henry Ward Beecher

816. Abstract art is a product of the untalented sold by the unprincipled to the utterly bewildered. -Al Capp

817. People would worry less about what others think of them if they only realized how seldom they do.

818. One reason why computers can do more work than people is that they never have to stop and answer the phone.

819. Nothing is more terrible than ignorance in action. -Johann von Goethe

820. As I would not be a slave so I would not be a master. This expresses my idea of democracy. -Abraham Lincoln

821. It takes twenty years to become an overnight success. - Eddie Cantor

822. Dispatch is the soul of business, and nothing contributes more to Dispatch than Method. - Lord Chesterfield

823. Observe due measure for right timing is in all things the most important factor. -Hesiod

824. The hand that hath made you fair hath made you good. -William Shakespeare

825. Possunt quia posse videntur. (They can because they think they can.) -Virgil

826. Do you know the three times that most people are in church? When they are hatched, matched and dispatched.

827. I prefer my oysters fried. That way I know my oysters died. -Roy G. Blount Jr.

828. By the time your life is finished you will have learned just enough to begin it well. -Eleanor Marx

829. Disconnecting from change does not recapture the past. It loses the future. -Kathleen Norris

830. Leadership is action, not position. -Donald H. McGannon

831. Smoking is one of the leading causes of statistics. -Fletcher Knebel

832. If a relationship is to evolve it must go through a series of endings. - Lisa Moriyama

833. Long years must pass before the truths we have made for ourselves become our very flesh. -Paul Valery

834. The hunger for love is much more difficult to remove than the hunger for bread. -Mother Theresa

835. It is not the answer that enlightens but the question. -Eugene Ionesco

836. Where there is joy there is creation. Where there is no joy there is no creation know the nature of joy. -Maitri Upanishad

837. The process of learning requires not only hearing and applying but also forgetting and then remembering again. -John Gray

838. The achievements of an organization are the results of the combined effort of each individual. -Vince Lombardi

839. History is the version of past events that people have decided to agree upon. -Napoleon

840. A good home must be made not bought. -Joyce Maynard

841. The person who will not stand for something will fall for anything. -Zig Ziglar

842. I think when the full horror of being fifty hits you, you should stay home and have a good cry. -Alan Bleasdale

843. Men show their characters in nothing more clearly than in what they think laughable. -Johann Wolfgang von Goethe

844. There is no more beautiful life than that of a student. - F. Albrecht

845. Time you enjoyed wasting is not wasted time. -T. S. Elliot

846. Praise youth and it will prosper. -Irish Proverb

847. Rest satisfied with doing well and leave others to talk of you as they please. -Pythagoras

848. The meek shall inherit the Earth but not its mineral rights. -J. Paul Getty

849. Leadership is practiced not so much in words as in attitude and in actions. -Harold S. Geneen

850. The direction in which education starts a man will determine his future life. -Plato

851. Next to knowing when to seize an opportunity the most important thing in life is to know when to forgo an advantage. -Benjamin Disraeli

852. If I take refuge in ambiguity I can assure you that it's quite conscious. -Frank Boyden

853. Deciding not to choose is still making a choice.

854. Magnificent promises are always to be suspected. -Theodore Parker

855. I'm not concerned about all hell breaking loose but that a PART of hell will break loose... it'll be much harder to detect. -George Carlin

856. As we acquire more knowledge, things do not become more comprehensible but more mysterious. -Albert Schweitzer

857. It is the job of thinking people not to be on the side of the executioners. -Albert Camus

858. You are indebted to your imagination for three-fourths of your importance. -David Garrick

859. Do not speak of your happiness to one less fortunate than yourself. -Plutarch

860. Life engenders life. Energy creates energy. It is by spending oneself that one becomes rich. -Sarah Bernhardt

861. There are two ways to write error-free programs. Only the third one works. -Anon.

862. Optimization hinders evolution. -Anon.

863. Ambition is a poor excuse for not having sense enough to be lazy. -Edgar Bergen

864. Saying goodbye doesn't mean anything. It's the time we spent together that matters not how we left it. -Trey and Matt Stone Parker

865. Have you got a problem? Do what you can where you are with what you've got. -Theodore Roosevelt

866. Death is not the greatest loss in life. The greatest loss is what dies inside us while we live. -Norman Cousins

867. As a housewife, I feel that if the kids are still alive when my husband gets home from work, then hey, I've done my job. -Roseanne Barr

868. He hasn't an enemy in the world - but all his friends hate him. -Eddie Cantor

869. It is not because things are difficult that we do not dare, it is because we do not dare that they are difficult. -Seneca

870. Quemadmodum gladius neminem occidit occidentis telum est. [A sword never kills anybody; it's a tool in the killer's hand.] -Seneca

871. Work and play are words used to describe the same thing under differing conditions. -Mark Twain

872. The highest love of all finds its fulfillment not in what it keeps but in what it gives. -Father Andrew SDC

873. Practice yourself what you preach. -Plautus

874. A good listener is not only popular everywhere but after a while he gets to know something. -Wilson Mizner

875. Always bear in mind that your own resolution to succeed is more important than any one thing. -Abraham Lincoln

876. Mountains cannot be surmounted except by winding paths. -Johann Wolfgang von Goethe

877. Where the speech is corrupted the mind is also. -Seneca

878. Knowledge is proud she knows so much; wisdom is humble that she knows no more. -Cowper

879. A man who lives in a glass house shouldn't throw stones.

880. Spotted on a desk: Of course I don't look busy ... I did it right the first time.

881. The people recognize themselves in their commodities; they find their soul in their automobile, hi-fi set, split-level home, kitchen equipment.

882. Life... is like a grapefruit. It's orange and squishy and has a few pips in it and some folks have half a one for breakfast. -Douglas Adams

883. Time is the scarcest resource and unless it is managed nothing else can be managed. -Peter Drucker

884. The object of education is to prepare the young to educate themselves throughout their lives. -Robert Hutchins

885. Art is everywhere, except it has to pass through a creative mind. -Louise Nevelson

886. Don't knock the weather nine-tenths of the people couldn't start a conversation if it didn't change once in a while. -Kin Hubbard

887. Tomorrow I'll think of some way . . . after all tomorrow is another day. -Scarlett O'Hara

888. Self-pity is our worst enemy and if we yield to it we can never do anything good in the world. -Helen Keller

889. They've taken the foot off Johnny Grubb. Uh they've taken the shoe off Johnny Grubb. -Jerry Coleman

890. What a blessing it would be if we could open and shut our ears as easily as we open and shut our eyes. -Georg Christoph Lichtenberg

891. It is easier to talk than to hold one's tongue. -Greek Proverb

892. Of all the properties which belong to honorable men, not one is so highly prized as that of character. -Henry Clary

893. Most everything in my brain someone else helped put there. -Unknown

894. We are shaped by our thoughts. We become what we think. -Buddha

895. A smiling face is half the meal. -Latvian Proverb

896. He not only overflowed with learning he stood in the slop. -Sydney Smith

897. There is no way to prosperity, prosperity is the way. -Wayne Dyer

898. Spoon feeding in the long run teaches us nothing but the shape of the spoon. -Edward Morgan Forster

899. Half the world is composed of idiots the other half of people clever enough to take indecent advantage of them. -Walter Kerr

900. People buy into the leader before they buy into the vision. -John C. Maxwell

901. For the most part fear is nothing but an illusion. When you share it with someone else it tends to disappear. -Marilyn C. Barrick

902. Whoso would be a man must be a nonconformist. -Ralph Waldo Emerson

903. Poetry often enters through the window of irrelevance. -M. C. Richards

904. Solitude is the beginning of all freedom. -William Orville Douglas

905. Talent is what you possess; genius is what possesses you. -Malcolm Cowley

906. It's not only the most difficult thing to know one's self but the most inconvenient. -Josh Billings

907. Those who live by the sword get shot by those who don't.

908. It is not how busy you are, but why you are busy- the bee is praised, the mosquito is swatted.

909. The highest courage is to dare to appear to be what one is. -John Lancaster Spalding

910. The great nations have always acted like gangsters and the small nations like prostitutes. -Stanley Kubrick

911. A book of quotations . . . can never be complete. -Robert M. Hamilton

912. The duty of helping one's self in the highest sense involves the helping of one's neighbors. -Samuel Smiles

913. Consumers are statistics. Customers are people. -Stanley Marcus

914. First we form habits, then they form us. Conquer your bad habits or they will conquer you. -Rob Gilbert

915. Silver's law: If Murphy's Law can go wrong, it will.

916. If a man destroys the eye of another man, they shall destroy his eye. -Hammurabi

917. Kevin McReynolds stops at third and he scores. -Ralph Kiner

918. Success seems to be largely a matter of hanging on after others have let go. -William Feather

919. Whoever cares to learn will always find a teacher. -German proverb

920. Forgive your enemies but never forget their names. -John Fitzgerald Kennedy

921. Reason is the substance of the universe. The design of the world is absolutely rational. -Georg Wilhelm Friedrich Hegel

922. Age is of no importance unless you are a cheese. -Billie Burke

923. God is at home, it's we who have gone out for a walk. -Meister Eckhart

924. You can accomplish by kindness what you cannot by force. -Publilius Syrus

925. In absence of clearly defined goals we become strangely loyal to performing daily acts of trivia. -Unknown

926. Success is a journey...not a destination. -Ben Sweetland

927. I don't think I can play any other way but all out. I enjoy the game so much because I'm putting so much into it. - George Brett

928. The person who is waiting for something to turn up might start with their shirtsleeves. -Garth Henrichs

929. In your life you will love someone so much you could eat them, then you will get married and wish you had.

930. Every man is ignorant - just on different subjects. -Will Rogers

931. The love of democracy is that of equality. -Charles de Montesquieu

932. Pride envy avarice - these are the sparks have set on fire the souls of man. -Alighieri Dante

933. Man is quite insane. He wouldn't know how to create a maggot and he creates Gods by the dozen. -Michel Eyquem de Montaigne

934. Count not him among your friends who will retail your privacies to the world. -Publilius Syrus

935. In archaeology you uncover the unknown. In diplomacy you cover the known. -Thomas Pickering

936. Beneath the rule of men entirely great, the pen is mightier than the sword. -Edward Bulwer-Lytton

937. Times don't change. Men do. -Sam Levenson

938. Alcohol preserves everything but not dignity.

939. A world without nuclear weapons would be less stable and more dangerous for all of us. -Margaret Hilda Thatcher

940. Friendship is like money easier made than kept. -Samuel Butler

941. Discretion is being able to raise your eyebrow instead of your voice.

942. Beat me with the truth, don't torture me with lies.

943. The trick is to make sure you don't die waiting for prosperity to come. -Lee Iacocca

944. Never let anyone steal your joy. -Mike Richards

945. A rose can say "I love you." Orchids can enthrall, but a weed bouquet in a chubby fist, yes, that says it all.

946. The hammer shatters glass but forges steel. -Assyrian Proverb

947. Chance never helps those who do not help themselves. -Sophocles

948. Life is so much simpler when you tell the truth.

949. All progress is based upon a universal innate desire on the part of every organism to live beyond its income. -Samuel Butler

950. Life is not meaningful to us unless serving an end beyond itself unless it is of value to someone else. -Abraham J. Herschel

951. Keep your head and your heart in the right direction and you will not have to worry about your feet.

952. Solitude is the best nurse of wisdom. -Laurence Sterne

953. Many difficulties which nature throws in our way may be smoothed away by the exercise of intelligence. -Titus Livius

954. Anger and intolerance are the enemies of correct understanding. -Mahatma Gandhi

955. Respect yourself and others will respect you. -Confucius

956. The soul would have no rainbow if the eyes had no tears. -Indian Proverb

957. If you can be well without health, you may be happy without virtue. -Edmund Burke

958. Leadership is the art of getting someone else to do something you want done because he wants to do it. -Dwight Eisenhower

959. Habit is habit and not to be flung out of the window by any man, but coaxed downstairs a step at a time. -Mark Twain

960. Don't point out your flaws because the world is not as sympathetic and nurturing as you think. -Jennifer Tilly

961. A thorough knowledge of the Bible is worth more than a college education. -Theodore Roosevelt

962. We never know the worth of water till the well is dry. -French Proverb

963. The very essence of leadership is that you have to have vision. You can't blow an uncertain trumpet. -Theodore M. Hesburgh

964. Meditation is the soul's perspective glass. -Owen Felltham

965. After silence that which comes nearest to expressing the inexpressible is music. -Aldous Huxley

966. To think is easy. To act is hard. But the hardest thing in the world is to act in accordance with your thinking. -Goethe

967. I've learned that although it's hard to admit it I'm secretly glad my parents are strict.

968. Lack of direction, not lack of time, is the problem. We all have twenty-four hour days. -Zig Ziglar

969. One great use of words is to hide our thoughts. - Voltaire

970. Love thy neighbor as yourself, but choose your neighborhood. -Louise Beal

971. Everything comes to him who hustles while he waits. -Thomas Edison

972. Greed is for amateurs. Disorder, chaos, anarchy, now that's fun. -Crow The Top Dollar

973. God creates men but they choose each other. -Niccolo Machiavelli

974. After three days without reading talk becomes flavorless. -Chinese Proverb

975. Any programming language is at its best before it is implemented and used.

976. Communication by empathy is a talent that few possess.

977. What do Windows and a handgun have in common? Both are harmless while not loaded.

978. Energy is the power that drives every human being. It is not lost by exertion by maintained by it. -Germaine Greer

979. Nature provides exceptions to every rule. -Margaret Fuller

980. I cannot say whether things will get better if we change what I can say is they must change if they are to get better. -G. C. Lichtenberg

981. We do not know what we want and yet we are responsible for what we are - that is the fact. -Jean-Paul Sartre

982. Christopher Columbus, as everyone knows, is honored by posterity because he was the last to discover America. -James Joyce

983. It requires wisdom to understand wisdom' the music is nothing if the audience is deaf. -Walter Lippmann

984. There is no reciprocity. Men love women. Women love children. Children love hamsters. -Alice Thomas Ellis

985. I know of no more encouraging fact than the unquestionable ability of man to elevate his life by conscious endeavor. -Henry David Thoreau

986. The greatest weakness of most humans is their hesitancy to tell others how much they love them while they're alive. -Orlando A. Battista

987. A little kindness from person to person is better than a vast love for all humankind. -Richard Dehmel

988. Big Ideas are so hard to recognize, so fragile, so easy to kill. Don't forget that, all of you who don't have them. -John Elliot, Jr.

989. Do one thing at time, with supreme excellence. -NASA proverb

990. Search others for their virtues thyself for thy vices. -Benjamin Franklin

991. Truth is the secret of eloquence and of virtue the basis of moral authority it is the highest summit of art and life. -Henri-Frederic Amiel

992. In a friend you find a second self. -Isabelle Norton

993. Prosperity is only an instrument to be used not a deity to be worshipped. -Calvin Coolidge

994. The woods are lovely, dark and deep, but I have promises to keep, and miles to go before I sleep. -Robert Frost

995. The course of human history is determined not by what happens in the skies but what takes place in our hearts. -Sir Arthur Keith

996. We will either find a way or make one -Hannibal

997. When a person wants to believe something, it doesn't take much to convince them.

998. Let us always greet each other with a smile for the smile is the beginning of love. -Mother Teresa

999. Forsan et haec olim meminisse iuvabit (Perhaps it will be pleasing sometime to have remembered these things from The Aeneid)-Virgil

1000. Great spirits have always encountered violent opposition from mediocre minds. - Albert Einstein

1001. The Great Spirit, when He made earth, never intended that it should be made merchandise -Native American.

1002. Here is a test to find out whether your mission in life is complete. If you're alive, it isn't. -Richard Bach

1003. Crime has already been organized. Now it's up to the police.

1004. Another unsettling element in modern art is that common symptom of immaturity the dread of doing what has been done before.-Edith Wharton

1005. I am glad that I paid so little attention to good advice; had I abided by it I might have been saved from some of my most valuable mistakes.

1006. Some succeed because they are destined to. But most succeed because they are determined to.

1007. We do not know the true value of our moments until they have undergone the test of memory. -Georges Duhamel

1008. Remember the greatest gift is not found in a store nor under a tree but in the hearts of true friends. -Cindy Lew

1009. Love is the immortal flow of energy that nourishes extends and preserves. Its eternal goal is life.-Smiley Blanton

1010. A newspaper consists of just the same number of words whether there be any news in it or not. -Henry Fielding

1011. A mouse trap, placed on top of your alarm clock, will prevent you from rolling over and going back to sleep when you hit the snooze button.

1012. Let me never fall into the vulgar mistake of dreaming that I am persecuted whenever I am contradicted. -Ralph Waldo Emerson

1013. If I did not laugh, I should die. -Abraham Lincoln

1014. Continental people have sex-lives the English have hot-water bottles. -George Mikes

1015. Even if you are on the right track, you'll get run over if you just sit there. - Will Rogers

1016. Success is simply a matter of luck. Ask any failure. -Earl Wilson

1017. There are three great friends: an old wife, an old dog, and ready money. -Benjamin Franklin

1018. No amount of study or learning will make a man a leader unless he has the natural qualities of one. -Archibald Wavell

1019. Listening, not imitation, may be the sincerest form of flattery. - Dr. Joyce Brothers

1020. Civilization is the art of living in towns of such size that everyone does not know everyone else. -Julian Jaynes

1021. The mysterious is always attractive. People will always follow a vail.-Bede Jarrett

1022. A man is a little soul carrying around a corpse. -Marcus Aurelius

1023. We are called to be architects of the future, not its victims. - Buckminster Fuller

1024. He's a real loser. He moved into a new neighborhood and got run over by the Welcome Wagon. -Red Buttons

1025. As the old proverb says. "Like readily consorts with like." - Cicero

1026. Democracy substitutes election by the incompetent many for appointment by the corrupt few. -George Bernard Shaw

1027. I meant what I said and I said what I meant. An elephant's faithful, one hundred percent. -Dr. Seuss

1028. To know just what has to be done, then to do it, comprises the whole philosophy of practical life. -Sir William Osler

1029. Some people are so much sunshine to the square inch. -Walt Whitman

1030. The only infallible criterion of wisdom to vulgar minds - success. -Edmund Burke

1031. Nothing succeeds like the appearance of success. -Christopher Lasch

1032. Do not say a little in many words but a great deal in a few. - Pythagoras

1033. The man who follows a crowd will never be followed by a crowd. -R. S. Donnell

1034. The next best thing to winning is losing At least you've been in the race. -Nellie Hershey Tullis

1035. Enlightened people seldom or never possess a sense of responsibility. -George Orwell

1036. No matter how old you are there's always something good to look forward to. -Lynn Johnston

1037. A man may learn wisdom, even from a foe. -Aristophanes

1038. Only your compassion and your loving kindness are invincible, and without limit. -Thich Nhat Hanh

1039. They say men are molded out of faults, and for the most, become much more the better; for being a little bad. -William Shakespeare

1040. Wise men talk because they have something to say; fools, because they have to say something. -Plato

1041. Love doesn't just sit there like a stone; it has to be made like bread, remade all the time made new. -Ursula K. LeGuin

1042.   Promise yourself to be just as enthusiastic about the success of others as you are about your own. -Christian Larson

1043.   Behind the phony tinsel of Hollywood lies the real tinsel. -Oscar Levant

1044.   A healthy male adult bore consumes each year one and a half times his own weight in other people's patience. -John Updike

1045.   To be positive is to be mistaken at the top of one's voice. -Ambrose Bierce

1046.   Love is the triumph of imagination over intelligence. - Dr. Karl Menninger

1047.   A good plan is like a road map: it shows the final destination and usually the best way to get there. -H. Stanley Judd

1048.   Rather fail with honor than succeed by fraud. -Sophocles

1049.   Life was a lot simpler when what we honored was father and mother rather than all major credit cards. -Robert Orben

1050.   Irony is the hygiene of the mind. -Elizabeth Bibesco

1051.   The cure for admiring the House of Lords is to go and look at it. - Walter Bagehot

1052.   Human beings must be known to be loved but Divine beings must be loved to be known. -Pascal

1053.   Sometimes the mind, for reasons we don't necessarily understand, just decides to go to the store for a quart of milk. -Andrew Schneider

1054.   You'll never find a better sparring partner than adversity. -Walt Schmidt

1055.   The happiest people seem to be those who have no particular cause for being happy except that they are so. -William Ralph Inge

1056.   Love is life. And if you miss love you miss life.

1057.   A single reason why you can do something is worth 100 reasons why you can't.

1058.   I feel that the greatest reward for going is the opportunity to do more. -Dr. Jonas Salk

1059.   Laughter is the brush that sweeps away the cobwebs of the heart.

1060.   Courage is the first of human qualities because it is the quality which guarantees all others. -Sir Winston Churchill

1061.   Laughter gives us distance. It allows us to step back from an event deal with it and then move on. -Bob Newhart

1062.   My only hobby is laziness which naturally rules out all others. — Gianni Nazzaro

1063.   There are no hopeless situations - only people who are hopeless about them. -Dinah Shore

1064.   To what extent is any given man morally responsible for any given act, we do not know. -Alexis Carrel

1065.   There smites nothing so sharp nor smelleth so sour as shame. - William Langland

1066.   Words do two major things: They provide food for the mind and create light for understanding and awareness. -Jim Rohn

1067.   The world is proof that God is a committee. -Bob Stokes

1068.   I was a vegetarian until I started leaning toward the sunlight. - Rita Rudner

1069.   It's hard to say who gets criticized the most; the successful person or the failure; but it's mighty close. -Joe Moore

1070.   If you reveal your secrets to the wind you should not blame the wind for revealing them to the trees. -Kahlil Gibran

1071.   There is no greater sorrow than to be mindful of the happy time in misery. -Dante Alighieri

1072.   Politics is the art of preventing people from taking part in affairs which properly concern them. -Paul Valery

1073.   Deep Thoughts: Sometimes I think I'd be better off dead. No wait. Not me, you. -Jack Handey

1074.   Fight for your opinions, but do not believe that they contain the whole truth, or the only truth. -Charles A. Dana

1075.   A better world shall emerge based on faith and understanding. - Douglas MacArthur

1076.   The trees that are slow to grow bear the best fruit. -Moliere

1077.   Happiness is not a reward - it is consequence. Suffering is not a punishment - it is a result. -Robert Green Ingersoll

1078.   Self-trust is the essence of heroism. -Ralph Waldo Emerson

1079.   Thou art gone from my gaze like a beautiful dream and I seek thee in vain by the meadow and stream. -George Linley

1080.   Success is not final; failure is not fatal; it is the courage to continue that counts. -Sir Winston Leonard Spenser Churchill

1081.   Well, you can take the girl outta the trailer park, but you can't take the trailer park outta the girl. -Swordfish Stan

1082.   There are no eternal facts as there are no absolute truths. -Friedrich Wilhelm Nietzsche

1083.   Never give a child a sword. -Latin Proverb

1084.   Oh, what a tangled web do parents weave, when they think that their children are naïve. -Ogden Nash

1085.   Sexual pleasure is, I agree, a passion to which all others are subordinate but in which they all unite. -Marquis de Sade

1086.   Nobody is bored when he is trying to make something that is beautiful, or to discover something that is true. -William Inge

1087.   Man cannot discover new oceans unless he has courage to lose sight of the shore.

1088.   The price of wisdom is eternal thought. - Frank Birch

1089.   We'll all be riding that streetcar of desire. -Robert Joseph Bob Dole

1090.   Brevis esse laboro obscurus fio.(When I labor to be brief I become obscure.) -Horace

1091.   Youth is a wonderful thing. What a crime to waste it on children. -George Bernard Shaw

1092.   No one would talk much in society if he knew how often he misunderstood others. -Johann von Goethe

1093.   Love will enter cloaked in friendship's name. -Ovid

1094.   A woman without a man is like a fish without a bicycle. -Gloria Steinem

1095.   Motivation is what gets you started. Habit is what keeps you going. -Jim Ryan

1096.   There are so many things that we wish we had done yesterday, so few that we feel like doing today. -Mignon McLaughlin

1097.   Sometimes too much to drink isn't enough.

1098.   Man is a gaming animal. He must always be trying to get the better in something or other. Charles Lamb

1099.   You only live once but if you live right, once is enough. - Unknown

1100.   Love looks through a telescope envy through a microscope. - Josh Billings

1101.   Evangelism is selling a dream. -Guy Kawasaki

1102.   Hope is itself a species of happiness and, perhaps, the chief happiness which this world affords. -Samuel Johnson

1103.   Silence will not betray your thoughts but the expression on your face will. Humor has a hundred faces tragedy only a few. -H. G. Mendelson

1104.   The crowd gives the leader new strength. -Evenius

1105.   To fall in love is to create a religion that has a fallible god. - Jorge Luis Borges

1106.   Support by United States rulers is rather in the nature of the support that the rope gives to a hanged man. -Nikita Khrushchev

1107.   With regard to excellence it is not enough to know but we must try to have and use it. -Aristotle

1108.   Nothing great was ever achieved without enthusiasm. -Ralph Waldo Emerson

1109.   Egotism is the anesthetic that dulls the pain of stupidity. -Frank Leahy

1110.   People that are really very weird can get into sensitive positions and have a tremendous impact on history. -Dan Quayle

1111.   Once a word has been allowed to escape it cannot be recalled - Horace

1112.   When a thing is done, it's done. Don't look back. Look forward to your next objective. -George C. Marshall

1113.   It is OK to let your mind go blank, but please turn off the sound.

1114.   I love my past. I love my present. I'm not ashamed of what I've had and I'm not sad because I have it no longer. -Colette

1115.   Creating success is tough but keeping it is tougher. -Pete Rose

1116.   We are what and where we are because we have first imagined it. -Donald Curtis

1117.   Beware of too much laughter for it deadens the mind and produces oblivion. -The Talmud

1118.   Curious things, habits. People themselves never knew they had them. -Agatha Christie

1119.   Don't go around saying the world owes you a living. The world owes you nothing. It was here first. -Mark Twain

1120.   To repeat what others have said requires education to challenge, it requires brains. -Mary Pettibone Poole

1121.   You can accomplish much if you don't care who gets the credit. -Ronald Reagan

1122.   Ever tried. Ever failed. No matter. Try again. Fail again. Fail better. -Samuel Beckett

1123.   He who knows enough is enough will always have enough. -Lao Tzu

1124.   There is no remedy for love but to love more. -Henry David Thoreau

1125.   William A. Orton If you keep your mind sufficiently open people will throw a lot of rubbish into it.

1126.   Talk not of wasted affection; affection never was wasted. -Henry Wadsworth Longfellow

1127.   You can never get enough of what you don't need to make you happy. -Eric Hoffer

1128.   There shall be eternal summer in the grateful heart. -Celia Thaxter

1129.   Parentage is a very important profession but no test of fitness for it is ever imposed in the interest of the children. -Sir Walter Besant

1130.   We made too many wrong mistakes. -Lawrence Peter Berra

1131.   It is only an auctioneer who can equally and impartially admire all schools of art. -Oscar Wilde

1132.   There is many a good man to be found under a shabby hat. -Chinese Proverb

1133. You make a living by what you get, but you make a life by what you give. -Unknown Author

1134. Pretty much all the honest truth telling there is in the world is done by children. -Oliver Wendell Holmes

1135. This time like all times is a very good one if we but know what to do with it -Ralph Waldo Emerson

1136. It is not what they say about you, it's what they whisper.

1137. It is not enough to aim; you must hit. -Italian Proverb

1138. Power does not corrupt. Fear corrupts, perhaps the fear of a loss of power. -John Ernst Steinbeck

1139. To err is human, to blame it on someone else is more human.

1140. The real problem is not whether machines think, but whether men do. -B. F. Skinner

1141. N.B. Fear itself. Franklin D. Roosevelt (See also H. D. Thoreau.)

1142. Let me tell you the secret that has led me to my goal. My strength lies solely in my tenacity. -Louis Pasteur

1143. There is no way to peace. Peace is the way. -J. Muste

1144. Get the best out of your body that you can get. -Pat Hall

1145. I have just about all I can take of myself. - S. Behrman

1146. It is the test of a good religion whether you can joke about it. -Gilbert Keith Chesterton

1147. Live with passion. -Anthony Robbins

1148. The only thing you take with you when you're gone is what you leave behind. -John Allston

1149. Nothing is easy to the unwilling. -Thomas Fuller

1150. Man is the only animal that can remain on friendly terms with the victims he intends to eat until he eats them. -Samuel Butler

1151. Children have neither a past nor a future. Thus they enjoy the present, which seldom happens to us.-Jean de la Bruyere

1152. People with true character show it when nobody else is present.

1153. Not even the gods fight against necessity. -Simonides

1154. There are some days I practice positive thinking. And other days I'm not positive, I am thinking.

1155.   Titus Livius We fear things in proportion to our ignorance of them.

1156.   I have learned that the Lord didn't do it all in one day. What makes me think I can?

1157.   The good man is the man who, no matter how morally unworthy he has been, is moving to become better. -John Dewey

1158.   There is no disguise which can hide love for long where it exists or simulate it where it does not. -La Rochefoucauld

1159.   Because I could not stop for death, He kindly stopped for me; The carriage held but just ourselves and immortality. -Emily Dickinson

1160.   Wise are those who learn that the bottom line doesn't always have to be their top priority. -William Arthur Ward

1161.   It is the habit of mediocre minds to condemn all that is beyond their grasp. -La Rochefoucauld

1162.   I wish they would only take me as I am. -Vincent Van Gogh

1163.   He is winding the watch of his wit by and by it will strike. -William Shakespeare

1164.   He who is not very strong in memory should not meddle with lying. -Michel de Montaigne

1165.   Better to rely on one powerful king than on many little princes. -Jean de La Fontaine

1166.   People need religion. It's a vehicle for a moral tradition. A crucial role. Nothing can take its place. -Irving Kristol

1167.   You can only find truth with logic if you have already found it without it. -Gilbert Keith Chesterton

1168.   I tended to place my wife under a pedestal. -Woody Allen

1169.   No one is listening until you make a mistake.

1170.   The beginning of anxiety is the end of faith. The beginning of true faith is the end of anxiety.

1171.   Saying what we think gives us a wider conversational range than saying what we know. -Cullen Hightower

1172.   To send a letter is a good way to go somewhere without moving anything but your heart. -Phyllis Theroux

1173.   It's deja vu all over again -Yogi Berra

1174.   He said true things but called them by wrong names. -Elizabeth Barrett Browning

1175.   The African is my brother, but he is my younger brother by several centuries.-Albert Schweitzer

1176.   I choose the likely man in preference to the rich man; I want a man without money rather than money without a man. - Themistocles

1177.   Happy families are all alike. Every unhappy family is unhappy in its own way. -Leo Tolstoy

1178.   The Promised Land always lies on the other side of a Wilderness. -Havelock Ellis

1179.   For it was not into my ear you whispered, but into my heart. It was not my lips you kissed, but my soul. - Judy Garland

1180.   The difference between the right word and the almost right word is the difference between lightning and the lightning bug. - Mark Twain

1181.   Crude classifications and false generalizations are the curse of the organized life. -H. G. Wells

1182.   The truth the hope of any time must always be sought in minorities. -Ralph Waldo Emerson

1183.   If all else fails, read the directions.

1184.   Habit is a cable; we spin a thread of it every day and at last we cannot break it.

1185.   If a cluttered desk signs a cluttered mind of what then is an empty desk a sign of? -Albert Einstein

1186.   Never chase a lie. Let it alone and it will run itself to death. - Lyman Beecher

1187.   The empires of the future are the empires of the mind. - Winston Churchill

1188.   The unnatural that too is natural. -Johann Wolfgang von Goethe

1189.   The lowest ebb is the turn of the tide. -Henry Wadsworth Longfellow

1190.   A loving person lives in a loving world. A hostile person lives in a hostile world. Everyone you meet is your mirror. -Ken Keys

1191.   We are usually the best men when in the worst health. -English Proverb

1192.   Art is not a handicraft; it is the transmission of feeling the artist has experienced. -Leo Tolstoy

1193.   Pascal keeps your hand tied. C gives you enough rope to hang yourself. -Anon.

1194.   Life can only be understood backwards but it must be lived forwards. -Johann Wolfgang von Goethe

1195.   Take away the miseries and you take away some folks reason for living. -Toni Cade Bambara

1196.   The politician is an acrobat; he keeps his balance by doing the opposite of what he says. -Maurice Barrs

1197.   You're in middle age when you realize you have more on your mind and less on your head.

1198.   Love and eggs are best when they are fresh. -Assyrian Proverb

1199.   The art of conversation is not only to say the right thing at the right time, but to leave the wrong thing unsaid at the most tempting moment

1200.   Listen to all, plucking a feather from every passing goose, but follow no one absolutely. -Chinese Proverb

1201.   If a little dreaming is dangerous, the cure for it is not to dream less but to dream more, to dream all the time. -Marcel Proust

1202.   Character is much easier kept than recovered. -Thomas Paine

1203.   Children in the back seats of cars cause accidents, but accidents in the back seats of cars cause children.

1204.   Many complain of their memory, few of their judgment. -Benjamin Franklin

1205.   Genius is the gold in the mine; talent is the miner who works and brings it out.-Countess of Marguerite Gardiner Blessington

1206.   As the eagle was killed by the arrow winged with his own feather, so the hand of the world is wounded by its own skill. -Helen Keller

1207.   A camel is a horse designed by committee. -Sir Alec Issigonis

1208.   It is fatal to enter any war without the will to win it. -Douglas Macarthur

1209.   Everything I did in my life that was worthwhile I caught hell for. -Earl Warren

1210.   Self-respect is the cornerstone of all virtue. -John Herschel

1211.   A perfect guest is one who makes his host feel at home.

1212.   We don't know a millionth of one percent about anything. -Thomas Alva Edison

1213.   The pot calls the kettle black. -Miguel de Cervantes

1214.   Yesterday's failures are today's seeds that must be diligently planted to be able to abundantly harvest tomorrow's success. -Unknown

1215.   I hear and I forget. I see and I remember. I do and I understand. -Chinese Proverb

1216.   Physicists like to think that all you have to do is say these are the conditions now what happens next. -Richard Feynman

1217.   Sign on restaurant window: Great food (50,000 flies can't be wrong.)

1218.   Trust enables you to put your deepest feelings and fears in the palm of your partner's hand, knowing they will be handled with care.

1219.   The book is here to stay. What we're doing is symbolic of the peaceful coexistence of the book and the computer. -Vartan Gregorian

1220.   No beast is more savage than man when possessed with power answerable to his rage. -Plutarch

1221.   Let not thy will roar when thy power can but whisper. -Thomas Fuller

1222.   The reward of one duty is the power to fulfill another. -George Eliot

1223.   The secret of being a bore is to tell everything. -Voltaire

1224.   Nurture your mind with great thoughts, for you will never go any higher than you think. -Benjamin Disraeli

1225.   People who work sitting down get paid more than people who work standing up. -Ogden Nash

- Liberty, Liberty how many crimes are committed in thy name. -Jeanne-Marie Roland

1226.   Many an opportunity is lost because a man is out looking for four-leaf clovers. -Unknown

1227.   If you want truly to understand something, try to change it. -Kurt Lewin

1228.   If we have no peace, it is because we have forgotten that we belong to each other. -Mother Teresa

1229.   Time and health are two precious assets that we don't recognize and appreciate until they have been depleted. -Denis Waitley

1230.   Never have children, only grandchildren. -Gore Vidal

1231.   Setting an example is not the main means of influencing others; it is the only means. -Albert Einstein

1232.   When speaking to your children: say what you mean, mean what you say, but don't be mean when you say it.

1233.   The Laws of Manu Depend not on another but lean instead on thyself...True happiness is born of self-reliance.

1234.   The art of dining well is no slight art the pleasure not a slight pleasure. -Michel de Montaigne

1235.   Always be ready to speak your mind and a base man will avoid you. -William Blake

1236.   Every vice has its excuse ready. -Publilius Syrus

1237.   Accident n. A condition in which presence of mind is good but absence of body is better. -Unknown

1238.   Those who restrain desire do so because theirs is weak enough to be restrained. -William Blake

1239.   The history of every country begins in the heart of a man or woman. -Willa Cather

1240.   Although gold dust is precious, when it gets in your eyes it obstructs your vision. -Hsi-tang

1241.   In America, sex is an obsession in other parts of the world it is a fact. -Marlene Dietrich

1242.   A failure is a man who has blundered, but is not able to cash in on the experience. -Elbert Hubbard

1243.   Most of life is choices, and the rest is pure dumb luck. -Marian Erickson

1244.   Man becomes a slave to his constantly repeated acts. What he at first chooses, at last compels. -Orison Swett Marden

1245.   Take off the blinders. You have to see opportunity before you can seize it. -Greg Hickman

1246.   The miracle is not to fly in the air, or to walk on the water; but to walk on the earth. -Chinese Proverb

1247.   Do not wait for extraordinary circumstances to do good try to use ordinary situations. -Jean Paul Richter

1248.   Virtue does not come from wealth but wealth and every other good thing which men have comes from virtue. -Socrates

1249.   Use no hurtful deceit think innocently and justly and if you speak, speak accordingly. -Benjamin Franklin

1250.   We know what happens to people who stay in the middle of the road. They get run over. -Aneurin Bevan

1251.   Happy the people whose annals are blank in the history books. -Thomas Carlyle

1252.   Deeds, not stones, are the true monuments of the great. -John L. Motley

1253.   Nothing worthwhile comes easily. Work, continuous work and hard work, is the only way to accomplish results that last. -Hamilton Holt

1254.   Journal writing is a voyage to the interior. -Christina Baldwin

1255.   I am a man and whatever concerns humanity is of interest to me. -Terence

1256.   I love acting. It is so much more real than life. -Oscar Wilde

1257.   I have nothing to offer but blood toil tears and sweat. -Sir Winston Leonard Spenser Churchill

1258.   It is a denial of justice not to stretch out a helping hand to the fallen; that is the common right of humanity. -Seneca

1259.   When we learn all the answers, they change the questions.

1260. Most books now say our sun is a star. But it still knows how to change back into a sun in the daytime.

1261. Your brain is that bodily organ which starts working the moment you awake and does not stop until you get into the office.

1262. What the mind of man can conceive and believe it can achieve. - Napoleon Hill

1263. The only new thing in this world, is the history you did not know. -Harry Truman

1264. Every calling is great when greatly pursued. -Oliver Wendell Holmes

1265. War never decides who is right, only who is left.

1266. The more the fruits of knowledge become accessible to men the more widespread is the decline of religious belief. -Sigmund Freud

1267. Shoot for the moon. Even if you miss, you'll land among the stars. -Les Brown

1268. A true artist doesn't change with the times. A true artist is already way ahead of the times. -Eric Pio

1269. There is a demand in these days for men who can make wrong appear right. -Terence

1270. You can't do anything, if you believe you can't.

1271. I am a part of all that I have seen. -Lord Alfred Tennyson

1272. There's nothing like a Catholic wedding to make you wish life had a fast forward button. - Daniel Chopin

1273. Do you know what happens when you give a procrastinator a good idea? Nothing! -Donald Gardner

1274. This fairy tale we're living is real inside our hearts. -Atlantic Starr

1275. It takes a long time to grow an old friend. -John Leonard

1276. The irrationality of a thing is no argument against its existence rather a condition of it. -Friedrich Wilhelm Nietzsche

1277. A good deed never goes unpunished. -Gore Vidal

1278. Be courteous to all but intimate with few, and let those few be well tried before you give them your confidence. -George Washington

1279.   Women have no sympathy and my experience of women is almost as large as Europe. - Florence Nightingale

1280.   I have against me the bourgeois, the military, and the diplomats, and for me, only the people who take the Metro. -Charles De Gaulle

1281.   It is better to be defeated on principle than to win on lies. - Arthur Calwell

1282.   The stupid neither forgive nor forget; the naive forgive and forget; the wise forgive but do not forget. -Thomas Szasz

1283.   Afflicted by love's madness all are blind. -Sextus Propertius

1284.   We'd never know how high we are till we are called to rise; and then, if we are true to plan, our statures touch the sky. -Emily Dickinson

1285.   Listening is a form of accepting. -Stella Terrill Mann

1286.   Don't ask what your community can do for you. Ask what you can do for your community. -Steve Andres

1287.   Live so that when your children think of fairness and integrity, they think of you. -H. Jackson Brown, Jr.

1288.   If a church wants a better pastor, it can get one by praying for the one it has. -Rev. Robert E. Harris

1289.   True knowledge exists in knowing that you know nothing. And in knowing that you know nothing that makes you the smartest of all. -Socrates

1290.   One must be poor to know the luxury of giving. -George Eliot

1291.   You are not superior just because you see the world in an odious light. —François-René de Chateaubriand

1292.   Some people take more care to hide their wisdom than their folly. -Jonathan Swift

1293.   You can't wait for inspiration. You have to go after it with a club. -Jack London

1294.   Since light travels faster than sound, isn't that why some people appear bright until you hear them speak?

1295.   Treasure the love you receive above all. It will survive long after your gold and good health have vanished. -Og Mandingo

1296.   The manager administers; the leader innovates. -Warren Bennis

1297.   The time to stop talking is when the other person nods his head affirmatively but says nothing. -Anon

1298.   Success is never permanent, and failure is never final. -Mike Ditka

1299.   When ideas fail, words come in very handy. -Johann von Goethe

1300.   Whatever you do will be insignificant but it is very important that you do it. -Mahatma Gandhi

1301.   The more I know about men the more I like dogs. -Gloria Allred

1302.   No man is too big to be kind...but many men are too little. -Matt Maguire

1303.   That's the good part of dying - when you've nothing to lose you run any risk you want. -Ray Douglas Bradbury

1304.   Early to rise and early to bed makes a male healthy and wealthy and dead. -James Thurber

1305.   Veni vidi vici. (I came. I saw. I conquered.) -Gaius Julius Caesar

1306.   Even if I knew that tomorrow the world would go to pieces, I would still plant my apple tree. -Martin Luther, German Theologian

1307.   It is very strange that the years teach us patience - that the shorter our time the greater our capacity for waiting. -Elizabeth Taylor

1308.   The obstacles you face are... mental barriers which can be broken by adopting a more positive approach. -Clarence Blasier

1309.   Love until it hurts. Real love is always painful and hurts; then it is real and pure. -Mother Teresa

1310.   The miracle is this - the more we share the more we have. -Leonard Nimoy

1311.   Human history becomes more and more a race between education and catastrophe. -H. G. Wells

1312.   Seeing is believing, but the feeling is the truth. -Thomas Fuller

1313.   If you would convince a man that he does wrong do right. Men will believe what they see. -Henry David Thoreau

1314.   Long invested at interest for years will become at which time it will be worth absolutely nothing. -Lazarus

1315.   All of life's great lessons present themselves again and again until mastered. -David Ashley Brewer

1316.   Communism is like one big phone company. -Lenny Bruce

1317.   I can't think of any sorrow in the world that a hot bath wouldn't help just a little bit. -Susan Glasee

1318.   People who are often in a hurry imagine they are energetic, when in most cases they are simply inefficient. -Sydney J. Harris

1319.   If you want to make certain a job gets done give it to somebody who is really busy. They'll have their secretary do it. -Joe Moore

1320.   Life is not an exact science; it is an art. -Samuel Butler

1321.   My wife met me at the door the other night in a sexy negligee. Unfortunately, she was just coming home. -Rodney Dangerfield

1322.   Faithless is he that says farewell when the road darkens. -J. R. R. Tolkien

1323.   To have respect for ourselves guides our morals and to have a deference for others governs our manners. -Lawrence Sterne

1324.   Our destiny rules over us even when we are not yet aware of it, it is the future that makes laws for us today. -Friedrich Wilhelm Nietzsche

1325.   If you tell the truth you don't have to remember anything. -Mark Twain

1326.   The optimist sees the rose and not its thorns; the pessimist stares at the thorns, oblivious of the rose. -Kahlil Gibran

1327.   One's real life is often the life that one does not lead. -Oscar Wilde

1328.   Good habits result from resisting temptation. -Ancient Proverb

1329.   If Karl, instead of writing a lot about capital, had made a lot of it ... it would have been much better. -Karl Marx's Mother

1330.   At my age the bones are water in the morning until food is given them. -Pearl Buck

1331.   He who is filled with love is filled with God himself. -Saint Augustine

1332.   Anything worth doing is worth doing poorly until you learn to do it well. -Steve Brown

1333. In life, as in football, you won't go far unless you know where the goalposts are. -Arnold H. Glasgow

1334. No one can possibly know what is about to happen; it is happening each time for the first time for the only time. -James Arthur Baldwin

1335. The objective of false prophets and teachers of whatever stripe is...the influence and control of the minds of men. -Ron Dart

1336. There is no exercise better for the heart than reaching down and lifting people up. -John Andrew Holmes

1337. Millions must plough and forge and dig in order that a few thousand may write and paint and study. -Heinrich Gotthard von Treitschke

1338. Make decisions from the strong part of you, not the weak. -Dr. Laura Schlessinger

1339. Freedom is nothing else but a chance to be better. -Albert Camus

1340. As long as I'm faced in the right direction, it does not matter the size of my steps.-Unknown

1341. The great use of life is to spend it for something that will outlast it. -Williams James

1342. The miserable have no other medicine, but only hope. - Friedrich Wilhelm Nietzsche

1343. The good befriend themselves. -Sophocles

1344. Say what you know; do what you must come what may. –Sofia Kovalevskaya

1345. I'm not dumb enough to be a goalie. -Brad Hull

1346. If you give a man a fish he will have a single meal. If you teach him how to fish he will eat all his life. -Kwan-Tzu

1347. The world has forgotten in its concern with "left" and "right" that there is an "above" and "below." -Glen Drake

1348. Courage is the price that life exacts for granting peace. -Amelia Earhart

1349. Nothing builds self-esteem and self-confidence like accomplishment. -Thomas Carlyle

1350.　I believe that every right implies a responsibility; every opportunity, an obligation; every possession, a duty. -John D. Rockefeller Jr.

1351.　Throwing a fastball to Henry Aaron is like trying to sneak the sun past a rooster. -Curt Simmons

1352.　Now hatred is by far the longest pleasure; men love in haste, but they detest at leisure. -George Gordon Byron

1353.　If you don't ask "why this" often enough, somebody will ask why you. -Tom Hirshfield

1354.　To become aware of the possibility of the search is to be onto something. -Walker Percy

1355.　Better to bend than to break. -Indian proverb

1356.　All great achievements require time. -David J. Schwartz

1357.　Moments of kindness and reconciliation are worth having, even if the parting has to come sooner or later. -Alice Munro

1358.　Gambling: The sure way of getting nothing from something. -Wilson Mizner

1359.　It is simplicity that makes the uneducated more effective than the educated when addressing popular audiences. -Aristotle

1360.　He who fears being conquered is sure of defeat. -Napoleon

1361.　A scholar who cherishes the love of comfort is not fit to be deemed a scholar. - Lao-Tzu

1362.　A man is related to all nature. -Ralph Waldo Emerson

1363.　A guest sees more in an hour than the host in a year. -Polish Proverb

1364.　If an injury has to be done to a man it should be so severe that his vengeance need not be feared. -Niccolo Machiavelli

1365.　You can't make someone else's choices. You shouldn't let someone else make yours. -Colin Powell

1366.　A sweet thing for whatever time to revisit in dreams the dear dad we have lost. -Euripides

1367.　Don't get suckered in by the comments ... they can terribly be misleading. -Dave Storer

1368.　Love in its essence is spiritual fire. -Swedenborg

1369. It is not the literal past that rules us save possibly in a biological sense. It is images of the past. -George Steiner

1370. Don't worry about people stealing an idea. If it's original you will have to ram it down their throats. -Howard Aiken

1371. Anger dwells only in the bosom of fools. - John Dryden

1372. Worry often gives a small thing a big shadow. -Swedish proverb

1373. Due to financial difficulties the light at the end of the tunnel has temporarily been switched off.

1374. A merely fallen enemy may rise again but the reconciled one is truly vanquished. -Johann Christian Friedrich von Schiller

1375. If we don't control our money, it will control us.

1376. There is always some madness in love. But there is also always some reason in madness. -Friedrich Nietzsche

1377. I hope our wisdom will grow with our power, and teach us, that the less we use our power the greater it will be. -Thomas Jefferson

1378. Income tax returns are the most imaginative fiction being written today. -Herman Wouk

1379. I'm not a teacher, only a fellow-traveler of whom you asked the way. I pointed ahead-ahead of myself as well as you.-George Bernard Shaw

1380. He felt about books as doctors feel about medicines or managers about plays - cynical but hopeful. - Dame Rose Macaulay

1381. The great leaders are like the best conductors - they reach beyond the notes to reach the magic in the players. -Blaine Lee

1382. Beauty is desired in order that it may be befouled; not for its own sake, but for the joy brought by the certainty of profaning it. - Georges Bataille

1383. It is our attitude at the beginning of a difficult task which, more than anything else, will affect its successful outcome. -William James

1384. Why? Why Not? Why Not You? Why Not Now? -Aslan

1385. I don't necessarily agree with everything I say. -Marshall McLuhan

1386.   You may have a fresh start any moment you choose, for this thing we call failure is not the falling down, but the staying down. - Mary Pickford

1387.   Heat cannot be separated from fire or beauty from The Eternal.- Alighieri Dante

1388.   Even in the bleakest times, there are gifts to be discovered. - Jann Mitchell

1389.   Organized crime constitutes nothing less than a guerilla war against society. -Lyndon B. Johnson

1390.   The advantage of the emotions is that they lead us astray and the advantage of science is that it is not emotional. -Oscar Wilde

1391.   Anger opens the mouth and shuts the mind.

1392.   Speak the truth, but leave immediately after. -Slovenian Proverb

1393.   Just remember, when you should grab something, grab it; when you should let go, let go. -Tao Saying

1394.   I am a strong believer in luck and I find the harder I work the more I have of it. -Benjamin Franklin

1395.   The secret to success is to know something nobody else knows. -Aristotle Onassis

1396.   A child will not spill on a dirty floor.

1397.   In attempts to improve your character know what is in your power and what is beyond it. -Francis Thompson

1398.   When it is dark enough, you can see the stars. -Charles Austin Beard

1399.   The definition of a recession is when your neighbor loses his job. A depression is when you lose yours. -US President Truman

1400.   If one sticks too rigidly to one's principles one would hardly see anybody. -Agatha Christie

1401.   They envy the distinction I have won let them therefore envy my toils my honesty and the methods by which I gained it. -Sallust

1402.   Be bold, be bold, and everywhere be bold. -Herbert Spencer

1403.   Whoso neglects learning in his youth, loses the past and is dead for the future. -Euripides

1404.　No one can make you feel inferior without your consent. -Eleanor Roosevelt

1405.　We must never forget that art is not a form of propaganda it is a form of truth. -John F. Kennedy

1406.　Fortune can for her pleasure fools advance, and toss them on the wheels of Chance. -Juvenal

1407.　Smell is a potent wizard that transports you across thousands of miles and all the years you have lived. -Helen Keller

1408.　Don't let the negativity given to you by the world disempower you. Instead give to yourself that which empowers you. -Les Brown

1409.　Oh darling let your body in, let it tie you in in comfort. -Anne Sexton

1410.　Live like you can look any man in the eye and tell him to go to hell. -Unknown

1411.　Education is not a preparation for life; education is life itself. -John Dewey

1412.　To love deeply in one direction makes us more loving in all others. -Anne-Sophie Swetchine

1413.　At least half the mystery novels published violate the law that the solution once revealed must seem to be inevitable. -Raymond Chandler

1414.　Money is in some respects life's fire; it is a very excellent servant but a terrible master. -P. Barnum

1415.　Oh what a tangled web we weave / When first we practice to deceive. -Sir Walter Scott

1416.　Enjoy the journey, enjoy every moment, and quit worrying about winning and losing. -Matt Biondi

1417.　Even God cannot change the past. -Agathon

1418.　Well I thought my razor was dull until I heard his speech. -Julius Henry Marx

1419.　Silence is golden but shouting is fun.

1420.　Great work is done by people who are not afraid to be great. -Fernando Flores

1421.   When we are born we die; our end is but the pendant of our beginning. -Manilius

1422.   The optimist says, "My cup runneth over, what a blessing." The pessimist says, "My cup runneth over, what a mess."

1423.   Ideas attract money, time, talents, skills, energy and other complementary ideas that will bring them into reality. -Mark Victor Hansen

1424.   While thou livest keep a good tongue in thy head. -William Shakespeare

1425.   Politics are usually the executive expression of human immaturity. -Vera Brittain

1426.   A merry Christmas to everybody. A happy New Year to all the world. -Charles Dickens

1427.   Learning to love yourself is the greatest love of all. -Michael Masser

1428.   You don't become a missionary by crossing the sea but by seeing the cross.

1429.   Thinking is the hardest work there is, which is probably the reason so few engage in it. -Henry Ford

1430.   Don't be content with being average. Average is as close to the bottom as it is to the top. -Unknown Author

1431.   If I have lost confidence in myself, I have the universe against me. -Ralph Waldo Emerson

1432.   As long as I have a want I have a reason for living. Satisfaction is death. -George Bernard Shaw

1433.   Sex is the tabasco sauce which an adolescent national palate sprinkles on every course in the menu.-Mary Day Winn

1434.   One word frees us of all the weight and pain of life: that word is love. - Sting

1435.   Do not fear to step into the unknown, for where there is risk there is also reward. -Lori Hard

1436.   We learn the rope of life by untying its knots. -Jean Toomer

1437.   Although the last, not least. -William Shakespeare

1438.   There is no substitute for victory. -Douglas MacArthur

1439.   I don't like to commit myself about heaven and hell; you see, I have friends in both places. -Mark Twain

1440.   Conceal a flaw and the world will imagine the worst. -Marcus Valerius Martialis

1441.   Love is everything it's cracked up to be. It really is worth fighting for being brave for risking everything for. -Erica Jong

1442.   Nothing is more difficult, and therefore more precious, than to be able to decide. -Napoleon Bonaparte

1443.   Evil, when we are in its power, is not felt as evil, but as a necessity or even a duty. -Simone Weil

1444.   He that never changes his opinions never corrects his mistakes will never be wiser on the morrow than he is today. -Tryon Edwards

1445.   It is well to think well; it is divine to act well. -Horace Mann

1446.   Chance favors the prepared mind. -Louis Pasteur

1447.   Others may argue your beliefs, but they can't refuse your love.

1448.   The goal of education is to replace an empty mind with an open mind. -Malcolm Forbes

1449.   The simple act of paying positive attention to people has a great deal to do with productivity. -Thomas Peters

1450.   Life is a succession of lessons which must be lived to be understood. -Ralph Waldo Emerson

1451.   Do everything with so much love in your heart that you would never want to do it any other way. -Yogi Desai

1452.   Refusing to have an opinion is a way of having one.

1453.   Spare your breath to cool your porridge. -Miguel de Cervantes

1454.   To philosophize is nothing else than to prepare oneself for death. -Michel Eyquem de Montaigne

1455.   Es tan corto el amor y tan largo el olvido. (Love is so short and so long forgotten.) -Pablo Neruda

1456.   Shared joy is double joy. Shared sorrow is half sorrow. -Swedish Proverb

1457.   Man is a make-believe animal - he is never so truly himself as when he is acting a part. -William Hazlitt

1458.   Don't be afraid your life will end; be afraid that it will never begin. -Grace Hansen

1459.   A pessimist is one who makes difficulties of his opportunities and an optimist is one who makes opportunities of his difficulties. -Harry Truman

1460.   Loyalty to petrified opinion never yet broke a chain or freed a human soul. -Mark Twain

1461.   You don't have to cook fancy or complicated masterpieces - just good food from fresh ingredients. -Julia Child

1462.   There are 10 types of people in the country, those who understand binary and those who don't.

1463.   Fainthearted animals move about in herds. The lion walks alone in the desert. Let the poet always walk thus. -Alfred Victor Vigny

1464.   The Lottery is a tax on people who are bad at math.

1465.   The brighter you are the more you have to learn. -Don Herold

1466.   But O the truth, the truth! The many eyes that look on it! The diverse things they see! -George Meredith

1467.   Yesterday's the past, and tomorrow's the future. Today is a gift, which is why they call it the present. -Bill Keane

1468.   Wealth is not his that has it but his who enjoys it. -Benjamin Franklin

1469.   To receive everything one must open one's hands and give. -Taisen Deshimaru

1470.   We must not always judge of the generality of the opinion by the noise of the acclamation. -Edmund Burke

1471.   I loathe people who keep dogs. They are cowards who haven't got the guts to bite people themselves. -August Strindberg

1472.   My mother buried three husbands and two of them were just napping. -Rita Rudner

1473.   Nothing is impossible. Some things are just less likely than others. -Jonathan Winters

1474.   What sees a blind man when he's dreaming?

1475.   You can never plan the future by the past. -Edmund Burke

1476. The way to combat noxious ideas is with other ideas. The way to combat falsehoods is with truth. -William O. Douglas

1477. When people are like each other they tend to like each other. -Anthony Robbins

1478. He who has injured thee was stronger or weaker than thee. If weaker spare him; if stronger spare thyself. - Seneca

1479. The man who never alters his opinions is like standing water and breeds reptiles of the mind. -William Blake

1480. One has to be able to count if only so that at fifty one doesn't marry a girl of twenty. -Maxim Gorky

1481. Trust your hunches. They're usually based on facts filed away just below the conscious level. -Joyce

1482. There is no pain so great as the memory of joy in present grief. -Aeschylus

1483. Everybody knows if you are too careful you are so occupied in being careful that you are sure to stumble over something. -Gertrude Stein

1484. The people and circumstances around me do not make me what I am, they reveal who I am. -Dr. Laura Schlessinger

1485. Ask not what your country can do for you, ask what you can do for your country. -John Fitzgerald Kennedy

1486. Ingenuity, plus courage, plus work, equals miracles. -Bob Richards

1487. Every decent man is ashamed of the government he lives under. -H.L. Mencken

1488. The only thing you will take through those pearly gates is what you have given away. -Marcia Moore

1489. To decide to be at the level of choice is to take responsibility for your life and to be in control of your life. -Arbie M. Dale

1490. If you haven't forgiven yourself for something, how can you forgive others? -Dolores Huerta

1491. We are here on Earth to do good to others. What the others are here for I don't know. -W. H. Auden

1492. No families take so little medicine as those of doctors except those of apothecaries. -Oliver Wendell Holmes

1493. If I had eight hours to chop down a tree I'd spend six sharpening my axe. -Abraham Lincoln

1494. I think and think for months and years. Ninety-nine times the conclusion is false. The hundredth time I am right. -Albert Einstein

1495. If the world should blow itself up the last audible voice would be that of an expert saying it can't be done. -Peter Ustinov

1496. You are what you think. You are what you go for. You are what you do. -Bob Richards

1497. We have two ears and one mouth so that we can listen twice as much as we speak. -Epictetus

1498. When you recover or discover something that nourishes your soul and bring joy, care enough about yourself to make room for it in your life.

1499. Love is a canvas furnished by nature and embroidered by imagination. -Voltaire

1500. It is Christmas in the heart that puts Christmas in the air. -W. T. Ellis

1501. Unless men see a beauty and delight in the worship of God they will not do it willingly. -John Owen

1502. If you gaze long into an abyss the abyss will gaze back into you. -Friedrich Wilhelm Nietzsche

1503. Young people are in a condition like permanent intoxication because youth is sweet and they are growing. -Aristotle

1504. A true friend is the greatest of all blessings and that which we take the least care of all to acquire. -François de La Rochefoucauld

1505. Truth needs no flower of speech.

1506. The lawyer's truth is not Truth but consistency or a consistent expediency. -Henry David Thoreau

1507. Nothing got him angrier than when people implied he was paranoid. It made him feel persecuted. -Robert Sheckley

1508. I have heard of your paintings too well enough God has given you one face and you make yourselves another. -William Shakespeare

1509. How things look on the outside of us depends on how things are on the inside of us. -Parks Cousins

1510. A man's character is his fate. -Heraclitus

1511. Difficulties are meant to rouse, not discourage. The human spirit is to grow strong by conflict. -William Ellery Channing

1512. True success is overcoming the fear of being unsuccessful. -Paul Sweeney

1513. Plant a seed of friendship; reap a bouquet of happiness. -Lois L. Kaufman

1514. Winter nights were made for warm snuggles and warmer hearts. - Anonymous

1515. I have a problem about being nearly 60; I keep waking up in the morning and thinking I'm 31. -Elizabeth Janeway

1516. Advice is what you ask for when you already know the answer but wish you didn't. -Erica Jong

1517. If crime fighters fight crime and fire fighters fight fire, what do freedom fighters fight?

1518. Misery loves company but company does not reciprocate. - Addison Mizner

1519. Epigrams succeed where epics fail. -Persian Proverb

1520. Formal education will earn you a living self-education make you a fortune. -Unknown

1521. Some people grow under responsibility, others merely swell. - Hubbell

1522. Carve your name in hearts, not marble. - Ben Franklin

1523. Go and never darken my towels again. -Groucho Marx

1524. And when he is out of sight quickly also is he out of mind. - Thomas Kempis

1525. Death in itself is nothing, but we fear to be we know not what we know not where. -John Dryden

1526. We need no wings to go in search of Him, but have only to find a place where we can be alone. -St. Teresa of Avila

1527. The only limits are as always those of vision. -James Broughton

1528.	An artist is a dreamer consenting to dream of the actual world. - George Santayana

1529.	He, who has health, has hope; and he who has hope has everything. -Arabian Proverb

1530.	Happiness is not something you have in your hands; it is something you carry in your heart.

1531.	If I am not worth the wooing I am surely not worth the winning. -Henry Wadsworth Longfellow

1532.	Luck is a loser's excuse for a winner's position!

1533.	Nothing is impossible for the man who doesn't have to do it himself.- H. Weiler

1534.	Those who do not plan for the future have to live through it anyway.

1535.	Your goal should be out of reach but not out of sight. -Anita Defrantz

1536.	If you want your dreams to come true don't sleep. -Yiddish Proverb

1537.	A man of great common sense and good taste meaning thereby a man without originality or moral courage. -Sir Walter Besant

1538.	Laugh and the world laughs with you. Cry and the world laughs at you. -J. M. Linsner

1539.	If a man knows not what harbor he seeks any wind is the right wind. -Seneca

1540.	Business is a lot like a game of tennis — those who serve well usually end up winning - Anonymous

1541.	Keep your face towards the sunshine and the shadows will fall behind you. - Unknown

1542.	Love is blind; friendship closes its eyes. -Friedrich Wilhelm Nietzsche

1543.	But in this world nothing can be said to be certain except death and taxes. -Benjamin Franklin

1544.	Only your real friends will tell you when your face is dirty. - Sicilian Proverb

1545.   Although the world is full of suffering, it is also full of the overcoming of it. -Helen Keller

1546.   You learn to put your emotional luggage where it will do some good, instead of using it to shit on other people, or blow up aeroplanes.

1547.   All is in the hands of man. Therefore wash them often. - Stanislaw Lec

1548.   Life's most urgent question is: What are you doing for others? - Martin Luther King, Jr.

1549.   The path to cheerfulness is to sit cheerfully and to act and speak as if cheerfulness were already there. -William James

1550.   We've removed the ceiling above our dreams. There are no more impossible dreams. -Libby Houston

1551.   How sweet the name of Jesus sounds in a believer's ear. It soothes his sorrows, heals his wounds, and drives away his fears. - John Newton

1552.   Even though you know a thousand things, ask the man who knows one. - Turkish Proverb

1553.   I am open to receive with every breath I breathe. -Michael Sun

1554.   I never think of the future - it comes soon enough. -Albert Einstein

1555.   My life needs a rewind/erase button. -Bill Watterson

1556.   Are you lost, daddy I asked tenderly. Shut up, he explained. - Ring Lardner

1557.   When I die, I want to go peacefully like my grandfather did - in his sleep. Not screaming like the passengers in his car.

1558.   A wise man can see more from the bottom of a well than a fool can from a mountain top. -Unknown

1559.   As scarce as truth is the supply has always been in excess of the demand. -Josh Billings

1560.   The only thing worse than a man you can't control is a man you can. -Margo Kaufman

1561.   The heart that is to be filled to the brim with holy joy must be held still. -George Seaton Bowes

1562. The chimerical pursuit of perfection is always linked to some important deficiency; frequently, the inability to love. -Bernard Grasset

1563. Kind words can be short and easy to speak but their echoes are truly endless. -Mother Teresa

1564. Enter any -digit prime number to continue... -Anon.

1565. I don't think of all the misery, but of all the beauty that still remains. -Anne Frank

1566. Children require guidance and sympathy far more than instruction. -Ambrose Bierce

1567. If my survival caused another to perish then death would be sweeter and more beloved. -Kahlil Gibran

1568. Come out of the circle of time and into the circle of love. -Jalal ud-Din Rumi

1569. If God didn't forgive Heaven would be empty.

1570. There is nothing more requisite in business than dispatch. -Joseph Addison

1571. The wisdom of the wise and the experience of ages may be preserved by quotation. -Benjamin Disraeli

1572. Some goals are so worthy, it's glorious even to fail.

1573. When it is a question of God's almighty Spirit, never say, "I can't." - Oswald Chambers

1574. The crux... is that the vast majority of the mass of the universe seems to be missing. -William J. Broad

1575. What we have to learn to do we learn by doing. -Aristotle

1576. Look around the habitable world; how few know their own good or knowing it pursue. -John Dryden

1577. The superfluous is very necessary. - Voltaire

1578. A child must learn early to believe that she is somebody worthwhile, and that she can do many praiseworthy things. - Benjamin Mays

1579. Self-conceit may lead to self-destruction. -Aesop

1580. He is happiest be he king or peasant who finds peace in his home. -Johann von Goethe

1581. When you talk you repeat what you already know when you listen you often learn something. -Jared Sparks

1582. To forgive calls upon our love - to forget calls upon our strength.

1583. The great secret of power is never to will to do more than you can accomplish. -Henrik Ibsen

1584. Making enemies out of friends is easy. Making friends out of enemies is difficult, but it is actually worthwhile.

1585. Learn from yesterday live for today hope for tomorrow. -Anon.

1586. One that hath wine as a chain about his wits such a one lives no life at all. -Alcaeus

1587. In man the things which are not measurable are more important than those which are measurable. -Alexis Carrel

1588. No sane man will dance. -Marcus Tullius Cicero

1589. If it takes a lot of words to say what you have in mind, give it more thought. -Dennis Roch

1590. The true miracle is not walking on water or walking in air but simply walking on this earth. -Thich Nhat Hanh

1591. You can build a throne with bayonets but you can't sit on it for long. -Boris Nikolayevich Yeltsin

1592. In music the passions enjoy themselves. -Friedrich Wilhelm Nietzsche

1593. One must learn by doing the thing. For though you think you know it, you have no certainty until you try. -Sophocles

1594. Better to light a candle than to curse the darkness. -Chinese Proverb

1595. If you can solve your problem, then what is the need of worrying? If you cannot solve it, then what is the use of worrying? - Shantideva

1596. Hear me my chiefs, I am tired. My heart is sick and sad. From where the sun now stands I will fight no more forever. -Chief Joseph

1597. Great indeed is the sublimity of the Creative to which all beings owe their beginning and which permeates all heaven. -I Ching

1598.   Man needs, for his happiness, not only the enjoyment of this or that, but hope and enterprise and change. -Bertrand Russell

1599.   Parenting is a negative thing. Keep your children from killing themselves or anyone else and hope for the best. -Erma Bombeck

1600.   Business was his aversion; Pleasure was his business. - Maria Edgeworth

1601.   If it's meant to be, it's up to me. -Terri Gulick

1602.   Keep thy eyes wide open before marriage and half-shut afterwards. -Benjamin Franklin

1603.   You can observe a lot just by watching. -Lawrence Peter Berra

1604.   The wages of sin are death, but by the time taxes are taken out, it's just sort of a tired feeling. -Paula Poundstone

1605.   Writing is easy. All you do is stare at a blank sheet of paper until drops of blood form on your forehead. -Gene Fowler

1606.   If you don't want to work you have to work to earn enough money so that you won't have to work. -Ogden Nash

1607.   Oh too convincing - dangerously dear - In woman's eye the unanswerable tear.

1608.   A man who dares to waste one hour of time has not discovered the value of life. -Charles Robert Darwin

1609.   This business will never hold water. - Colley Cibber

1610.   History is a vast early warning system. -Norman Cousins

1611.   All life is an experiment. -Ralph Waldo Emerson

1612.   Speak to me as to thy thinkings as thou dost ruminate and give thy worst of thoughts the worst of words. -William Shakespeare

1613.   Oh come on. If you can't laugh at the walking dead who can you laugh at? -Dan Fielding

1614.   But every thyng which schyneth as the gold, Nis nat gold, as that I have herd it told. - Geoffrey Chaucer

1615.   To be feared is to fear no one has been able to strike terror into others and at the same time enjoy peace of mind. -Seneca

1616.   There are truths which are not for all men nor for all times. - Francois Marie Arouet Voltaire

1617. The greatest things are accomplished by individual people, not by committees or companies. -Alfred A. Montapert

1618. One's destination is never a place but rather a new way of looking at things. -Henry Miller

1619. Ideas are funny little things, they won't work unless you do.

1620. Suicidal glory is the luxury of the irresponsible. We're not giving up. We're waiting for a better opportunity to win. -Lois McMaster Bujold

1621. Computers make very fast, very accurate mistakes.

1622. Law stands mute in the midst of arms. -Cicero

1623. To feel valued to know even if only once in a while that you can do a job well is an absolutely marvelous feeling. -Barbara Walters

1624. I believe that people would be alive today if there were a death penalty. -Nancy Reagan

1625. When we die we leave behind us all that we have and take with us all that we are.

1626. Chance corrects us of many faults that reason would not know how to correct. -François de La Rochefoucauld

1627. I wash my hands of those who imagine chattering to be knowledge, silence to be ignorance, and affection to be art. -Kahlil Gibran

1628. A small rock holds back a great wave. -Homer

1629. Television has done much for psychiatry by spreading information about it as well as contributing to the need for it. -Alfred Hitchcock

1630. There is only one good knowledge and one evil ignorance. - Socrates

1631. Why call it a building if it's already been built?

1632. I didn't attend the funeral but I sent a nice letter saying that I approved of it. -Mark Twain

1633. The man least dependent upon the morrow goes to meet the morrow most cheerfully.-Epicurus

1634. Crimes of which a people is ashamed constitute its real history. The same is true of man. -Jean Genet

1635.   Those who love deeply never grow old. - Anonymous

1636.   Man plans and God laughs. -Hebrew Proverb

1637.   Always leave loved ones with loving words, it may be the last time you see them.

1638.   The beginning is always today. -Mary Wollstonecraft Shelley

1639.   Talk of nothing but business and dispatch that business quickly. -Aldus Manutius

1640.   There are more pleasant things to do than beat up people. - Muhammad Ali

1641.   The only true happiness comes from squandering ourselves for a purpose. -William Cowper

1642.   Why is lemonade made with artificial flavoring, while dishwasher soap is made with real lemons?

1643.   It takes less time to do things right than to explain why you did it wrong. -Henry Wadsworth Longfellow

1644.   Think like a wise man but communicate in the language of the people. -William Butler Yeats

1645.   A meeting is an event at which the minutes are kept and the hours are lost.

1646.   By failing to prepare, you are preparing to fail. -Benjamin Franklin

1647.   What you give you get ten times over. -Yoruba Proverb

1648.   If we have the opportunity to be generous with our hearts ourselves, we have no idea of the depth and breadth of love's reach. - Margaret Cho

1649.   A seafood diet is the best: whenever you see food, eat it.

1650.   If you should put even a little on a little and should do this often, soon this would become big. -Hesiod

1651.   We learn simply by the exposure of living and what we learn most natively is the tradition in which we live. -David P Gardner

1652.   The cure for boredom is curiosity. There is no cure for curiosity. -Ellen Parr

1653.   How you think when you lose determines how long it will be until you win. -G.K. Chesterton

1654. An ounce of prevention is worth a pound of cure. -Henry de Bracton

1655. Character is not made in a crisis - it is only exhibited. - Robert Freeman

1656. It is much easier to try one's hand at many things than to concentrate one's powers on one thing. -Quintilian

1657. The future belongs to those who believe in the beauty of their dreams. -Eleanor Roosevelt

1658. A giving church is a living church.

1659. They consider me to have sharp and penetrating vision because I see them through the mesh of a sieve. -Kahlil Gibran

1660. An actor's a guy who if you ain't talking about him ain't listening. -Marlon Brando

1661. When I was born I was so surprised I didn't talk for a year and a half. -Gracie Allen

1662. You can plant a dream. -Anne Campbell

1663. Death is not the worst than can happen to men. -Plato

1664. Worry is simply an unhealthy and destructive mental habit. - Norman Vincent Peale

1665. There is a fullness of all things even of sleep and love. -Homer

1666. All the flowers of all the tomorrows are in the seeds of today and yesterday.

1667. Hot heads and cold hearts never solved anything. -Billy Graham

1668. To be successful the first thing to do is to fall in love with your work. -Sister Mary Lauretta

1669. I know all except myself. -Francois Villon

1670. Be free all worthy spirits, and stretch yourselves, for greatness and for height. -George Chapman

1671. Everyone who receives the protection of society owes a return for the benefit. -John Stuart Mill

1672. Religion is what keeps the poor man from murdering the rich. - Napoleon Bonaparte

1673. The absence of alternatives clears the mind marvelously. -Henry Kissinger

1674. The Congress is a strange place where people get up and speak, nobody listens, and then everyone disagrees at the top of their lungs.

1675. If at first you don't succeed failure may be your style. -Quentin Crisp

1676. Time discovers truth.-Seneca

1677. Effort only fully releases its reward after a person refuses to quit. -Napoleon Hill

1678. It is better to be hated for what you are than loved for what you are not. -Andre Gide

1679. Man's most valuable trait is a judicious sense of what not to believe. -Euripides

1680. People would enjoy life more if, once they got what they wanted, they could remember how much they wanted it.

1681. Any simple problem can be made insoluble if enough meetings are held to discuss it. -Mitchell's Law of Committees

1682. The Universe may be as great as they say. But it wouldn't be missed if it didn't exist. -Piet Hein

1683. What doesn't kill us makes us stronger -Friedrich Nietzsche

1684. As blushing will sometimes make a whore pass for a virtuous woman so modesty may make a fool seem a man of sense. -Jonathan Swift

1685. Knock: Please don't ring bell. -Sign at the Pavlov Institute:

1686. Advice is like snow; the softer it falls the longer it dwells upon, and the deeper it sinks into the mind. - Samuel Taylor Coleridge

1687. General Failures Fault. Not Yours. -Anon.

1688. A vacuum is a hell of a lot better than some of the stuff that nature replaces it with. -Tennessee Williams

1689. It is fast approaching the point where I don't want to elect anyone stupid enough to want the job. -Erma Bombeck

1690. Earn as much as you can. Save as much as you can. Invest as much as you can. Give as much as you can."—John Wesley

1691. Someone's boring me. I think it's me. -Dylan Thomas

1692. To waken interest and kindle enthusiasm is the sure way to teach easily and successfully. -Tryon Edwards

1693. It is better to ask some of the questions than to know all the answers. -James Grover Thurber

1694. Only sick music makes money today. -Friedrich Nietzsche

1695. Maturity is only a short break in adolescence. -Jules Feiffer

1696. He who kneels the most stands best. -D.L. Moody

1697. A true friend walks in when the world walks out.

1698. Sooner or later everyone sits down to a banquet of consequences. -Robert Louis Stephenson

1699. In politics, it is necessary either to betray one's country of the electorate. I prefer to betray the electorate. -Charles De Gaulle

1700. Three o'clock is always too late or too early for anything you want to do. -Jean-Paul Sartre

1701. You are making progress if each mistake is a new one.

1702. Unless you try to do something beyond what you have already mastered, you will never grow. -Ronald E. Osborn

1703. Why do they have ear piercing while you wait? Is there some shop where you can drop them off and pick them up later?

1704. Women want mediocre men, and men are working hard to become as mediocre as possible. -Margaret Mead

1705. The medium is the message. -Marshall McLuhan

1706. Drive carefully! Remember, it's not only a car that can be recalled by its maker.

1707. It is possible to store the mind with a million facts and still be entirely uneducated. -Alec Bourne

1708. Give me the luxuries of life and I will willingly do without the necessities. -Frank Lloyd Wright

1709. Common sense in an uncommon degree and is what the world calls wisdom. -Samuel Taylor Coleridge

1710. He that is down can fall no lower. -Samuel Butler

1711. Play is the exultation of the possible. -Martin Buber

1712. Walter Lippmann Love endures only when the lovers love many things together and not merely each other.

1713. Fail your way to the top. -Jeff Olsen

1714.   I have only one superstition. I touch all the bases when I hit a homerun. -Babe Ruth

1715.   There are many things worth living for, there are a few things worth dying for, but there is nothing worth killing for. -Tom Robbins

1716.   There are two things that are hard to hit and see, that's a spooky ghost and Muhammed Ali. -Muhammed Ali

1717.   A politician is a person who can make waves and then make you think they are the only one who can save the ship.

1718.   The soul without imagination is what an observatory would be without a telescope. -Henry Ward Beecher

1719.   In every friend we lose a part of ourselves and the best part. -Alexander Pope

1720.   Don't fall before you're pushed. -English Proverb

1721.   The Mets have gotten their leadoff batter on only once this inning. -Ralph Kiner

1722.   Horse sense is the thing a horse has which keeps it from betting on people. -W. C. Fields

1723.   Man can learn nothing unless he proceeds from the known to the unknown. -Claude Bernard

1724.   It is surprising what a man can do when he has to, and how little most men will do when they don't have to. -Walter Linn

1725.   You can clutch the past so tightly to your chest that it leaves your arms too full to embrace the present. -Jan Glidwell

1726.   To travel hopefully is a better thing than to arrive and the true success is to labor. -Robert Louis Stevenson

1727.   Censor a self-appointed snoop hound who sticks his nose in other people's business. -Bennett Alfred Cerf

1728.   To be able to be caught up into the world of thought - that is being educated.-Edith Hamilton

1729.   Life must be understood backward. But it must be lived forward. -Soren Kierkegaard

1730.   Fear defeats more people than any other one thing in the world. -Ralph Waldo Emerson

1731. Be careful what you set your heart upon - for it will surely be yours. -James Arthur Baldwin

1732. Hating hate does not mean you love love.--Unknown

1733. Ability is of little account without opportunity. -Napoleon Bonaparte

1734. The South Wind has for the evening donned jasmine scent. -Saiom Shriver

1735. Darkness is only driven out with light, not more darkness. -Martin Luther King Jr.

1736. The best way to beat your enemy is to beat him at politeness.

1737. Things may come to those who wait, but only things left by those who hustle. -Abraham Lincoln

1738. Mire Hacia Las Estrellas. Look At The Stars. -Raul E. Sanchez

1739. The imagination is never governed, it is always the ruling and divine power. -John Ruskin

1740. Pet owner: Every time a bell rings my dog goes and sits in the corner. Veterinarian: That's perfectly normal; he's a boxer.

1741. Music is the vernacular of the human soul. -Geoffrey Latham

1742. Do not regret growing older. It's a privilege denied to many. -Unknown

1743. Real meaningful endeavors, the biggies in human existence, often require the sacrifice of others.—Diane Frolov

1744. To one extent if you've seen one city slum you've seen them all. -Spiro Agnew

1745. Happiness is nothing more than good health and a bad memory. -Albert Schweitzer

1746. Oxymoron: Microsoft Works.

1747. Being powerful is like being a lady. If you have to tell people you are - you aren't. -Margaret Thatcher

1748. In all pleasures hope is a considerable part. -Samuel Johnson

1749. Failure is opportunity in disguise.

1750. Fear not that thy life shall come to an end but rather fear that it shall never have a beginning. -John Henry Cardinal Newman

1751.   Man "If I could see you naked, I'd die happy." Woman "Yeah, but if I saw you naked, I'd probably die laughing."

1752.   The longer I live the more beautiful life becomes. -Frank Lloyd Wright

1753.   I find my familiarity with thee has bred contempt. -Miguel de Cervantes

1754.   A bird does not sing because it has an answer. It sings because it has a song. -Chinese Proverb

1755.   Some books are to be tasted, others swallowed, and some few to be chewed and digested. -Francis Bacon

1756.   If you are going to walk on thin ice, you might as well dance. -Unknown Author

1757.   To lose one parent, Mr. Worthing, may be regarded as a misfortune. To lose both looks like carelessness. -Oscar Wilde

1758.   The mark of a good leader is to know when it's time to follow. -Susie Switzer

1759.   No person is your friend who demands your silence or denies your right to grow. -Alice Walker

1760.   The indispensable first step to getting the things you want out of life is this: decide what you want. -Ben Stein

1761.   Studies serve for delight, for ornaments, and for ability. -Francis Bacon

1762.   Kindness and honesty can only be expected from the strong. -Unknown

1763.   Statistician: A man who believes figures don't lie but admits that under analysis some of them won't stand up either. -Evan Esar

1764.   To reform a man, you must begin with his grandmother. -Victor Hugo

1765.   If you want something said, ask a man; if you want something done, ask a woman. -Margaret Hilda Thatcher

1766.   Teenagers express their burning desires to be different by dressing exactly alike.

1767.   Don't talk unless you can improve the silence. -Jorge Luis Borges

1768.   When she stopped conforming to the conventional picture of femininity she finally began to enjoy being a woman. -Betty Naomi Friedan

1769.   Some problems are so complex that you have to be highly intelligent and well informed just to be undecided about them. - Laurence J. Peter

1770.   Only two classes of books are of universal appeal. The very best and the very worst. -Ford Maddox

1771.   He who has a why to live for can bear almost any how. - Friedrich Nietzsche

1772.   Your imagination, my dear fellow, is worth more than you imagine. -Louis Aragon

1773.   Love one another and you will be happy. It's as simple and as difficult as that. -Michael Leuning

1774.   "Whom are you?" he asked, for he had attended business college.—George Ade

1775.   It's not your salary that makes you rich, it's your spending habits. - Charles A. Jaffe

1776.   Life is consciousness. -Emmet Fox

1777.   The secret of happiness is something to do. -John Burroughs

1778.   Honesty is the cornerstone of all success, without which confidence and ability to perform shall cease to exist. -Mary Kay Ash

1779.   A person must stand very tall to see their own fate. -Danish Proverb

1780.   Duty over desire - may that inspire.

1781.   Knowledge is like money the more he gets the more he craves. - Josh Billings

1782.   To harken to evil conversation is the road to wickedness... - Anonymous

1783.   I see God in every human being. -Mother Theresa

1784.   He who is plenteously provided for from within, needs but little from without. -Johann Wolfgang Von Goethe

1785.   Power works best in the hands of those who don't want it.

1786.   Enjoy the little things, for one day you may look back and realize they were the big things. -Robert Brault

1787.   Nothing is particularly hard if you divide it into small jobs. -Henry Ford

1788.   God heals and the doctor takes the fees. -Benjamin Franklin

1789.   Experience is not what happens to you; it's what you do with what happens to you. -Aldous Huxley

1790.   Happiness is that state of consciousness which proceeds from the achievement of one's values. -Ayn Rand

1791.   It is better to be 5 minutes late than dead for 5 minutes. -John Leighton

1792.   Don't you wish there were a knob on the TV to turn up the intelligence? There's one marked "brightness," but it doesn't work. -Gallagher

1793.   If you are out to describe the truth leave elegance to the tailor. -Albert Einstein

1794.   I've often wondered how some people in positions of this kind ... manage without having had any acting experience. -Ronald Reagan

1795.   Time is like money: you can either spend, waste, or invest!

1796.   Teachers open the door, but you must enter by yourself. -Chinese proverb

1797.   If you can't control the wind, adjust your sail.

1798.   Do no dishonor to the earth lest you dishonor the spirit of man. -Henry Beston

1799.   Human salvation lies in the hands of the creatively maladjusted. -Martin Luther King Jr.

1800.   Challenges are what make life interesting overcoming them is what makes life meaningful. -Joshua J. Marine

1801.   We cannot command nature except by obeying her. -Francis Bacon

1802.   The universe is full of magical things, patiently waiting for our wits to grow sharper. -Eden Phillpotts

1803.   I'm a controversial figure. My friends either dislike me or hate me. -Toni Morrison

1804.	Nothing can cause turmoil and the defeat of accomplishment as quickly as disorganization. -Unknown

1805.	Defining consultancy is a bit like defining the upper class; every possible candidate draws the line just below himself. -John Peet

1806.	We grow great by dreams. All big men are dreamers. -Woodrow T. Wilson

1807.	Tis our true policy to steer clear of permanent alliances with any portion of the foreign world. -George Washington

1808.	In faith there is enough light for those who want to believe and enough shadows to blind those who don't. -Blaise Pascal

1809.	There is no security on this earth, there is only opportunity. -General Douglas Macarthur

1810.	You always pass failure on the way to success. -Mickey Rooney

1811.	Desultory reading is delightful but to be beneficial our reading must be carefully directed. -Seneca

1812.	Child Age: I've learned that when I wave to people in the country they stop what they are doing and wave back.

1813.	A good friend can shield you from the storm. -Rhea Olsen

1814.	Do not fear to be eccentric in opinion for every opinion now accepted was once eccentric. -Bertrand Russell

1815.	Well I wouldn't say I was in the great class but I had a great time while I was trying to be great. -Harry S. Truman

1816.	Anger manages everything badly. - Statius

1817.	The path of precept is long that of example short and effectual. -Seneca

1818.	Who gossips to you will gossip of you. -Turkish proverb

1819.	You can always get the truth from a politician after he has turned seventy or given up all hope of the Presidency. -Joe Moore

1820.	Many receive advice, only the wise profit from it. -Syrus

1821.	A man's life consisteth not in the abundance of the things which he possesseth. [Luke 12:15]. - Bible

1822.	Fortune and love befriend the bold. -Ovid

1823.	We confide in our strength without boasting of it we respect that of others without fearing it. -Thomas Jefferson

1824. If you would persuade you must appeal to interest rather than intellect. -Benjamin Franklin

1825. As iron sharpens iron so a man sharpens the countenance of his friend. -Proverbs Bible

1826. Come for the House of Hope is built on sand bring wine for the fabric of life is as weak as the wind. -Wilfred Wilson Gibson

1827. He who wishes to be rich in a day will be hanged in a year. -Leonardo Da Vinci

1828. A good conscience is a soft pillow.

1829. This one step - choosing a goal and sticking to it - changes everything. -Scott Reed

1830. Most turkeys taste better the day after. My mother's tasted better the day before. -Rita Rudner

1831. Those who flee temptation generally leave a forwarding address. -Lane Olinghouse

1832. Don't judge each day by the harvest you reap but by the seeds that you plant. -Robert Louis Stevenson

1833. If you suspect a man don't employ him, and if you employ him don't suspect him. -Chinese Proverb

1834. Experience is the worst teacher it gives the test before presenting the lesson. -Vernon Law

1835. My masculinity isn't hinged on whether or not I knit. -Robin Green

1836. The man who reads nothing at all is better educated than the man who reads nothing but newspapers. -Thomas Jefferson

1837. Even if happiness forgets you a little bit never completely forget about it. -Donald Robert Perry Marquis

1838. The NeXT Computer The hardware makes it a PC the software makes it a workstation the unit sales makes it a mainframe. -Anon.

1839. Patriotism is often an arbitrary veneration of real estate above principles. -George Jean Nathan

1840. There are no office hours for leaders. -Cardinal J. Gibbons

1841. Mastering others is strength. Mastering yourself is true power. -Tao Te Ching

1842. Married couples tell each other a thousand things without speech. -Chinese Proverb

1843. Do as most do and men will speak well of you. -Thomas Fuller

1844. Blade: There are worse things out tonight than vampires. Dr. Karen Jenson: Like what? Blade: Like me. -Blade

1845. The dynamics of capitalism is postponement of enjoyment to the constantly postponed future. -Norman O. Brown

1846. Noble Hope is nature's veil for hiding truth's nakedness. -Alfred Bernhard

1847. Logic is in the eye of the logician. -Gloria Steinem

1848. Gardens and flowers have a way of bringing people together drawing them from their homes. -Clare Ansberry

1849. Leadership is a combination of strategy and character. If you must be without one, be without the strategy. -Gen. H. Norman Schwarzkopf

1850. Invite the man that loves thee to a feast but let alone thine enemy. -Hesiod

1851. Liberty is one of the most valuable blessings that Heaven has bestowed upon mankind. -Miguel de Cervantes

1852. When you give a man a dole you deny him his dignity, and when you deny him his dignity you rob him his destiny. -Zig Ziglar

1853. If you stay in Beverly Hills too long you become a Mercedes. -Robert Redford

1854. He who can suppress a moment's anger may prevent a day of sorrow. -Tryon Edwards

1855. Cyberspace: A consensual hallucination experienced daily by billions of legitimate operators in every nation. -William Gibson

1856. I am a part of all that I have seen. -Alfred Lord Tennyson

1857. The price of liberty is eternal vigilance. -Thomas Jefferson

1858. Rules without relationship equals rebellion.

1859. Nearly all men can stand adversity, but if you want to test a man's character, give him power. -Abraham Lincoln

1860. When you put somebody down, you have to be down there to hold him down. You could soar high otherwise.

1861. I prefer to be a dreamer among the humblest with visions to be realized than lord among those without dreams and desires. -Kahlil Gibran

1862. I was going to waste, but Jesus recycled me.

1863. The great aim of education is not knowledge but action.-Herbert Spencer

1864. Peace visits not the guilty mind. -Juvenal

1865. Maps encourage boldness. They're like cryptic love letters. They make anything seem possible. -Mark Jenkins

1866. What lies behind us and what lies before us are tiny matters compared to what lies within us. -Oliver Wendell Holmes

1867. Businesses planned for service are apt to succeed businesses planned for profit are apt to fail. -Nicholas Murray Butler

1868. By learning to obey, you will know how to command. -Italian Proverb

1869. Never look a gift horse in the mouth. -Saint Jerome

1870. I have always depended on the kindness of strangers. -Tennessee Williams

1871. Don't learn the tricks of the trade, learn the trade.

1872. Earth's the right place for love. I don't know where it's likely to go better. -Robert Frost

1873. What's money? A man is a success if he gets up in the morning and goes to bed at night and in between does what he wants to do. -Bob Dylan

1874. The universe is made of stories not atoms. -Muriel Rukeyser

1875. A good plan today is better than a perfect plan tomorrow. -George S. Patton

1876. Swine fever. Click here for the latest, and no doubt we will sell you something.-Unknown

1877. Reference Manual: Object that raises the monitor to eye level. Also used to compensate for that short table leg.

1878. It is better to be feared than loved if you cannot be both. -Niccolo Machiavelli

1879.   No facts are to me sacred, none are profane, I simply experiment an endless seeker with no Past at my back. -Ralph Waldo Emerson

1880.   The secret to managing is to keep the guys who hate you away from the guys who are undecided. -Casey Stengel

1881.   What people say you cannot do you try and find that you can. -Henry David Thoreau

1882.   A wise man gets more use from his enemies than a fool from his friends. -Baltasar Gracian

1883.   The idle mind knows not what it wants. -Ennius

1884.   Tis not love's going hurts my days, but that it went in little ways. —Edna St. Vincent Millay

1885.   No one is responsible for all the things that happen to him, but he is responsible for the way he acts when they do happen.

1886.   Look alive. Here comes a buzzard. - Lady Stella Reading

1887.   Our bodies communicate to us clearly and specifically if we are willing to listen to them. -Shakti Gawain

1888.   Any American who is prepared to run for president should automatically by definition be disqualified from ever doing so. -Gore Vidal

1889.   I learned that if you want to make it bad enough, no matter how bad it is, you can make it. -Gale Sayers

1890.   Pursue some path, however narrow and crooked, in which you can walk with love and reverence. -Henry David Thoreau

1891.   Anarchy is not chaos, but order without control. -David Layson

1892.   It's a Sicilian message. It means Luca Brasi sleeps with the fishes. -The Godfather, The Tessio

1893.   A man's word and his intestinal fortitude are two of the most honorable virtues known to mankind. -Jim Nantz

1894.   There are some things so serious you have to laugh at them. -Niels Henrik David Bohr

1895.   As large as life, and twice as natural. - Lewis Carroll (pseudonym of Rev. Charles L. Dodgson)

1896.   The defining function of the artist is to cherish consciousness. -Max Eastman

1897.   He who cannot forgive breaks the bridge over which he himself must pass. -George Herbert

1898.   The historian is a prophet in reverse. -Friedrich von Schlegel

1899.   Never Never Never Say NEVER. -Gary Thadani

1900.   Leave no stone unturned. -Euripides

1901.   We have the power to do any damn fool thing we want to do and we seem to do it about every 10 minutes. -William Fullbright

1902.   A journey of a thousand miles must begin with a single step. -Lao Tzu

1903.   Children are a poor man's wealth. -Danish proverb

1904.   Life is like a dogsled team. If you ain't the lead dog, the scenery never changes.-Lewis Grizzard

1905.   Opportunity may knock only once, but temptation leans on the doorbell. -Anonymous

1906.   A hypocrite is a person who - but who isn't? -Don Marquis

1907.   I wonder how much deeper the ocean would be without sponges?

1908.   Ambition is like love, impatient both of delays and rivals. -Sir John Denham

1909.   In order to be irreplaceable, one must always be different. -Coco Chanel

1910.   Our intention creates our reality. -Wayne Dyer

1911.   As the kindled fire consumes the fuel so in the flame of wisdom the embers of action are burnt to ashes. -Bhagavad Gita

1912.   The art of mothering is to teach the art of living to children. -Elain Heffner

1913.   Do not wrong or hate your neighbor for it is not he that you wrong but yourself. -American Indian Proverb

1914.   Equal opportunity means everyone will have a fair chance at being incompetent. -Laurence J. Peter

1915.   Fortune does not change men it unmasks them. -Suzanne Necker

1916.   What is the difference between a happy husband and a jilted lover? One kisses his missus, and, the other misses the kisses.

1917. Cultivate money and you grow rich. Cultivate mind and you raise culture.

1918. Facts in books, statistics in encyclopedias, the ability to use them in men's heads. - Fogg Brackell

1919. When I stopped seeing my mother with the eyes of a child, I saw the woman who helped me give birth to myself. -Nancy Friday

1920. Efficiency is intelligent laziness. -David Dunham

1921. Time sneaks up on you like a windshield on a bug. -Jon Lithgow

1922. Helps Wise sayings often fall on barren ground but a kind word is never thrown away. -Sir Arthur

1923. Education is when you read the fine print. Experience is what you get if you don't. -Pete Seeger

1924. A liar should have a good memory. -Quintilian

1925. Avoid having your ego so close to your position that when your position falls your ego goes with it. -Colin Powell

1926. Information is the currency of democracy. -Thomas Jefferson

1927. Love is friendship set on fire. -Jeremy Taylor

1928. I saw a girl wearing a sweatshirt with "Guess" on it. I said, "Thyroid problem?"

1929. Do just once what others say you can't do and you will never pay attention to their limitations again. -James R. Cook

1930. Now I know what love is. -Virgil Lat

1931. I had rather be right than be President. -Henry Clay

1932. Whatever it is, I fear Greeks, even when they bring gifts. -Virgil

1933. Where there is no vision the people perish. -Proverbs Bible

1934. He who shall introduce into public affairs the principles of primitive Christianity will change the face of the world. -Benjamin Franklin

1935. Possession is eleven points in the law. -Colley Cibber

1936. Concentration comes out of a combination of confidence and hunger. -Arnold Palmer

1937. I don't give a damn for a man that can only spell a word one way. -Mark Twain

1938.   The task of the educator lies in seeing that the child does not confound good with immobility and evil with activity. -Maria Montessori

1939.   It is hard to understand how a cemetery raised its burial charges and blamed it on the cost of living.

1940.   No matter where you go or what you do, you live your entire life within the confines of your head. -Terry Josephson

1941.   Children have to be educated but they have also to be left to educate themselves. -Ernest Dimnet

1942.   If a man is proud of his wealth, he should not be praised until it is known how he employs it. - Socrates

1943.   Neither irony or sarcasm is argument. - Rufus Choate

1944.   When the going still gets tough, the tough, pray.

1945.   The barb in the arrow of childhood suffering is this-- it's intense loneliness; it's intense ignorance. -Akhenaton

1946.   Computer programmers do it byte by byte.

1947.   You can live a lifetime and at the end of it know more about other people than you know about yourself. -Beryl Markham

1948.   Looking back, I have this to regret, that too often when I loved, I did not say so. - David Grayson

1949.   Some open minds should be closed for repairs.

1950.   If a small thing has the power to make you angry, does that not indicate something about your size? - Sydney J. Harris

1951.   Life itself can't give you joy, unless you really will it. Life just gives you time and space, it's up to you to fill it. -Anonymous

1952.   Feeling passionate about something is like getting a peek at your soul smiling back at you. -Amanda Medinger

1953.   I went to a store and asked if they had anything to put under coasters. -Steven Wright

1954.   A smile is a fortune, but you can't sell it, you can't buy it and you can't steal it, but it isn't good to anyone until it is given away.

1955.   Patience and perseverance have a magical effect before which difficulties disappear and obstacles vanish. -John Quincy Adams

1956.   He altered the image of the Jew from that of rabbi, merchant, wanderer, to that of scientist, farmer, and soldier. -Shimon Peres

1957.   The secret of happiness is to make others believe they are the cause of it. -Al Batt

1958.   There is nothing worse in this world then wasted talent. - Unknown

1959.   I do not want a friend who smiles when I smile, who weeps when I weep, for my shadow in the pool can do better than that. - Confucius

1960.   Life is a tragedy for those who feel, and a comedy for those who think. -Jean de la Bruyère

1961.   Life is a great big canvas; throw all the paint on it you can. - Danny Kaye

1962.   True happiness... arises in the first place from the enjoyment of one's self. -Joseph Addison

1963.   Vitality shows not only in the ability to persist, but in the ability to start over. -F. Scott Fitzgerald

1964.   A hit, a very palpable hit. -William Shakespeare

1965.   There must be quite a few things a hot bath won't cure, but I don't know many of them. -Sylvia Plath

1966.   Economics is extremely useful as a form of employment for economists. -John Kenneth Galbraith

1967.   When asked by his boss why he only worked four days a week, the employee replied, "Because I can't manage on three days a week."

1968.   We must overcome the notion that we must be regular. It robs us of the chance to be extraordinary and leads us to the mediocre. - Uta Hagan

1969.   There is a difference between knowing the path and walking the path! -Morpheus

1970.   What makes humility so desirable is the marvelous thing it does to us; it creates in us a capacity for the closest possible intimacy with God.

1971.   Stupidity consists in wanting to reach conclusions. We are a thread and we want to know the whole cloth. -Gustave Flaubert

1972. A successful man is one who can lay a firm foundation with the bricks others throw at him. -David Brinkley

1973. The most important work you and I will ever do will be within the wall of our own homes. -Harold B. Lee

1974. Web users ultimately want to get at data quickly and easily. They don't care as much about attractive sites and pretty design. -Tim Berners-Lee

1975. Retirement at sixty-five is ridiculous. When I was sixty-five I still had pimples. -George Burns

1976. He who can no longer pause to wonder and stand rapt in awe is as good as dead his eyes are closed. -Albert Einstein

1977. Absence diminishes small loves and increases great ones as the wind blows out the candle and blow up the bonfire. -La Rochefoucauld

1978. The penalty of success is to be bored by the attentions of people who formerly snubbed you. -Mary Wilson Little

1979. Nothing takes the taste out of peanut butter quite like unrequited love. -Charles M. Schulz

1980. If men can run the world, why can't they stop wearing neckties? How smart is it to start the day by tying a little noose around your neck?

1981. The biggest man you ever did see once was a baby.

1982. To understand the heart and mind of a person, look not at what he has already achieved but at what he aspires to. -Kahlil Gibran

1983. The greatest thing in the world is to know how to belong to oneself. -Michel de Montaigne

1984. The penalty for success is to be bored by the people who used to snub you. -Nancy Astor

1985. Success isn't a result of spontaneous combustion. You must set yourself on fire. -Arnold H. Glasgow

1986. The love of truth lies at the root of much humor. -Robertson Davies

1987. The tears that you spill the sorrowful are sweeter than the laughter of snobs and the guffaws of scoffers. -Kahlil Gibran

1988. Big doesn't necessarily mean better. Sunflowers aren't better than violets.

1989. The mark of a good action is that it appears inevitable in retrospect. -Robert Louis Stevenson

1990. Positive thinking will let you do everything better than negative thinking will. -Zig Ziglar

1991. A friend hears the song in my heart and sings it to me when my memory fails. -Readers Digest

1992. Hold a true friend with both your hands. -Friedrich Wilhelm Nietzsche

1993. What is originality? Undetected plagiarism. -William Ralph Inge

1994. Wealth is not in making money, but in making the man while he is making money. -John Wicker

1995. The bravest thing that men do is love women. -Mort Sahl

1996. Be careful - with quotations you can damn anything. -Andre Malraux

1997. Teaching kids to count is fine but teaching them what counts is best. -Bob Talbert

1998. Art is a word which summarizes the quality of communication. -L. Ron Hubbard

1999. Opportunity is often difficult to recognize we usually expect it to beckon us with beepers and billboards. -William Arthur Ward

2000. It is impossible for a man to learn what he thinks he already knows. -Epictetus

2001. Planning is bringing the future into the present so that you can do something about it now. -Alan Lakein

2002. Be careful about reading health books. You may die of a misprint. -Mark Twain

2003. Rumor travels faster but it don't stay put as long as truth. -Will Rogers

2004. Real valor consists not in being insensible to danger; but in being prompt to confront and disarm it. -Sir Walter Scott

2005. Better keep yourself clean and bright; you are the window through which you must see the world. -George Bernard Shaw

2006. Everybody likes a kidder but nobody lends him money. -Arthur Miller

2007. Quoting the act of repeating erroneously the words of another. -Ambrose Gwinett Bierce

2008. Some people reach the top of the ladder of success only to find it is leaning against the wrong wall.

2009. The definition of an upgrade: Take old bugs out, put new ones in.

2010. Nothing is so dangerous as an ignorant friend. A wise enemy is worth more. -Jean de La Fontaine

2011. Success in marriage does not come merely through finding the right mate but through being the right mate. -Barnett Brickner

2012. Perseverance alone does not assure success. No amount of stalking will lead to game in a field that has none. -I Ching

2013. We must believe in luck. For how else can we explain the success of those we don't like? -Jean Cocteau

2014. A great NOW will be a great WAS A bad NOW will always be a bad WAS and all you can hope for is a Great GONNA BE. -Sid Caesar

2015. The hardest thing about any political campaign is how to win without proving that you are unworthy of winning. -Theodor Wiesengrund Adorno

2016. Hate the sin and love the sinner. -Mohandas Karamchand Gandhi

2017. Once I had the strength but no wisdom now I have the wisdom but no strength. -Persian Proverb

2018. Every advantage in the past is judged in the light of the final issue. -Demosthenes

2019. The person who seeks all their applause from outside has their happiness in another's keeping. - Claudius Claudianus

2020. Fat people are harder to kidnap.

2021. A man's dreams are an index to his greatness. -Zadok Rabinwitz

2022. Needless to say, since Christ's expiation, not one single Christian has been known to sin or die. - Voltaire

2023. But be as you have been my happiness... -Randall Jarrell

2024. Doing easily what others find difficult is talent; doing what is impossible for talent is genius. -Henri-Frederic Amiel

2025. Courage is what it takes to stand up and speak Courage is also what it takes to sit down and listen. -Carl Hermann Voss

2026. Hope is the worst of evils, for it prolongs the torments of man. -Friedrich Wilhelm Nietzsche

2027. Leadership has a harder job to do than just choose sides. It must bring sides together. -Jesse Louis Jackson

2028. To accomplish great things, we must dream as well as act. -Anatole France

2029. The most beautiful thing we can experience is the mysterious. -Albert Einstein

2030. Religion is a bandage that man has invented to protect a soul made bloody by circumstance. -Theodore Herman Albert Dreiser

2031. Money is like a sixth sense without which you cannot make a complete use of the other five. -W. Somerset Maugham

2032. Do not go where the path may lead, go instead where there is no path and leave a trail. -Ralph Waldo Emerson

2033. It is preoccupation with possessions more than anything else that prevents us from living freely and nobly. -Bertrand Russell

2034. Do what you know best; if you're a runner, run, if you're a bell, ring - Unknown

2035. Most people, once they graduate from the School of Hard Knocks, automatically enroll in the University of Adversity. -Peter McWilliams

2036. In the middle of the journey of our life I came to myself within a dark wood where the straight way was lost. -Dante Alighieri

2037. In the right light at the right time everything is extraordinary. -Aaron Rose

2038. Originality is simply a pair of fresh eyes. -Thomas W. Higginson

2039.   Men are wise in proportion, not to their experience, but to their capacity for experience. -Samuel Johnson

2040.   When you want to believe in something you also have to believe in everything that's necessary for believing in it. -Ugo Betti

2041.   Years and sins are always more than owned.-Italian Proverb

2042.   When unhappy, one doubts everything; when happy, one doubts nothing. -Joseph Roux

2043.   Eat one live toad the first thing in the morning and nothing worse will happen to you the rest of the day.

2044.   Fools take to themselves the respect that is given to their office. - Aesop

2045.   The more things a man is ashamed of, the more respectable he is. -George Bernard Shaw

2046.   If he was any slower, he'd be going in reverse.

2047.   Power never takes a back step - only in the face of more power. -Malcolm X

2048.   Seeing yourself as you want to be is the key to personal growth. -Unknown Author

2049.   I know you know what I think I said, but I'm not sure you realize that what you heard is not what I meant.

2050.   There are a thousand thoughts lying within a man that he does not know till he takes up a pen to write. -William Makepeace Thackeray

2051.   Stress is an ignorant state. It believes that everything is an emergency. Nothing is that important. -Natalie Goldberg

2052.   Often an entire city has suffered because of an evil man. -Hesiod

2053.   Compromise: the art of dividing a cake so that everybody believes he or she got the biggest piece.

2054.   Always hold your head up but be careful to keep your nose at a friendly level. -Max L. Forman

2055.   A decent boldness ever meets with friends. -Homer

2056.   Life is 10 percent what you make it and 90 percent how you take it. -Irving Berlin

2057.   It is the customary fate of new truths to begin as heresies and to end as superstitions. -Aldous Huxley

2058.   He fishes well who uses a golden hook. -Latin Proverb

2059.   Action is only coarsened thought-thought becomes concrete obscure and unconscious. -Henri-Frederic Amiel

2060.   The power of accurate observation is commonly called cynicism by those who have not got it. -George Bernard Shaw

2061.   No opera plot can be sensible for people do not sing when they are feeling sensible. -W. H. Auden

2062.   Good timber does not grow with ease; the stronger the wind, the stronger the trees. -J. Willard Marriott

2063.   I once said cynically of a politician, "He'll double-cross that bridge when he comes to it." -Oscar Levant

2064.   The choice you make today will usually affect tomorrow.

2065.   Science is a wonderful thing if one does not have to earn one's living at it. -Albert Einstein

2066.   Feel the fear and do it anyway. -Susan Jeffers

2067.   Freeman's Extension: "...but you can get everything dirty without getting anything clean."

2068.   Go confidently in the direction of your dreams. Live the life you've imagined. -Henry David Thoreau

2069.   I'll sleep when I'm dead. -Warren Zevon

2070.   The quieter you become the more you can hear. -Baba Ram Dass

2071.   Never trust the man who tells you all his troubles but keeps from you all his joys. -Jewish Proverb

2072.   Failure is success if we learn from it. -Malcom S. Forbes

2073.   Advertising is the modern substitute for argument its function is to make the worse appear the better. -George Santayana

2074.   Old age and sickness bring out the essential characteristics of a man. - Felix Frankfurter

2075.   You know Lake Eerie actually caught on fire once from all the crap floating around in it. I wish I could've seen that. -Crow The T-Bird

2076. Blessed are the cracked, for they shall let in the light. - Unknown

2077. One of the greatest pieces of economic wisdom is to know what you do not know. -John Kenneth Galbraith

2078. Nature does not loathe virtue; it is unaware of its existence. - Françoise Mallet-Joris

2079. No trumpets sound when the important decisions of our life are made. Destiny is made known silently. -Agnes De Mille

2080. I have had dreams, and I have had nightmares. I overcame the nightmares because of my dreams. -Dr. Jonas Salk

2081. People don't understand the virtue of time until their clock stops ticking. -Steve Goodman

2082. The wit makes fun of other persons the satirist makes fun of the world the humorist makes fun of himself. -James Thurber

2083. Never pretend to a love which you do not actually feel for love is not ours to command. -Alan Watts

2084. Love is the only thing that can be divided without being diminished.

2085. Give me the children until they are seven and anyone may have them afterward. -Saint Francis Xavier

2086. I favor the Civil Rights Act of and it must be enforced at gunpoint if necessary. -Ronald Reagan

2087. Forget about all the reasons why something may not work. You only need to find one good reason why it will. -Dr. Robert Anthony

2088. Why fools are endowed by nature with voices so much louder than sensible people possess is a mystery. It's a fact emphasized throughout history.

2089. Give to a pig when it grunts and a child when it cries and you will have a fine pig and a bad child. -Danish proverb

2090. The idea is not responsible for the people who believe in it.

2091. When two men share an umbrella, both of them get wet. - Michael Isenberg

2092. Music has charms to soothe the savage breast-- To soften rocks or bend a knotted oak. -William Congreve

2093.   Nothing but blackness above, and nothing that moves but the cars... God, if you wish for our love, Fling us a handful of stars!—Louis Untermeyer

2094.   In the business world, everyone is paid in two coins: cash and experience. Take the experience first; the cash will come later. -Harold S. Geneen

2095.   The only truly happy people are children and the creative minority. -Jean Caldwell

2096.   Beta. Software undergoes beta testing shortly before it's released. Beta is Latin for "still doesn't work."

2097.   I will permit no man to narrow and degrade my soul by making me hate him. -Booker T. Washington

2098.   The voice of the people is the voice of God. -Alcuin

2099.   Ful wys is he that can himselven knowe (Very wise is he that can know himself.) -Geoffrey Chaucer

2100.   Live among men as if God beheld you speak to God as if men were listening. -Seneca

2101.   You bluffed me I don't like it when people bluff me. It makes me question my perception of reality. -Andrew Schneider

2102.   I hate and I love. Perhaps you ask why I do so. I do not know but I feel it and am in agony. -Catullus

2103.   When we do the best that we can we never know what miracle is wrought in our life or in the life of another. -Helen Keller

2104.   Rough work, iconoclasm, but the only way to get at truth. -Oliver Wendell Holmes

2105.   A classic is something that everybody wants to have read and nobody has.

2106.   Make sure to be in with your equals if you're going to fall out with your superiors. -Jewish Proverb

2107.   You can't build a reputation on what you're going to do. -Henry Ford

2108.   Man needs difficulties; they are necessary for health. -Carl Gustav Jung

2109.   Never interrupt your enemy when he is making a mistake. - Napoleon Bonaparte

2110.   To find a fault is easy to do; better may be difficult. -Plutarch

2111.   Death comes to all But great achievements raise a monument which shall endure until the sun grows old. -George Fabricius

2112.   A cathedral, a wave of storm, a dancer's leap, never turn out to be as high as we had hoped. —Marcel Proust

2113.   Until he extends his circle of compassion to include all living things man will not himself find peace. -Albert Schweitzer

2114.   A cat does not want all the world to love her - only those she has chosen to love. -Helen Thomson

2115.   A dinner lubricates business.-Lord William Stowell

2116.   A university is what a college becomes when the faculty loses interest in students. -John Anthony Ciardi

2117.   Most people are about as happy as they make up their minds to be. -Abraham Lincoln

2118.   It's how you deal with failure that determines how you achieve success. -David Feherty

2119.   Deaf rage that hears no leader. [Ger., Dem tauben Grimm, der keinen Fuhrer hort.] - Johann Christoph Friedrich von Schiller

2120.   Love consists in this that two solitudes protect and touch and greet each other. -Rainer Maria Rilke

2121.   The only real prison is fear and the only real freedom is freedom from fear. -Aung San Suu Kyi

2122.   The abuse of greatness is when it disjoins remorse from power. - Mary Bertone

2123.   The universe is full of magical things patiently waiting for our wits to grow sharper. -Eden Phillpotts

2124.   On the whole human beings want to be good but not too good and not quite all the time. -George Orwell

2125.   A wise man among the ignorant is as a beautiful girl in the company of blind men. -Saadi, Persian poet

2126.   Winter lies too long in country towns, hangs on until it is stale and shabby old and sullen. -Willa Cather

2127.	When one shuts one eye, one does not hear everything. -Swiss Proverb

2128.	Art is born of the observation and investigation of nature. -Cicero

2129.	Never mistake knowledge for wisdom. One helps you make a living; the other helps you make a life. -Sandra Carey

2130.	Two rules to follow: 1) Don't sweat the small stuff. 2) It's all small stuff. -Robert Elliot

2131.	It is better to be happy for a moment and be burned up with beauty than to live a long time and be bored all the while. -Helen Keller

2132.	The secret of greatness is simple do better work than any other man in your field - and keep on doing it. -Wilfred A. Peterson

2133.	Those who race through life finish first. -Darrel Hunsbedt

2134.	Live your beliefs and you can turn the world around. -Henry David Thoreau

2135.	In the first place God made idiots. That was for practice. Then he made school boards. -Mark Twain

2136.	Anything not worth doing is worth not doing well. Think about it. -Elias Schwartz

2137.	The mind of man is capable of anything - because everything is in it all the past as well as all the future. -Joseph Conrad

2138.	Food, love, career, and mothers: the four major guilt groups. -Cathy Guisewite

2139.	The goal of revival is conformity to the image of Christ not imitation of animals. -Richard F. Lovelace

2140.	Nothing gives one person so much advantage over another as to remain always cool and unruffled under all circumstances. -Thomas Jefferson

2141.	The glorious gifts of the gods are not to be cast aside. -Homer

2142.	To improve is to change; to be perfect is to change often. -Winston Churchill

2143.	Gluttony is an emotional sign that something is eating us. -Peter Devries

2144.   Candy is dandy but liquor is quicker. -Roald Dahl

2145.   I like pigs. Dogs look up to us. Cats look down on us. Pigs treat us as equals. -Sir Winston Churchill

2146.   We are each of us angels with only one wing, and we can only fly by embracing one another. -Luciano De Crescenzo

2147.   Gratitude is merely the secret hope of further favors. -François de La Rochefoucauld

2148.   Ah music. A magic beyond all we do here. -J. K. Rowling

2149.   Rich Folkers is throwing up in the bullpen. -Jerry Coleman

2150.   Let the punishment match the offense. -Cicero

2151.   I was brought up to believe that how I saw myself was more important than how others saw me. -Anwar el Sadat

2152.   A man's feet should be planted in his country but his eyes should survey the world. -George Santayana

2153.   Violence is the last refuge of the incompetent. Never let your morals stop you from doing what is right. -Isaac Asimov

2154.   By following the concept of one country, two systems, you don't swallow me up, nor I you. -Deng Xiaoping

2155.   Whether you think you can or whether you think you can't, you're right. -Henry Ford

2156.   Dwell as near as possible to the channel in which your life flows. -Henry David Thoreau

2157.   It is destruction to the weak man to attempt to imitate the powerful. -Phaedrus

2158.   Live with men as if God saw you converse with God as if men heard you. -Seneca

2159.   The worth of a book is to be measured by what you can carry away from it. -James Bryce

2160.   You don't get harmony when everybody sings the same note. -Doug Floyd

2161.   Man is the only creature that refuses to be what he is. -Albert Camus

2162.   For all the advances in medicine, there is still no cure for the common birthday. -John Herschel Glenn Jr.

2163.   The little foolery that wise men have makes a great show. - William Shakespeare

2164.   In all things of nature there is something of the marvelous. - Aristotle

2165.   I quit therapy because my analyst was trying to help me behind my back. -Richard Lewis

2166.   We have only this moment, sparkling like a star in our hand - and melting like a snowflake. -Marie B. Ray

2167.   Some people don't get it when I'm being sarcastic. -Leonardo DiCaprio

2168.   I am a mushroom on whom the dew of heaven drops now and then. -John M. Ford

2169.   America is a young country with an old mentality. -George Santayana

2170.   To keep a lamp burning we have to keep putting oil in it. - Mother Theresa

2171.   Without an acquaintance with the rules of propriety, it is impossible for the character to be established. -Confucius

2172.   Republicans understand the importance of bondage between a mother and child. -Dan Quayle

2173.   I don't think you have to teach people how to be human. I think you have to teach them how to stop being inhumane. -Eldridge Cleaver

2174.   If we would build on a sure foundation in friendship, we must love friends for their sake rather than for our own. -Charlotte Bronte

2175.   It is not against the law to be stupid, but it is stupid to be against the law.

2176.   Perhaps even these things one day will be pleasing to remember. -Virgil

2177.   I used to be indecisive, but now I'm not so sure.

2178.   No, Ernest don't talk about action. It is the last resource of those who know not how to dream. -Oscar Wilde

2179.   Life just isn't worth living unless you're willing to take some big chances and go for broke. Eliot Wiggington

2180. What sculpture is to a block of marble education is to the soul. -Joseph Addison

2181. You see what power is - holding someone else's fear in your hand and showing it to them. -Amy Tan

2182. If I can only be with you in my dreams, then I want to sleep forever.

2183. Talent develops in tranquility; character in the full current of human life. -Johann Wolfgang von Goethe

2184. Dietrich Bonhoeffer If you do a good job for others you heal yourself at the same time because a dose of joy is a spiritual cure.

2185. The only limits are, as always, those of vision. -James Broughton

2186. Every revolution evaporates and leaves behind only the slime of a new bureaucracy. -Franz Kafka

2187. An unexamined life is not worth living. - Socrates

2188. Of life's two chief prizes, beauty and truth I found the first in a loving heart and the second in a laborers' hand. -Kahlil Gibran

2189. No great deed private or public had ever been undertaken in a bliss of certainty. -Leon Wieseltier

2190. We must all hang together or most assuredly we shall all hang separately. -Benjamin Franklin

2191. When you exercise your freedom to express yourself at the lowest level, you ultimately condemn yourself to live at that level. - Zig Ziglar

2192. If you live to be a hundred, I want to live to be a hundred minus one day so I never have to live without you. -Winnie the Pooh

2193. Make money your god and it will plague you like the devil. - Henry Fielding

2194. God's delays are not God's denials. -Robert Schuller

2195. I have found out in later years that we were very poor, but the glory of America is that we didn't know it then. -Dwight D Eisenhower

2196. It is dangerous to be sincere unless you are also stupid. -George Bernard Shaw

2197.   I hate mankind, for I think myself to be one of them and I know how bad I am. -Samuel Johnson

2198.   I don't care what anybody says about me as long as it isn't true. -Truman Capote

2199.   Do giraffes get sore throats?

2200.   Our nettlesome task is to discover how to organize our strength into compelling power. -Martin Luther King, Jr.

2201.   Opportunities are like sunrises. If you wait too long, you miss them. -William Arthur Ward

2202.   May you live all the days of your life. -Jonathan Swift

2203.   It is easier to fight for one's principles than to live up to them. -Alfred Adler

2204.   I am not bound to please thee with my answers. -William Shakespeare

2205.   We will always tend to fulfill our own expectation of ourselves. -Brian Tracy

2206.   The more I want to get something done, the less I call it work. -Richard Bach

2207.   Most of the change we think we see in life is due to truths being in and out of favor. -Robert Frost

2208.   You have to have confidence in your ability, and then be tough enough to follow through. -Rosalynn Carter

2209.   A happy life consists in tranquility of mind. -Cicero

2210.   The man who makes no mistakes does not usually make anything. -Bishop W. C. Magee

2211.   In order to truly master the comfort zone, you have to learn to love it. -Peter McWilliams

2212.   As far as we know, our computer has never had an undetected error.

2213.   Enjoyment is not a goal; it is a feeling that accompanies important ongoing activity. -Paul Goodman

2214.   A cucumber would be well sliced, and dressed with pepper and vinegar, and then thrown out as good for nothing. -Samuel Johnson

2215.   If you can't make it better you can laugh at it. -Erma Bombeck

2216.   To err is human; to forgive infrequent. -Franklin P. Adams

2217.   I figure you have the same chance of winning the lottery whether you play or not. -Fran Lebowitz

2218.   It is not fair to ask of others what you are not willing to do yourself. -Eleanor Roosevelt

2219.   Never let the fear of striking out get in your way. -Babe Ruth

2220.   Everyone is unique. Compare not yourself with anyone else lest you spoil God's curriculum. -Baal Shem Tov

2221.   There is no passion like that of a functionary for his function. -Georges Clemenceau

2222.   Take good hold of instruction and don't let her go, keep her for she is your life. - Bible

2223.   As long as we separate this oneness into two, we won't achieve realization. -Bruce Lee

2224.   A successful man is one who can lay a firm foundation with the bricks that others throw at him. -Sidney Greenberg

2225.   Happiness is more a state of health than of wealth. -Frank Tyger

2226.   Deep Thoughts: It's too bad that whole families have to be torn apart by something as simple as wild dogs. -Jack Handey

2227.   It is not the speaker who controls communication, but the listener.

2228.   The hard way is the right way. -John Alves

2229.   If at first you don't succeed; you are running about average. - M. H. Alderson

2230.   Humanity has only scratched the surface of its real potential. -Pilgrims

2231.   If you're not failing every now and again, it's a sign you're not doing anything very innovative. -Woody Allen

2232.   Welcome anything that comes to you but do not long for anything else. -Andre Gide

2233.   When a stupid man is doing something he is ashamed of he always declares that it is his duty. -George Bernard Shaw

2234. God loved the birds and invented trees. Man loved the birds and invented cages. -Jacques Deval

2235. Tommy, if I wanted a kiss I'd call your mother. -Tommy Boy

2236. I've learned that sometimes all a person needs is a hand to hold, and a heart to understand. - Andy Rooney

2237. All human actions have one or more of these seven causes: Chance, nature, compulsion, habit, reason, passion, and desire. - Aristotle

2238. The Los Angeles riots were not caused by the Rodney King verdict. The Los Angeles riots were caused by rioters. -Rush Limbaugh

2239. A great many people think they are thinking when they are merely re-arranging their prejudices. -William James

2240. Those who bring sunshine to the lives of others cannot keep it from themselves. -James Barrie

2241. Life can only be understood backwards but it must be lived forwards. -Kierkegaard

2242. My imagination makes me human and makes me a fool it gives me all the world and exiles me from it. -John Fitzgerald Kennedy

2243. Everything has its beauty but not everyone sees it. -Confucius

2244. What was once thought can never be unthought. - Carl J. Friedrich

2245. An eye for an eye makes the whole world blind. -Mahatma Gandhi

2246. It is our responsibilities, not ourselves, that we should take seriously. -Peter Ustinov

2247. And virtue, though in rags, will keep me warm. -John Dryden

2248. Where fear is, happiness is not. -Seneca

2249. Art, like morality, consists of drawing the line somewhere. -G. K. Chesterton

2250. If it sounds good, you'll hear it. If it looks good, you'll see it. If it's marketed right, you'll buy it. But if it's real, you'll feel it. -Kid Rock

2251. I can hire one half of the working class to kill the other half. - Jay Gould

2252. Rejoicing is clearly a spiritual command. To ignore it I need to remind you is disobedience. -Charles R. Swindoll

2253. They are able because they think they are able. -Virgil

2254. A home without books is a body without soul. -Marcus Tullius Cicero

2255. Justice cannot be for one side alone but must be for both. - Eleanor Roosevelt

2256. Good nonsense is good sense in disguise. -Josh Billings

2257. Perfection is a road not a destination. Every time I live I get an education. -Burk Hudson

2258. The doctor is not able to operate the notable, because he has no table!

2259. My wife is a light eater ... as soon as its light she starts to eat. - Henny Youngman

2260. The cynics are right nine times out of 10. -Henry Louis Mencken

2261. Virtue extends our days he live two lives who relives his past with pleasure. -Marcus Valerius Martialis

2262. Deep Thoughts: I hope they never find out that lightning has a lot of vitamins in it because do you hide from it or not. -Jack Handey

2263. A man has reached middle age when he is cautioned to slow down by his doctor instead of by the police.

2264. The one who says it cannot be done should never interrupt the one who is doing it.

2265. Peace comes from within. Do not seek it without. -Buddha

2266. Build for your team a feeling of oneness of dependence on one another and of strength to be derived by unity. -Vince Lombardi

2267. The superior man makes the difficulty to be overcome his first interest; success only comes later. -Confucius

2268. Ability is what you're capable of doing. Motivation determines what you do. Attitude determines how well you do it. -Lou Holtz

2269. I've been on a calendar, but I've never been on time. -Marilyn Monroe

2270. Someday we'll look back on this moment and plow into a parked car. -Evan Davis

2271. I like work; it fascinates me. I can sit and look at it for hours. -Jerome K. Jerome

2272. Kids go where there is excitement. They stay where there is love. -Zig Ziglar

2273. Happiness is the only sanction of life where happiness fails; existence remains a mad and lamentable experiment. -George Santayana

2274. Educate the heart - educate the heart. Let us have good men. -Hiram Powers

2275. The highest result of education is tolerance. -Helen Keller

2276. Lord grant that I might always desire more than I can accomplish. -Michelangelo

2277. There is no more miserable human being than one in whom nothing is habitual but indecision. -William James

2278. If courage wasn't a standard result of aging it meant that the young could somehow acquire it as well. -Lawana Blackwell

2279. Royalty has always been an unconscious but all-consuming goal of the European immigrant. -Vine Deloria Jr.

2280. He who fears he will suffer already suffers because of his fear. -Michel Eyquem de Montaigne

2281. Feel for others - in your pocket. -Charles Haddon Spurgeon

2282. Never leave that till tomorrow which you can do today. -Benjamin Franklin

2283. America is a land where citizens vote for Democrats but hope to live like Republicans.

2284. We may affirm absolutely that nothing great in the world has ever been accomplished without enthusiasm. -Georg Hegel

2285. Such praise coming from so degraded a source was degrading to me, its recipient. -Cicero

2286.   We make a living by what we get we make a life by what we give. -Sir Winston Churchill

2287.   If you don't know what to do, call the media and at least give the appearance of doing something. -David Peterson

2288.   One only needs two tools in life WD- to make things go and duct tape to make them stop. -G. Weilacher

2289.   If you die in an elevator be sure to push the up button. -Sam Levenson

2290.   The superior man is modest in his speech but exceeds in his actions. -Confucius

2291.   A 'wish' changes nothing. A 'decision' changes everything!

2292.   Smash forehead on keyboard to continue. -Anon.

2293.   The great roe is a mythological beast with the head of a lion and the body of a lion, though not the same lion. -Woody Allen

2294.   I can't listen to that much Wagner. I start getting the urge to conquer Poland. -Woody Allen

2295.   One should not lose one's temper unless one is certain of getting more and more angry to the end. - William Butler Yeats

2296.   One who condones evil is just as guilty as the one who perpetrates it. -Martin Luther King Jr.

2297.   The artist is nothing without the gift but the gift is nothing without work. -Emile Zola

2298.   Often it does seem a pity that Noah and his party did not miss the boat. -Mark Twain

2299.   It is not the years in your life, but the life in your years that count. -Adlai Stevenson

2300.   Even though a number of people have tried no one has yet found a way to drink for a living. -Jean Kerr

2301.   Many a man is praised for his reserve and so-called shyness when he is simply too proud to risk making a fool of himself. -J. B. Priestley

2302.   The reason of a resolution is more to be considered than the resolution itself. -John Holt

2303.	Do not seek evil gains evil gains are the equivalent of disaster. - Hesiod

2304.	The heavy is the root of the light. The tranquil is the ruler of the hasty. -Lao Tzu

2305.	Making your good times count and not forgetting your bad times makes a man successful.

2306.	From the cradle to the coffin underwear comes first. - Bertolt Brecht

2307.	A well written life is almost as rare as a well spent one. -Thomas Carlyle

2308.	Charity begins at home. Success begins at work.

2309.	You never see what you want to see, forever playing to the gallery. - Robertson Davies

2310.	If beef comes from a cow and ham from a pig, why do they put beef in hamburgers?

2311.	Success is getting what you want. Happiness is wanting what you get. -Dale Carnegie

2312.	Whatever the mind of man can conceive and believe, it can achieve. -W. Clement Stone

2313.	My basic principle is that you don't make decisions because they are cheap; you make them because they're right. -Theodore Hesburgh

2314.	And come he slow or come he fast, it is but death who comes at last. -Sir Walter Scott

2315.	The lion and the calf will lay down together, but the calf won't get much sleep. - Woody Allen

2316.	The ability to convert ideas to things is the secret of outward success. -Henry Ward Beecher

2317.	Don't ask God to guide your footsteps if you're not willing to move your feet.

2318.	They can expect nothing, but their labor for their pains. - Miguel de Cervantes

2319.	Pray that success will not come any faster than you are able to endure it. -Benjamin Nnamdi Azikiwe

2320. Common sense and education are highly compatible in fact neither is worth much without the other. -Donald G. Smith

2321. Most of what we call management consists of making it difficult for people to get their work done. - Peter F. Drucker

2322. What is written without effort is in general read without pleasure. -Samuel Johnson

2323. It ain't a bad plan to keep still occasionally even when you know what you're talking about. -Kim Hubbard

2324. Reset Universe (Y/N) ?

2325. Our constitution works. Our great republic is a government of laws not of men. -Gerald R. Ford

2326. If a man die shall he live again All the days of my appointed time will I wait till my change come. -Job, The Hebrew Bible

2327. Within your heart, keep one still, secret spot where dreams may go. -Louise Driscoll

2328. You become a champion by fighting one more round. When things are tough, you fight one more round. -James J. Corbett

2329. For those who love it cooking is at once child's play and adult joy. And cooking done with care is an act of love. -Craig Claiborne

2330. If you aim at nothing, you'll hit it every time.

2331. Not to be absolutely certain is, I think, one of the essential things in rationality. -Bertrand Russell

2332. All riches have their origin in mind. Wealth is in ideas - not money. -Robert Collier

2333. One man's religion is another man's belly laugh. -Robert Anson Heinlein

2334. You don't always win your battles but it's good to know you fought. -Lauren Bacall

2335. If your computer says, "Printer out of Paper," this problem cannot be resolved by continuously clicking the "OK" button.

2336. Compassion is the antitoxin of the soul: where there is compassion even the most poisonous impulses remain relatively harmless. - Eric Hoffer

2337. Call no man foe but never love a stranger. -Stella Benson

2338. Don't look now, but there's one too many in this room, and I think it's you. -Julius Henry Marx

2339. Do a little more each day than you think you possibly can. -Lowell Thomas

2340. Nature gave us one tongue and two ears so we could hear twice as much as we speak. -Epictetus

2341. Some people grin and bear it. Others smile and change it.

2342. No one is exempt from talking nonsense; the mistake is to do it solemnly. -Michel Eyquem de Montaigne

2343. We need not think alike to love alike. -Francis David

2344. In literature, as in love, we are astonished at what is chosen by others. -Andre Maurois

2345. Doctrine is nothing but the skin of truth set up and stuffed. -Henry Ward Beecher

2346. If you can imagine it, you can achieve it. If you can dream it, you can become it. -William Arthur Ward

2347. Dream no small dreams for they have no power to move the hearts of men. -Johann Wolfgang Von Goethe

2348. The person who can bring the spirit of laughter into a room is indeed blessed. -Bennett Alfred Cerf

2349. That's the way things come clear. All of a sudden. And then you realize how obvious they've been all along. -Madeleine L'Engle

2350. I don't know what will be used in the next world war, but the fourth will be fought with stones. -Albert Einstein

2351. The controlled person is a powerful person. He who always keeps his head will get ahead. -Norman Vincent Peale

2352. Tears will get you sympathy. Sweat will get you results.

2353. No trumpets sound when the important decisions of our life are made. Destiny is made known silently. -Agnes DeMille

2354. One friend in a lifetime is much, two are many, three are hardly possible. -Henry Adams

2355. Nurture your mind with great thoughts. -Benjamin Disraeli

2356. A closed mind is like a closed book just a block of wood.-Chinese Proverb

2357.   Education is the best provision for old age. -Aristotle

2358.   Be your character what it will, it will be known; and nobody will take it upon your word. -Philip Dormer Shanhope, Lord Chesterfield

2359.   True wisdom comes to each of us when we realize how little we understand about life, ourselves, and the world around us. -Socrates

2360.   It is no wonder that people are so horrible when they start their life as children. -Kingsley Amis

2361.   You become a champion by fighting one more round. When things are tough, you fight one more round. -Joseph J. Corbett

2362.   There's no business like show business. - Irving Berlin

2363.   Appearances are a glimpse of the unseen. - Aeschylus

2364.   Treat a person as he is and he will remain as he is. Treat him as he could be and he will become what he should be. -Jimmy Johnson

2365.   Many a crown of wisdom is but the golden chamber pot of success worn with pompous dignity. -Joey Adams

2366.   People forget how fast you did a job- but they remember how well you did it.

2367.   Who puts the thin ice sign in the middle of the thin ice?

2368.   If I am not free to fail, I'm not free to take risks, and everything in life that's worth doing involves a willingness to risk failure.

2369.   A mere friend will agree with you, but a real friend will argue. - Assyrian Proverb

2370.   When in doubt, tell the truth. -Mark Twain

2371.   The art of love ... is largely the art of persistence. -Albert Ellis

2372.   Safeguarding the rights of others is the most noble and beautiful end of a human being. -Kahlil Gibran

2373.   If speaking is silver, then listening is gold. -Turkish Proverb

2374.   Smile.... it makes others wonder what you're thinking.

2375.   Alimony: funds which allow a woman who lived unhappily married to live happily unmarried.

2376.   When people keep telling you that you can't do a thing, you kind of like to try it. -Margaret Chase Smith

2377.   There are never enough hours in a day, but always too many days before Saturday.

2378. The whole life of man is but a point of time, let us enjoy it. -Plutarch

2379. Silence is the perfectest herald of joy; I were but little happy if I could say how much. -William Shakespeare

2380. People who get nostalgic about childhood were obviously never children. -Bill Watterson

2381. Show me a man who cannot bother to do little things and I'll show you a man who cannot be trusted to do big things. -Lawrence Bell

2382. What breaks in a moment may take years to mend. -Swedish Proverb

2383. The essential conditions of everything you do must be choice, love, and passion. -Nadia Boulanger

2384. The surest way to make a monkey of a man is to quote him. -Robert Benchley

2385. Delay is preferable to error. -Thomas Jefferson

2386. It is not unseemly for a man to die fighting in defense of his country. -Homer

2387. If you haven't all the things that you want, be thankful for all the things that you don't have that you didn't want.

2388. People forget how fast you did a job-but they remember how well you did it. -Howard W. Newton

2389. To flee vice is the beginning of virtue and to have got rid of folly is the beginning of wisdom. -Horace

2390. All theory, dear friend is gray, but the golden tree of life springs ever green. -Johann Wolfgang von Goethe

2391. In War: Resolution. In Defeat: Defiance. In Victory: Magnanimity. In Peace: Goodwill. -Sir Winston Leonard Spencer Churchill

2392. Nothing is stronger than habit. -Ovid

2393. Depression loses its power when fresh vision pierces the darkness. -Peter Sinclair

2394. If there is Magic on this planet it is contained in water. -Loren

2395.   Learning to dislike children at an early age saves a lot of expense and aggravation later in life. -Robert Byrne

2396.   The beginning of faith is the beginning of fruitfulness but the beginning of unbelief however glittering is empty. -Johann von Goethe

2397.   Don't seek to follow in the footsteps of the wise: seek what they sought. -Basho

2398.   I never did anything alone. Whatever was accomplished in this country was accomplished collectively. -Golda Meir

2399.   Cherish that which is within you and shut off that which is without. -Chuang-Tzu

2400.   What difference does it make how much you have What you do not have amounts to much more. -Seneca

2401.   A man's dreams are an index to his greatness. -Zadok Rabinwitz

2402.   Little birdie in the sky, dropped a poopie in my eye I didn't scream, I didn't cry, But I thanked the Lord cows can't fly!

2403.   You can't ever be really free if you admire somebody too much. -Tove Jansson

2404.   Write the bad things that are done to you in sand, but write the good things that happen to you on a piece of marble. - Arabic Parable

2405.   Those who do not do politics will be done in by politics. - French Proverb

2406.   Mediocrity requires aloofness to preserve its dignity. -Charles Gates Dawes

2407.   Modesty and unselfishness - these are the virtues which men praise - and pass by. -Andre Maurois

2408.   Do not worry about your difficulties in Mathematics. I can assure you mine are still greater. -Albert Einstein

2409.   What is food to one man is bitter poison to others. -Lucretius

2410.   Despise the enemy strategically but take him seriously tactically. -Mao Zedong

2411.   There is nothing more frightful than ignorance in action. - Johann von Goethe

2412. Whatever you may look like marry a man your own age - as your beauty fades so will his eyesight. -Phyllis

2413. You never find yourself until you face the truth. -Pearl Bailey

2414. Life beats down and crushes the soul and art reminds you that you have one. -Stella Adler

2415. The first lady is and always has been an unpaid public servant elected by one person - her husband. -Claudia Alta Taylor Johnson

2416. The truth is more important than the facts. -Frank Lloyd Wright

2417. Persistence is the twin sister of excellence. One is a matter of quality, the other a matter of time -Marabel Morgan .

2418. Jack was out kissing babies while I was out passing bills. Someone had to tend the store. -Lyndon B. Johnson

2419. Ultimately the only power to which man should aspire is that which he exercises over himself. -Elie Wiesel

2420. Every man I meet is in some way my superior. -Ralph Waldo Emerson

2421. Adapt or perish now as ever is nature's inexorable imperative. - H. G. Wells

2422. If you want to be respected you must respect yourself. -Spanish Proverb

2423. Call it Nature, Fate, Fortune; all these are names of the one and selfsame God. -Seneca

2424. We can't take any credit for our talents. It's how we use them that counts. -Madeleine L'Engle

2425. The job of buildings is to improve human relations architecture must ease them, not make them worse. -Ralph Erskine

2426. Science when well digested is nothing but good sense and reason. -Stanislaw I. Leszczynski

2427. Golf and sex are about the only things you can enjoy without being good at. -Jimmy Demaret

2428. It's not enough that I should succeed - others should fail. - David Merrick

2429. Worry is the darkroom in which 'negatives' are developed.

2430. The greatest discovery of my generation is that human beings can alter their lives by altering their attitudes of mind. -William James

2431. Success is liking yourself liking what you do and liking how you do it. -Maya Angelou

2432. A man who does not know foreign language is ignorant of his own. -Johann von Goethe

2433. What is not good for the swarm is not good for the bee. -Marcus Aurelius

2434. Blindness and error can change a life as surely as judgment and reason can. -M. Morris

2435. All mankind is divided into three classes: those who are immovable, those who are movable; and those who move. -Benjamin Franklin

2436. Success and rest don't sleep together. -Russian proverb

2437. Great necessities call out great virtues. -Abigail Adams

2438. An unbreakable toy is useful for breaking other toys.

2439. The computing field is always in need of new clichés. -Alan Perlis

2440. It is better to be hated for who you are than to be loved for what you are not. -Andre Gide

2441. Castles in the air - they are so easy to take refuge in. And so easy to build too. -Henrik Ibsen

2442. I am careful not to confuse excellence with perfection. Excellence, I can reach for; perfection is God's business. -Michael J. Fox

2443. People seem not to see that their opinion of the world is also a confession of their character. -Ralph Waldo Emerson

2444. To die for an idea is to set a rather high price upon conjecture. -Anatole France

2445. You will face many defeats in your life, but never let yourself be defeated. -Maya Angelou

2446. The mind is no match with the heart in persuasion; constitutionality is no match with compassion. - Everett M. Dirksen

2447.   If you have time to worry, you have time to pray.

2448.   Don't worry about people stealing your ideas. If your ideas are any good you'll have to ram them down people's throats. -Howard Aiken

2449.   The highest happiness of man ... is to have probed what is knowable and quietly to revere what is unknowable. -Johann Wolfgang von Goethe

2450.   The world is wide and I will not waste my life in friction when it could be turned into momentum. -Frances Willard

2451.   Some books are undeservedly forgotten; none are undeservedly remembered. -Wystan Hugh Auden

2452.   If a nation loses its storytellers, it loses its childhood. -Peter Handke

2453.   There are two ways to be contented: one is liking what you do, and the other is doing what you like.

2454.   He does not preach what he practices till he has practiced what he preaches. -Confucius

2455.   Know the right moment. -Pittacus

2456.   People forget what you said. People forget what you did. But people never forget how you made them feel.

2457.   One lives in the hope of becoming a memory. -Antonio Porchia

2458.   That is what learning is. You suddenly understand something you've understood all your life but in a new way. -Doris Lessing

2459.   It is extraordinary how extraordinary the ordinary person is. -George Will

2460.   Happiness in intelligent people is the rarest thing I know. -Ernest Hemingway

2461.   Acting childish seems to come naturally, but acting like an adult, no matter how old we are, just doesn't come easy to us. -Edith Ann

2462.   He is great enough that is his own master. -Joseph Hall

2463.   Do more than you're supposed to do and you can have or be or do anything you want. -Bill Sands

2464. Bad planning on your part does not necessarily constitute an automatic emergency on my part.

2465. He was so narrow-minded he could see through a keyhole with two eyes. -Black Elk

2466. Earn but don't burn. -B. J. Gupta

2467. What really matters is what happens in us- not to us.

2468. Great lives are the culmination of great thoughts followed by great actions. -Peter Sinclair

2469. Experience teaches only the teachable. -Aldous Huxley

2470. Love is a fire. But whether it is going to warm your hearth or burn down your house, you can never tell. - Fr. Jerome Cummings

2471. It's more important to do the right thing than to do things right. -Peter Drucker

2472. The genius of the American system is that we have created extraordinary results from plain old ordinary people. -Phil Gramm

2473. A disbelief in God does not result in a belief in nothing; disbelief in God usually results in a belief in anything.

2474. I was teaching my 6-year-old daughter how to unbuckle her seat belt. She asked me, "Single click or double click?"

2475. The true measure of a man is how he treats someone who can do him absolutely no good. -Ann Landers

2476. You can only flap your arms so much before gravity catches up to you. -J & A Foundation

2477. Procrastination is the art of keeping up with yesterday. -Don Marquis

2478. Happiness is the harvest of a quiet eye. -Austin O'Malley

2479. Money is power, freedom, a cushion, the root of all evil, the sum of all blessings. -Carl Sandburg

2480. Too many people are thinking of security instead of opportunity. They seem more afraid of life than death. -James F. Byrnes

2481. It is an interesting question how far men would retain their relative rank if they were divested of their clothes. -Henry David Thoreau

2482.   When someone is having a bad day, be silent, sit close by and nuzzle them gently.

2483.   Many of life's failures are people who did not realize how close they were to success when they gave up. -Thomas Edison

2484.   Hate no one; hate their vices, not themselves. -Henry James

2485.   Zeal without knowledge is the sister of folly. - Sir John Davies

2486.   Everything in the world may be endured except continued prosperity. -Johann Wolfgang von Goethe

2487.   A man with a watch knows what time it is. ... A man with two watches is never sure.

2488.   Treat the other man's faith gently; it is all he has to believe with. -Athenus

2489.   A magician pulls rabbits out of hats. An experimental psychologist pulls habits out of rats. -Anonymous

2490.   If one desires a change, one must be that change before that change can take place. -Gita Bellin

2491.   You didn't have to say it was gone. It was gone before it got outta here. It was gonna that fast. -Jerry Coleman

2492.   I've learned that you can't have everything and do everything at the same time. -Oprah Winfrey

2493.   Ask not what you can do for your country. Ask what's for lunch. -Orson Welles

2494.   With a written agreement you have a prayer; with a verbal agreement you have nothing but air. -Robert Ringer

2495.   You can do what you want, but saving love doesn't bring any interest. - Mae West

2496.   It is not giving children more that spoils them; it is giving them more to avoid confrontation. -John Gray

2497.   The century which we are entering can be and must be the century of the common man. -Henry Wallace

2498.   It is always the best policy to speak the truth, unless, of course, you are an exceptionally good liar. - Jerome K. Jerome

2499.   Life is a state of consciousness. -Emmett Fox

2500. It has been said that man is a rational animal. All my life I have been searching for evidence which could support this. -Bertrand Russell

2501. What you spend years building may be destroyed overnight. Build anyway. -Mother Theresa

2502. Life is always a tightrope or a feather bed. Give me the tightrope. -Edith Newbold Jones Wharton

2503. Money is a poor man's credit card. -Herbert Marshall McLuhan

2504. There is no loneliness greater than the loneliness of a failure. The failure is a stranger in his own house. -Eric Hoffer

2505. Instruction does much, but encouragement does everything. -Johann Wolfgang Von Goethe

2506. Quit now, you'll never make it. If you disregard this advice you'll be halfway there. -David Zucker

2507. A verbal contract isn't worth the paper it's written on. -Samuel Goldwyn

2508. It's so easy to be wicked without knowing it, isn't it? -L. M. Montgomery

2509. Television is bubble gum for the eyes. -Frank Lloyd Wright

2510. It was the greatest feeling I ever had. Followed abruptly by the worst feeling I ever had. -Blow George

2511. Lasciate ogni speranza voi chentrate. (Abandon all hope all ye who enter here)-Dante

2512. We cannot truly face life until we face the fact that it will be taken away from us. -Billy Graham

2513. As I said before, I never repeat myself.

2514. The only way to have a friend is to be one. -Ralph Waldo Emerson

2515. If you make people think they're thinking they'll love you, but if you really make them think, they'll hate you. -Don Marquis

2516. If you want to play, practice. If you want to win, practice harder.

2517. Confidence is the companion of success. -Unknown Author

2518. Prejudice is the child of ignorance. -Samuel Hoffenstein

2519.   Speak when you are angry and you will make the best speech you will ever regret. - Ambrose Bierce

2520.   The world is blessed most by men who do things, not by those who merely talk about them. -James Oliver

2521.   Character is like a tree and a reputation like a shadow. The shadow is what we think of it; the tree is the real thing. -Abraham Lincoln

2522.   Kisses are like tears, the only real ones are the ones you can't hold back.

2523.   Courage is the power to let go of the familiar. -Raymond Lindquist

2524.   It's innocence when it charms us; ignorance when it doesn't. - Mignon McLaughlin

2525.   3 nails + 1 cross = 4 given.

2526.   One does not sell the earth upon which the people walk. –Crazy Horse

2527.   The poor wish to be rich, the rich wish to be happy, the single wish to be married, and the married wish to be dead. -Ann Landers

2528.   The great consolation in life is to say what one thinks. - Voltaire

2529.   Deep Thoughts: If you wear a toupee, why not let your friends try it on for a while? Come on, we're not going to hurt it. -Jack Handey

2530.   The discipline of desire is the background of character. -John Locke

2531.   Friends are like melons. Shall I tell you why? To find one good you must a hundred try. -Unknown

2532.   Success... it's what you do with what you've got. - Leroy Van Dyke

2533.   It's a very funny thing about life; if you refuse to accept anything but the best, you very often get it. -William Somerset Maugham

2534.   One learns to itch where one can scratch. - Ernest Bramah

2535.   Forget not that the earth delights to feel your bare feet and the winds long to play with your hair. -Kahlil Gibran

2536. You can't make war in the Middle East without Egypt and you can't make peace without Syria. -Robert Francis Kennedy

2537. The Fear of Death often proves Mortal and sets People on Methods to save their Lives which infallibly destroy them. -Joseph Addison

2538. There are two perfect men: one dead and the other unborn. -Chinese Proverb

2539. Nothing in education is so astonishing as the amount of ignorance it accumulates in the form of facts. -Henry Adams

2540. A good newspaper, I suppose, is a nation talking to itself. -Arthur Miller

2541. Count your rainbows, not your thunderstorms.

2542. It is a good thing God chose me before I was born, because he surely would not have afterwards. =C.H. Spurgeon

2543. A poem is never finished, only abandoned.-Paul Valery

2544. Some editors are failed writers, but so are most writers. -T. S. Eliot

2545. Triumph is "umph" added to try.

2546. Friendship make prosperity more shining and lessens adversity by dividing and sharing it. -Cicero

2547. Painting is silent poetry and poetry is painting with the gift of speech. -Simonides

2548. Never speak more clearly than you think. -Jeremy Bernstein

2549. Things that are not at all are never lost. -Christopher Marlowe

2550. The strongest man in the world is he who stands alone. -Henrik Ibsen

2551. In a world where there is so much to be done. I felt strongly impressed that there must be something for me to do. -Dorothea Dix

2552. All slang is a metaphor and all metaphor is poetry. -G. K. Chesterton

2553. Wit makes its own welcome and levels all distinctions. -Ralph Waldo Emerson

2554. All truly great thoughts are conceived by walking. -Friedrich Nietzsche

2555.   You are seeking joy and peace in far-off places. But the spring of joy is in your heart. The haven of peace is in yourself. -Satya Sai Baba

2556.   You've got to keep fighting; you've got to risk your life every six months to stay alive. -Elia Kazan

2557.   Help others get ahead. You will always stand taller with someone else on your shoulders. -Bob Moawad

2558.   Many could forgo heavy meals, a full wardrobe, a fine house, etc.; it is the ego they cannot forgo. - Gandhi

2559.   I never vote for anyone; I always vote against. -W. C. Fields

2560.   Hate is not a feeling toward another but a feeling of defeat by another. -Kristen Ashley Roth

2561.   To err is human - and to blame it on a computer is even more so. -Robert Orben

2562.   The way to develop self-confidence is to do the thing you fear. - William Jennings Bryan

2563.   The trouble with most people is that they think with their hopes or fears or wishes, rather than with their minds. -Lady Nancy Astor

2564.   I know nothing about sex because I was always married. -Zsa Zsa Gabor

2565.   Waste no more time talking about great souls and how they should be. Become one yourself. -Marcus Aurelius

2566.   I made my money by selling too soon. -Bernard Baruch

2567.   Work consists of whatever a body is obliged to do. Play consists of whatever a body is not obliged to do. -Mark Twain

2568.   Marital problems? You don't need a new wife, you need a new life!

2569.   Shah is a kind of magic word with the Persian people. - Mohammed Reza Pahlavi

2570.   In a few years there will be only five kings in the world - the King of England and the four kings in a pack of cards. - Farouk I

2571.   The harder you work the luckier you get. -Plato

2572.   Those who are lifting the world upward and onward are those who encourage more than criticize. -Elizabeth Harrison

2573.   The past is a guidepost, not a hitching post. -Thomas Holcroft

2574.   There is no human problem which could not be solved if people would simply do as I advise. -Gore Vidal

2575.   Basic research is what I am doing when I don't know what I am doing. -Wernher von Braun

2576.   The hardness of the butter is proportional to the softness of the bread.

2577.   Nothing can be created from nothing. -Lucretius

2578.   The better part of one's life consists of his friendships. - Abraham Lincoln

2579.   People begin to become successful the minute they decide to be. -Harvey Mackay

2580.   My house isn't dirty.

2581.   Do not trust to the cheering, for those persons would shout as much if you and I were going to be hanged. - Oliver Cromwell

2582.   I am certain of nothing but the holiness of the heart's affections and the truth of imagination. -Joseph Joubert

2583.   Although golf was originally restricted to wealthy overweight Protestants, today it's open to anybody who owns hideous clothing. - Dave Barry

2584.   If you want to make an apple pie from scratch you must first create the universe. -Carl Sagan

2585.   Are there any guys out there who are JUST NORMAL? -Road Trip, Beth

2586.   The whole being of any Christian is faith and love. Faith brings the man to God, love brings him to men. -Martin Luther

2587.   You're never beaten until you admit it. -George S. Patton

2588.   Life is the childhood of our immortality. -Johann von Goethe

2589.   The things taught in schools and colleges are not an education, but the means to an education. -Ralph Waldo Emerson

2590.   No man is justified in doing evil on the ground of expediency. - Theodore Roosevelt

2591.   There is nothing that fear and hope does not permit men to do. -Marquis De Vauvenargues

2592. You don't get to control any outcome, only every choice you make along the way. -Stephen C. Paul

2593. Grief is the agony of an instant, the indulgence of grief the blunder of a life. -Benjamin Disraeli

2594. It is dangerous to be right in matters on which the established authorities are wrong. -Francois Marie Arouet Voltaire

2595. Most people ignore most poetry because most poetry ignores most people. -Adrian Mitchell

2596. The United States is a nation of laws badly written and randomly enforced. -Frank Zappa

2597. Discipline is the refining fire by which talent becomes ability. -Roy L. Smith

2598. Perhaps the angels who fear to tread where fools rush in used to be fools who rushed in. -Franklin P. Jones

2599. Humor brings insight and tolerance. Irony brings a deeper and less friendly understanding. -Agnes Repplier

2600. Second thoughts are ever wiser. -Euripides

2601. Wit is educated insolence. -Aristotle

2602. Last night I dreamed I ate a ten-pound marshmallow and when I woke up the pillow was gone. -Tommy Cooper

2603. He who wishes to secure the good of others has already secured his own. -Confucius

2604. Money the root of all evil...but the cure for all sadness. -Mike Gill

2605. It is amazing how much people can get done if they do not worry about who gets the credit. -Sandra Swinney

2606. If you smile when no one else is around, you really mean it. -Andrew A. Rooney

2607. A woman never shot a man while he was doing dishes.

2608. There's a certain slant of light winter afternoons that oppresses like the heft of cathedral tunes. -Emily Dickinson

2609. The marble not yet carved can hold the form of every thought the greatest artist has. -Michelangelo

2610. The pursuit of perfection often impedes improvement. -George F. Will

2611. Children love to be alone because alone is where they know themselves and where they dream. -Roger Rosenblatt

2612. Church is the only place I know, where I can arrive late and get the best seats in the house!

2613. The lessons taught in great books are misleading. The commerce in life is rarely so simple and never so just. -Anita Brookner

2614. Experience is what allows us to repeat our mistakes, only with more finesse. -Derwood Fincher

2615. If we resist our passions, it is more from their weakness than from our strength. -La Rochefoucauld

2616. When the blind man carries the lame man both go forward. -Swedish Proverb

2617. The life of every man is a diary in which he means to write one story and writes another. -James Barrie

2618. Keyboard not connected, press F1 to continue.

2619. Men keep agreements when it is to the advantage of neither to break them. -Solon

2620. What is life? It is the flash of a firefly in the night. It is the breath of a buffalo in the winter time. -Crowfoot

2621. I must respect the opinions of others even if I disagree with them. - Herbert Henry Lehman

2622. It a letter contains a misleading impression not a lie. It was being economical with the truth. -Robert Armstrong

2623. The great accomplishments of man have resulted from the transmission of ideas of enthusiasm. -Thomas J. Watson

2624. An entrepreneur tends to bite off a little more than he can chew hoping he'll quickly learn how to chew it. -Roy Ash

2625. If I eat equal amounts of dark chocolate and white chocolate, is that a balanced diet?

2626. Democracy is the name we give the people whenever we need them.

2627.   Johann Wolfgang von Goethe My poor head is in such a whirl my mind is all in bits. –Robert de Flers

2628.   No man is lonely while eating spaghetti. It requires so much attention. -Christopher Morley

2629.   It is no use saying, "We are doing our best." You have got to succeed in doing what is necessary. -Winston Churchill

2630.   Sometimes even to live is an act of courage. - Seneca

2631.   Tenderness and kindness are not signs of weakness and despair, but manifestations of strength and resolution. -Kahlil Gibran

2632.   Asking a writer what he thinks about criticism is like asking a lamppost what it feels about dogs. -John Osborne

2633.   Our lives begin to end the day we become silent about things that matter. -Martin Luther King, Jr.

2634.   Shallow men believe in luck. Strong men believe in cause and effect. -Ralph Waldo Emerson

2635.   Dusty bibles lead to dirty lives.

2636.   When two men in business always agree, one of them is unnecessary. -William Jr. Wrigley

2637.   A poor report card has one good thing in its favor: at least you know the student is not cheating.

2638.   Genius will live and thrive without training but it does not the less reward the watering pot and the pruning knife. -Margaret Fuller

2639.   Shared joys make a friend not shared sufferings. -Friedrich Wilhelm Nietzsche

2640.   Hard work has future payoff. Laziness pays off now.

2641.   I don't want to describe the hate mail we've gotten. (on why she was fearful of her husband running for president) -Alma Powell

2642.   Wisdom is knowing what to do next, skill is knowing how to do it, and virtue is doing it. -David Starr Jordan

2643.   Bias against the Negro is the worst disease from which the society of our nation suffers. -Albert Einstein

2644.   Comedy is tragedy plus time. -Carol Burnett

2645. Because I could not stop for Death - He kindly stopped for me - The carriage held but just ourselves and immortality. -Emily Dickinson

2646. What you choose to focus your mind on is critical because you will become what you think about most of the time. -Noel Peebles

2647. There is no time for cut-and-dried monotony. There is time for work. And time for love. That leaves no other time! - Coco Chanel

2648. It is cruel to discover one's mediocrity only when it is too late. - W. Somerset Maugham

2649. Power tends to corrupt and absolute power corrupts absolutely. –John Emerich Edward Dalberg Acton

2650. If you really do put a small value upon yourself, rest assured that the world will not raise your price. -Anonymous

2651. There are only 3 colors, 10 digits, and 7 notes; it's what we do with them that's important. -Ruth Ross

2652. Never tell people how to do things. Tell them what to do and they will surprise you with their ingenuity. -George S. Patton

2653. One worthwhile task carried to a successful conclusion is worth half-a-hundred half-finished tasks. -Malcolm S. Forbes

2654. Wheresoever you go, go with all your heart. -Confucius

2655. The bravest thing you can do when you are not brave is to profess courage and act accordingly. -Corra Harris

2656. Why is it new and improved? If it's new, how can it be an improvement of something, and if it's improved how can it be something new?

2657. Before I got married, I had six theories about bringing up children. Now I have six children and no theories. -John Wilmot

2658. People say I've had brushes with the law. That's not true. I've had brushes with overzealous prosecutors. -Mark Duffy

2659. Trust men and they will be true to you; treat them greatly, and they will show themselves great. -Ralph Waldo Emerson

2660. Knowledge speaks, wisdom listens.

2661. Freedom from the desire for an answer is essential to the understanding of a problem. -Jiddu Krishnamurti

2662. Having your lawyer pay for lunch will be very expensive in the end.

2663. Being entirely honest with oneself is a good exercise. -Sigmund Freud

2664. The artist alone sees spirits. But after he has told of their appearing to him everybody sees them. -Johann von Goethe

2665. Watch what people are cynical about and one can often discover what they lack. -Harry Emerson Fosdick

2666. I like neither new clothes nor new kinds of food. -Albert Einstein

2667. The fear of becoming a 'has-been' keeps some people from becoming anything. - The Passionate State of the Mind, 1954. - Eric Hoffer

2668. Music is the movement of sound to reach the soul for the education of its virtue. -Plato

2669. Strive for excellence, not perfection. -H. Jackson Jr. Brown

2670. Insanity doing the same thing over and over again and expecting different results. -Albert Einstein

2671. Literature should not be suppressed merely because it affects the moral code of the censor. -William Orville Douglas

2672. Desire! That's the one secret of every man's career. Not education. Not being born with hidden talents. Desire. -Bobby Unser

2673. Integrity without knowledge is weak and useless and knowledge without integrity is dangerous and dreadful. -Samuel Johnson

2674. To the man who only has a hammer in the toolkit, every problem looks like a nail. -Abraham Maslow

2675. It is a pain in the ass waiting around for someone to try to kill you. -Roger Zelazny

2676. Good better best never let it rest till your good is better and your better is best. -Anon.

2677. Round numbers are always false. -Samuel Johnson

2678. On a front door: Everyone on the premises is a vegetarian except the dog.

2679. People with integrity do what they say they are going to do. Others have excuses. -Dr. Laura Schlessinger

2680. We are made to persist. That's how we find out who we are. -Tobias Wolff

2681. State intelligence, like military intelligence and woman friend, is a contradiction in terms. -Niall MacDermot

2682. Hope is a waking dream. -Aristotle

2683. Reading transports me. I can go anywhere and never leave my chair. It lets me shake hands with new ideas. -Rolfe Neill

2684. The surest way to get rid of a bore is to lend money to him. -Paul Louis Courier

2685. No one can be right all of the time but it helps to be right most of the time. -Robert Half

2686. Lying is done with words and also with silence. -Adrienne Rich

2687. All commend patience, but none can endure to suffer. - Thomas Fuller

2688. Either you run the day or the day runs you. -Jim Rohn

2689. The part can never be well unless the whole is well. -Saul Bellow

2690. Wisdom oft lurks beneath a tattered coat. -Caecilius Statius

2691. If we don't change, we don't grow. If we don't grow, we aren't really living. -Gail Sheehy

2692. Tomorrow is only found in the calendar of fools. -Og Mandino

2693. One man with courage makes a majority. -Andrew Old Hickory Jackson

2694. We are where we are, as we are, because of what we are. -Earle J. Glade

2695. To truly hear you must quiet the mind.

2696. There are always those who think they know what is your responsibility better than you do. -Ralph Waldo Emerson

2697. History is littered with the wars which everybody knew would never happen. -Enoch Powell

2698. Parents learn a lot from their children about coping with life. -Muriel Spark

2699. The American lives even more for his goals for the future than the European. Life for him is always becoming never being. -Albert Einstein

2700. Looks like I picked the wrong week to stop sniffing glue. - *Airplane,* Steve McCroskey

2701. It is no use walking anywhere to preach unless our walking is our preaching. -St. Francis Assisi

2702. Real freedom lies in wildness, not in civilization. -Charles Lindbergh

2703. No one should live by the early bird policy without finding out whether he classifies as a bird or a worm.

2704. I wonder if other dogs think poodles are members of a weird religious cult. -Rita Rudner

2705. Never believe anything until it has been officially denied. -Claud Cockburn

2706. I'm a great believer in luck, and I find the harder I work, the more luck I have. -Thomas Jefferson

2707. Honest criticism is hard to take particularly from a relative, a friend, an acquaintance, or a stranger. -Franklin P. Jones

2708. You have to do what others won't. To achieve what others don't. -Anonymous

2709. Judges don't age; time decorates them. -Enid Bagnold

2710. There are no secrets to success. It is the result of preparation hard work and learning from failure. -Colin Powell

2711. Many are called but few get up. -Oliver Herford

2712. Let your life lightly dance on the edges of Time like dew on the tip of a leaf. -Tagore

2713. How is it that little children are so intelligent and men so stupid? It must be education that does it. -Alexandre Dumas

2714. Weekends are a bit like rainbows; they look good from a distance, but disappear when you get up close to them. -John Shirley

2715. You couldn't even prove the White House staff sane beyond a reasonable doubt. -Ed Meese

2716.　We are born into the world of nature; our second birth is into the world of spirit. -Bhagavad-Gita

2717.　Many of life's failures are people who did not realize how close they were to success when they gave up. -Thomas Alva Edison

2718.　As I get older, I've learned to listen to people rather than accuse them of things. -Po Bronson

2719.　Hope is the ability to hear the music of the future. Faith is having the courage to dance to it today.

2720.　The soul has this proof of its divinity that divine things delight in it. -Seneca

2721.　Questions are the creative acts of intelligence. -Frank Kingdon

2722.　We must hang together, gentlemen...else, we shall most assuredly hang separately. -Benjamin Franklin, 1776

2723.　When you have eliminated the impossible that which remains however improbable must be the truth. -Frederick Douglas

2724.　I can tell you honest friend what to believe. Believe life. It teaches better than book or orator. -Johann von Goethe

2725.　One doesn't discover new lands without consenting to lose sight of the shore for a very long time. -Andre Gide

2726.　It usually takes more than three weeks to prepare a good impromptu speech. -Mark Twain

2727.　A wrongdoer is often a man that has left something undone, not always he that has done something. -Marcus Aurelius

2728.　No answer is also an answer.

2729.　All sins cast long shadows. -Irish Proverb

2730.　Never trust anybody who says trust me. Except just this once of course. *Steel Beach*, John Varley

2731.　A wife encourages her husband's egoism in order to encourage her own. -Russel Green

2732.　He that maketh haste to be rich shall not be innocent. -Biblical Proverb

2733.　We hate some persons because we do not know them, and we will not know them because we hate them. -Charles Caleb Colton

2734. When you understand one thing through and through you understand everything. -Shunryu Suzuki

2735. Remember that failure is an event - not a person.

2736. Most people would like to be delivered from temptation but would like it to keep in touch. -Robert Orben

2737. Many count their chickens before they are hatched, and where they expect bacon, meet with broken bones. -Miguel de Cervantes

2738. Talent does what it can, genius does what it must. -Unknown

2739. Opinions founded on prejudice are always sustained with the greatest of violence. -Francis Jeffrey

2740. Before he sets out the traveler must possess fixed interests and facilities to be served by travel. -George Santayana

2741. Our deeds determine us as much as we determine our deeds. - George Eliot

2742. Love rules without rules. -Italian proverb

2743. Slow but sure moves the might of the gods. -Euripides

2744. Friendship without self-interest is one of the rare and beautiful things of life. -James F. Byrnes

2745. Better to do something imperfectly than to do nothing perfectly. -Robert Schuller

2746. Never fall out with your bread and butter. -English Proverb

2747. I tell you the past is a bucket of ashes. -Carl Sandburg

2748. Realism...has no more to do with reality than anything else. - Hob Broun

2749. If we don't believe in freedom of expression for people we despise, we don't believe in it at all. Noam Chomsky

2750. When spiders unite, they can tie down a lion. -Ethiopian Proverb

2751. People with courage and character always seem sinister to the rest. -Hermann Hesse

2752. Start by doing what's necessary, then do what's possible, and suddenly you are doing the impossible. -Saint Francis of Assisi

2753. Why? Is the query of a skeptic; How? Is the question of a person who wants to believe. -J. Tilse

2754. When I was young, I admired clever people. Now that I am old, I admire kind people. -Abraham Joshua Heschel

2755. Passion makes the world go round. Love just makes it a safer place. -Ice T

2756. Men at sometime are the masters of their fate. -William Shakespeare

2757. Every human is an artist. The dream of your life is to make beautiful art. -Don Miguel Ruiz

2758. I have often depended on the blindness of strangers. -Adrienne E. Gusoff

2759. Success depends on your backbone, not your wishbone. - Unknown Author

2760. If there's one thing I know; it's God does love a good joke. - Hugh Elliott

2761. What's in a name? That which we call a rose by any other name would smell as sweet. -William Shakespeare

2762. Either war is obsolete or men are. -Richard Buckminster Fuller

2763. Better never to have met you in my dream than to wake and reach for hands that are not there. -Otomo No Yakamochi

2764. He that is discontented in one place will seldom be happy in another. -Aesop

2765. Every child is an artist. The problem is how to remain an artist once he grows up. -Pablo Picasso

2766. Culture makes all men gentle. -Menander

2767. How else but through a broken heart May Lord Christ enter in? -Oscar Wilde

2768. We always like those who admire us we do not always like those whom we admire. -François de La Rochefoucauld

2769. Once all struggle is grasped miracles are possible. -Mao Zedong

2770. Some men see things as they are and say why? I dream things that never were and say Why not? -Robert Francis Kennedy

2771. Beauty is in the heart of the beholder. - Al Bernstein

2772. Self-sacrifice enables us to sacrifice other people without blushing. -George Bernard Shaw

2773. Cicero Force overcome by force.

2774. A weed is a plant whose virtues have not yet been discovered. - Ralph Waldo Emerson

2775. I do not believe in doing for pleasure things I do not like to do. -Norman R. Augustine

2776. If you want your eggs hatched sit on them yourself. -Haitian Proverb

2777. It doesn't matter where you are coming from. All that matters is where you are going. -Brian Tracy

2778. Pity is the virtue of the law and none but tyrants use it cruelly. - William Shakespeare

2779. Were I a nightingale, I would act the part of a nightingale; were I a swan, the part of a swan. -Epictetus

2780. When I do good, I feel good. When I do bad, I feel bad, and that is my religion. -Abraham Lincoln

2781. Talents are best nurtured in solitude character is best formed in the stormy billows of the world. -Johann Wolfgang von Goethe

2782. What you see and hear depends a great deal on where you are standing; it also depends on what sort of person you are. -C. S. Lewis

2783. The obscure we see eventually. The completely obvious, it seems, takes longer. -Edward R. Murrow

2784. Yeah, baby, yeah. -Austin Powers, *International Man of Mystery: Austin Powers*

2785. Nothing is as simple as we hope it will be. -Jim Horning

2786. Though a man be wise, it is no shame for him to live and learn. -Sophocles

2787. Don't go through life GROW through life. -Eric Butterworth

2788. Education is a state-controlled manufactory of echoes. -Norman Douglas

2789. In a hierarchy every employee tends to rise to his level of incompetence. -Laurence J. Peter

2790. Stop thinking in terms of limitations and start thinking in terms of possibilities. -Terry Josephson

2791.	When you get through all the phony tinsel of Hollywood, you find the genuine tinsel underneath. -Fred Allen

2792.	We all have the extraordinary coded within us waiting to be released. -Jean Houston

2793.	The secret of success is constancy of purpose. -Benjamin Disraeli

2794.	People seem to get nostalgic about a lot of things they weren't so crazy about the first time around.

2795.	May your trouble be like the old man's teeth...few and far between.

2796.	Don't worry about the world coming to an end today. It's already tomorrow in Australia. -Charles M. Schulz

2797.	Diplomacy is the art of saying, "Nice doggie" until you can find a rock. -Will Rogers

2798.	Eighty percent of success is showing up. -Woody Allen

2799.	Life is a succession of lessons which must be lived to be understood. -Helen Keller

2800.	If you live to be a hundred, I want to live to be a hundred minus one day, so I never have to live without you. -Winnie the Pooh

2801.	Music expresses that which cannot be put into words and that which cannot remain silent. -Victor Hugo

2802.	Adversity is the diamond dust Heaven polishes its jewels with. -Robert Leighton

2803.	Poverty is a veil that obscures the face of greatness. An appeal is a mask covering the face of tribulation. -Kahlil Gibran

2804.	The younger brother hath the more wit. -John Ray

2805.	Every situation properly perceived becomes an opportunity. -Helen Schucman

2806.	Man "Is this seat empty?" Woman "Yes, and this one will be too if you sit down."

2807.	Life is what happens to you when you're making other plans. -Betty Talmadge

2808.	The squeaking wheel doesn't always get the grease. Sometimes it gets replaced. -Vic Gold

2809.   If it is your time, love will track you down like a cruise missile. -Lynda Barry

2810.   I trust that everything happens for a reason even when we're not wise enough to see it. -Oprah Winfrey

2811.   The trouble with the world is that the stupid are cocksure and the intelligent are full of doubt. -Bertrand Russell

2812.   Our own heart, and not other men's opinions, forms our true honor. -Samuel Taylor Coleridge

2813.   Singularity shows something wrong in the mind. - Clarissa

2814.   The world at large does not judge us by who we are and what we know it judges us by what we have. -Joyce Brothers

2815.   Forget regret or life is yours to miss. -Jonathan Larson

2816.   There is nothing either good or bad but thinking makes it so. -William Shakespeare

2817.   Why love if losing hurts so much? We love to know that we are not alone. -C.S. Lewis

2818.   The snow goose need not bathe to make itself white. Neither need you do anything but be yourself. - Lao-Tzu

2819.   If loving the Lord is wrong, I don't want to be right. -Coming to America, Rev. Brown

2820.   All marriages are mixed marriages. -Chantal Saperstein

2821.   Statistics are like bikinis. What they reveal is suggestive but what they conceal is vital. -Aaron Levenstein

2822.   Lawyers-a profession it is to disguise matters. -Sir Thomas More

2823.   If you love someone put their name in a circle because hearts can be broken but circles never end. -Unknown

2824.   I don't believe anything. I only know some things to a greater degree of certainty than others. -John Ryman, from When Galaxies Collide

2825.   Why do people point at their wrists when they ask what time it is? Do I point at my crotch when I ask where the bathroom is?

2826.   Our opinions do not really blossom into fruition until we have expressed them to someone else. -Mark Twain

2827. Despair in short seeks its own environment as surely as water finds its own level. -Alvarez

2828. The journey is the reward. -Taoist Saying

2829. I don't even butter my bread. I consider that cooking. -Katherine Cebrian

2830. There are too many mediocre things to deal with. Love shouldn't be one of them.

2831. Our friends should be companions who inspire us, who help us rise to our best. -Joseph B. Wirthlin

2832. You cannot be really first-rate at your work if your work is all you are. -Anna Quindlen

2833. The tragedy of life is not that man loses but that he almost wins. -Heywood

2834. When the mouth stumbles it is worse than the foot. -African Proverb

2835. When we speak of the commerce with our colonies, fiction lags after truth, invention is unfruitful, and imagination cold and barren.

2836. You have to learn that if you start making sure you feel good everything will be okay. -Ruben Studdard

2837. The expectations of life depend upon diligence; the mechanic that would perfect his work must first sharpen his tools. -Confucius

2838. The fact that when we die we are nothing more than worm meat - I just don't think about it. -Robin Green

2839. We must walk consciously only part way toward our goal and then leap in the dark to our success. -Henry David Thoreau

2840. I don't understand Christianity, nor do I understand electricity, but I don't intend to sit in the dark until I do!

2841. We all have ability. The difference is how we use it. -Stevie Wonder

2842. Sex is emotion in motion. -Mae West

2843. There's one good kind of writer - a dead one. -James T. Farrell

2844. The test of a vocation is the love of the drudgery it involves. -Logan Pearsall Smith

2845.　The key to happiness is not fixing your problems but changing your attitude towards your problems.

2846.　Sow an act...reap a habit Sow a habit...reap a character Sow a character...reap a destiny. -George Dana Boardman

2847.　Of all noises I think music is the least disagreeable. -Samuel Johnson

2848.　A storm broke loose in my mind. -Albert Einstein

2849.　History is the discovering of the constant and universal principles of human nature. -David Hume

2850.　Any plan is bad which is incapable of modification. -Publilius Syrus

2851.　A boy becomes an adult three years before his parents think he does and about two years after he thinks he does. -Lewis Blaine Hershey

2852.　He that cannot reason is a fool. He that will not is a bigot. He that dare not is a slave. -Andrew Carnegie

2853.　Character is the result of two things: Mental attitude and the way we spend our time. -Elbert Hubbard

2854.　Every man should have a fair-sized cemetery in which to bury the faults of his friends. -Henry Brooks Adams

2855.　If you commit a crime, you're guilty. -Rush Limbaugh

2856.　The go-between wears out a thousand sandals. -Japanese Proverb

2857.　My salad days, when I was green in judgment. -William Shakespeare

2858.　Seek ye first the good things of the mind and the rest will either be supplied or its loss will not be felt. -Francis Bacon

2859.　Great spirits have always encountered violent opposition from mediocre minds. -Albert Einstein

2860.　He who can no longer pause to wonder and stand rapt in awe is as good as dead; his eyes are closed. -Albert Einstein

2861.　You have to see the pattern, understand the order and experience the vision. -Michael E. Gerber

2862.　Events are less important than our response to them.

2863.   Every man has one thing he can do better than anyone else -
and usually its reading his own handwriting. -G. Norman Collie

2864.   Set all things in their own peculiar place and know that order is
the greatest grace. -John Dryden

2865.   I was the kid next door's imaginary friend. -Emo Phillips

2866.   The perfecting of one's self is the fundamental base of all
progress and all moral development. -Confucius

2867.   I wouldn't ever set out to hurt anyone deliberately unless it was
you know important like a league game or something. -Dick Butkus

2868.   After people have repeated a phrase a great number of times
they begin to realize it has meaning and may even be true. -H. G.
Wells

2869.   Believe one who has proved it. Believe an expert. -Virgil

2870.   Anger dwells only in the bosom of fools. -Albert Einstein

2871.   The only thing we have to fear is fear itself. -Franklin D
Roosevelt

2872.   I love living. I have some problems with my life, but living is the
best thing they've come up with so far. -Neil Simon

2873.   I've got all the money I'll ever need, if I die by four o'clock. -
Henny Youngman

2874.   In the civilization a new law of hostility prevails. And to call it
the law of the jungle is unfair to the jungle. -Colin Wilson

2875.   A friend is known when needed. -Arabian proverb

2876.   Who are you and how did you get in here? I'm a locksmith. And
I'm a locksmith. -Leslie Nielsen

2877.   Bad habits are like chains that are too light to feel until they are
too heavy to carry. -Warren Buffett

2878.   The dynamics that are required to make any relationship work:
Just keep putting your love out there. - Anonymous

2879.   There is no security on earth; there is only opportunity. -
Douglas MacArthur

2880.   In the choice of a horse and a wife, a man must please himself
ignoring the opinion and advice of friends. -George John Whyte-
Melville

2881. Where there are no swamps, there are no frogs. -German proverb

2882. Always be a little kinder than necessary. -James Barrie

2883. Sometimes it's good to contrast what you like with something else. It makes you appreciate it even more. -Darby Conley

2884. In what concerns you much do not think that you have companions know that you are alone in the world. -Henry David Thoreau

2885. When everything seems to be going against you, remember the airplane takes off against the wind, not with it. -Henry Ford

2886. I love my country too much to be a nationalist. -Albert Camus

2887. Rage is the only quality which has kept me or anybody I have ever studied writing columns for newspapers. -Jimmy Breslin

2888. Good people do not need laws to tell them to act responsibly, while bad people will find a way around the laws. -Plato

2889. Winning isn't everything but wanting to win is. -Vince Lombardi

2890. Life is too short to settle for anything less than an effort. -Unknown

2891. In the night all cats are gray. -Miguel de Cervantes

2892. Some people are about as helpful as a porcupine in a balloon factory. -Donna Early

2893. Where we're going, we don't need roads? -*Back to the Future*, Dr. Emmett Brown Roads

2894. Deep Thoughts: If any man says he hates war more than I do he better have a knife, that's all I have to say. -Jack Handey

2895. The Anglo-Saxon conscience doesn't keep you from doing anything. It just keeps you from enjoying it. -Salvador de Madariaga

2896. There are no great things, only small things with great love. Happy are those. -Mother Theresa

2897. Irrational barriers and ancient prejudices fall quickly when the question of survival itself is at stake. -John Fitzgerald Kennedy

2898. There is no way to be completely happy without being oblivious to the world around you. -Meredith Close

2899. Nothing surely is so disgraceful to society and to individuals as unmeaning wastefulness. -Count Benjamin Thompson Rumford

2900. I found Rome a city of bricks and left it a city of marble. -Caesar Augustus

2901. This is how God showed His love among us He sent His one and only Son into the world that we might live through Him. -John NIV Bible

2902. An army of sheep led by a lion would defeat an army of lions led by a sheep. -Arab Proverb

2903. Show class, have pride and display character. If you do, winning takes care of itself. -Paul Bryant

2904. Passion costs me too much to bestow it on every trifle. -Thomas Adams

2905. The earth has music for those who listen. -William Shakespeare

2906. People seldom refuse help, if one offers it in the right way. - A. C. Benson

2907. To be, or not to be, those are the parameters.

2908. Remember that there is nothing stable in human affairs; therefore avoid undue elation in prosperity, or undue depression in adversity. - Socrates

2909. Disability is a matter of perception. If you can do just one thing well, you're needed by someone. -Martina Navratilova

2910. Don't think you are going to conceal thoughts by concealing evidence that they ever existed. -Dwight D Eisenhower

2911. The wise man is he who knows the relative value of things. - William Ralph Inge

2912. The main thing needed to make men happy is intelligence. - Bertrand Russell

2913. Always be nice to your children because they are the ones who will choose your rest home. -Phyllis Diller

2914. Some days you're a bug; some days you're a windshield. -Price Cobb

2915. Riches and power are but gifts of blind fate whereas goodness is the result of one's own merits. -Heloise

2916. The enjoyment of life would be instantly gone if you removed the possibility of doing something. -Chauncey Depew

2917. I do most of my work sitting down that's where I shine. -Robert Charles Benchley

2918. I'm writing a book. I've got the page numbers done.

2919. A neurotic is a man who builds a castle in the sky. A psychotic is the man who lives in it. And a psychiatrist collects the rent.

2920. You shall know the truth and the truth shall make you mad. -Aldous Huxley

2921. Success is the child of audacity. -Benjamin Disraeli

2922. I'm tired of Love. I'm still more tired of Rhyme. But Money gives me pleasure all the time. -Hilaire Belloc

2923. Old programmers never die. They just branch out to a new address. -Anon.

2924. It is undesirable to believe a proposition when there is no ground whatsoever for supposing it is true. -Bertrand Russell

2925. Forgive O Lord my little jokes on Thee and I'll forgive Thy great big one on me. -Robert Frost

2926. It is what you do about what happens that counts. -Jim Rohn

2927. He who knows others is learned; he who knows himself is wise. -Lao-Tzu

2928. We protest against unjust criticism but we accept unearned applause. -Jose Narosky

2929. Trying to squash a rumor is like trying to unring a bell. -Shana Alexander

2930. Oh for a book and a shady nook... -John Wilson

2931. How many ages hence Shall this our lofty scene be acted over In states unborn and accents yet unknown. -William Shakespeare

2932. The virtuous man is never a novice in worldly things. -Marcus Valerius Martialis

2933. Don't worry about anything. Worrying never solved anything. All it does is distort your mind. -Milton Garland

2934. Wise men make proverbs but fools repeat them. -Samuel Palmer

2935.   Action without a name, a "who" attached to it, is meaningless.—Jerome

2936.   Good people do not need laws to tell them to act responsibly while bad people will find a way around the laws. -Plato

2937.   A classic is something that everybody wants to have read and nobody wants to read. -Mark Twain

2938.   Definition of a Statistician: A man who believes figures don't lie, but admits than under analysis some of them won't stand up either. -Evan Esar

2939.   One boy is more trouble than a dozen girls. -English Proverb

2940.   Great opportunities to help others seldom come but small ones surround us every day. -Sally Koch

2941.   Every great player has learned to two C's: how to concentrate and how to maintain composure. -Byron Nelson

2942.   The mind is like the stomach. It is not how much you put into it that counts but how much it digests. -J. Nock

2943.   By perseverance the snail reached the ark. -Charles Haddon Spurgeon

2944.   A friend is one who believes in you when you have ceased to believe in yourself. -Unknown

2945.   Action springs not from thought, but from a readiness for responsibility. - Dietrich Bonhoeffer

2946.   Think to yourself that every day is your last; the hour to which you do not look forward will come as a welcome surprise. -Horace

2947.   Whatever happens, it all happens as it should. Thou wilt find this true if thou shouldst watch closely. -Marcus Aurelius

2948.   If the desire to need is measured by the value of something, then you my darling are quite simply priceless. -Derek Breslin

2949.   Hard work brings prosperity; playing around brings poverty. -Bible

2950.   It's hard for me to answer a question from someone who really doesn't care about the answer. -Charles Grodin

2951.   Excellence is the gradual result of always striving to do better. -Pat Riley

2952. An injury is much sooner forgotten than an insult. -Lord Chesterfield

2953. One of the most important things in communication is to hear what is not being said. -Peter Drucker

2954. Marriage is a book of which the first chapter is written in poetry and the remaining chapters in prose. -Beverly Nichols

2955. Art washes away from the soul the dust of everyday life.-Pablo Picasso

2956. Inside yourself or outside, you never have to change what you see, only the way you see it. -Thaddeus Golas

2957. Early to rise and early to bed makes a man healthy, wealthy, and dead.—James Thurber

2958. Gratitude is not only the greatest of virtues but the parent of all others. -Cicero

2959. Hardware: The parts of a computer system that can be kicked.

2960. Unless you believe you will not understand. -Saint Augustine

2961. No sin is small. -Jeremy Taylor

2962. Let him who desires peace prepare for war. -Vegetius

2963. Human beings can alter their lives by altering their attitudes. -Norman Vincent Peale

2964. Poets have been mysteriously silent on the subject of cheese. -G. K. Chesterton

2965. Compassion is the basis of all morality. -Arthur Schopenhauer

2966. Once conform, once do what others do because they do it, and a kind of lethargy steals over all the finer senses of the soul. -Montaigne

2967. The truth is cruel but it can be loved and it makes free those who have loved it. -George Santayana

2968. Be like a postage stamp. Stick to one thing until you get there. -Josh Billings

2969. Drunkenness is temporary suicide. -Bertrand Russell

2970. The only true love is love at first sight; second sight dispels it. -Israel Zangwill

2971.   At any given point of time you are exactly what you wanted to be. -Vinny Nayak

2972.   A man can stand anything except a succession of ordinary days. -Johann Wolfgang von Goethe

2973.   It may be said with a degree of assurance that not everything that meets the eye is as it appears. -Rod Serling

2974.   For every action there is an equal and opposite government program. -Bob Wells

2975.   Writing is hard work and bad for the health. -E. B. White

2976.   It is foolish and wrong to mourn the men who died. Rather we should thank God that such men lived. -George Smith Patton Jr.

2977.   A mind, like a home, is furnished by its owner, so if one's life is cold and bare he can blame none but himself. -Louis L'Amour

2978.   There's two heads to every coin. -Jerry Coleman

2979.   The eyes are not responsible when the mind does the seeing. -Publilius Syrus

2980.   I believe in Christianity as I believe that the sun has risen. Not only because I see it, but because by it I see everything else.

2981.   There is no flying without wings. -French Proverb

2982.   Accustom yourself continually to make many acts of love for they enkindle and melt the soul. -Saint Teresa of Avila

2983.   Only he who can see the invisible can do the impossible. -Frank Gaines

2984.   Natural selection, as it has operated in human history, favors not only the clever but the murderous. -Barbara Ehrenreich

2985.   I think it's more important to be fit so that you can be healthy and enjoy activities than it is to have a good body. -Rachel Blanchard

2986.   We cannot change anything unless we accept it. Condemnation does not liberate it oppresses. -Carl Jung

2987.   Being cool, is not trying to be cool.

2988.   Reality can be beaten with enough imagination. -Anon.

2989.   Failure is only postponed success as long as courage coaches ambition. The habit of persistence is the habit of victory. -Herbert Kaufman

2990. There is none who cannot teach somebody something and there is none so excellent but he is excelled. -Baltasar Gracian

2991. All paid jobs absorb and degrade the mind. -Aristotle

2992. I'd rather give my life than be afraid to give it. -Lyndon B. Johnson

2993. Laughter is the shortest distance between two people. -Victor Borge

2994. For all sad words of tongue and pen, the saddest are these, "It might have been." -John Greenleaf Whittier

2995. Property has its duties as well as its rights. -Thomas Brummond

2996. Did you ever walk into a room and forget why you walked in? I think that is how dogs spend their lives. -Sue Murphy

2997. The only certain means is to render more and better service than is expected of you no matter what your task may be. -Og Mandino

2998. I've decided to stick with love. Hate is too great a burden to bear. -Martin Luther King, Jr.

2999. Republicans believe every day is the Fourth of July, but Democrats believe every day is April 15. -Ronald Reagan

3000. A wise person has something to say, a fool has to say something.

3001. Even Popeye didn't eat his spinach until he absolutely had to.

3002. A word of encouragement during a failure is worth more than an hour of praise after success. -Author unknown

3003. Love is not the dying moan of a distant violin... it's the triumphant twang of a bedspring. -S. J. Perelman

3004. I shall curse you with book and bell and candle. -Sir Thomas Malory

3005. When you have eliminated the impossible, whatever remains, however improbable, must be the truth. -Sir Arthur Conan Doyle

3006. Until lions have their historians, tales of the hunt shall always glorify the hunter. -African Proverb

3007. The hand cannot reach higher than does the heart. -Orison Swett Marden

3008. Character matters; leadership descends from character. -Rush Limbaugh

3009.   Some people grin and bear it; others smile and do it. - Anonymous

3010.   The main dangers in this life are the people who want to change everything - or nothing. -Lady Nancy Astor

3011.   He turns all of his injuries into strengths; that which does not kill him makes him stronger; he is superman. -Friedrich Wilhelm Nietzsche

3012.   Education is a kind of continuing dialogue, and a dialogue assumes, in the nature of the case, different points of view. -Robert Hutchins

3013.   What we need are more people who specialize in the impossible. -Theodore Roethke

3014.   Economics is war pursued by other means. -Raymond F. DeVoe Jr.

3015.   The unexpected always comes at the most awkward times. - Larry Niven

3016.   In a mirror last place becomes first place... Just depends on how you wish to look at it. -Debbie Skelly

3017.   People often say that motivation doesn't last. Well, neither does bathing-that's why we recommend it daily. -Zig Ziglar

3018.   No degree of dullness can safeguard a work against the determination of critics to find it fascinating. -Harold Rosenberg

3019.   Mr. Attlee is a very modest man. Indeed, he has a lot to be modest about. -Winston Churchill

3020.   Talent develops in tranquility character in the full current of human life. -Johann von Goethe

3021.   He was a man take him for all in all I shall not look upon his like again. -William Shakespeare

3022.   There's no point in burying the hatchet if you're going to put up a marker on the site. -Sydney Harris

3023.   I do not pretend to know where many ignorant men are sure-that is all that agnosticism means. -Clarence Darrow

3024.   Whatever limits us we call fate. -Ralph Waldo Emerson

3025.   Honor has not to be won; it must only not be lost. - Arthur
Schopenhauer

3026.   The principle is: competing against yourself. It's about self-
improvement, about being better than you were the day before. -
Steve Young

3027.   Getting ideas is like shaving if you don't do it every day you're a
bum. -Alex Kroll

3028.   An idea is salvation by imagination. -Frank Lloyd Wright

3029.   If suffer we must, let's suffer on the heights. -Victor Hugo

3030.   The way to final freedom is within thy self. -The Book of the
Golden Precepts

3031.   Everything has two handles - one by which it may be borne
another by which it cannot. -Epictetus

3032.   Indeed man wishes to be happy even when he so lives as to make
happiness impossible. -Saint Augustine

3033.   The art of love ... is largely the art of persistence. - Albert Ellis

3034.   Riches, like glory or heath, have no more beauty or pleasure
than their possessor is pleased to lend them. -Michel Eyquem de
Montaigne

3035.   Motivation is like food for the brain. You cannot get enough in
one sitting. It needs continual and regular top ups. -Peter J. Davies

3036.   No idea is so antiquated that it was not once modern. No idea is
so modern that it will not someday be antiquated. -Ellen Glasgow

3037.   When we seek to discover the best in others, we somehow bring
out the best in ourselves. -William Arthur Ward

3038.   Passion costs me too much to bestow it on every trifle. -
Thomas Adams

3039.   Too little liberty brings stagnation and too much brings chaos. -
Bertrand Russell

3040.   I can't change the direction of the wind. But I can adjust my
sails. -Unknown Author

3041.   Fall down seven times, stand up eight. -Japanese Proverb

3042.   A person can fail many times, but they are not really a failure
until they start to blame someone else.

3043. It is unfortunate, considering that enthusiasm moves the world, that so few enthusiasts can be trusted to tell the truth. -Stanley Baldwin

3044. Every step toward Christ kills a doubt. Every thought word and deed for Him carries you away from discouragement. -Theodore Ledyard Cuyler

3045. He who cannot rest cannot work; he who cannot let go cannot hold on; he who cannot find footing cannot go forward. -Richard Willard Armour

3046. I don't have anything against work. I just figure, why deprive somebody who really loves it. -Dobie Gillis

3047. The thing I hate about an argument is that it always interrupts a discussion. -G. K. Chesterton

3048. He hath eaten me out of house and home. -William Shakespeare

3049. Criminal: A person with predatory instincts who has not sufficient capital to form a corporation. -Howard Scott

3050. To err is dysfunctional, to forgive co-dependent. -Berton Averre

3051. Where there are friends; there is wealth. -Titus Maccius Plautus 250-184 BC

3052. We know accurately only when we know little; with knowledge, doubt increases. -Johann von Goethe

3053. One can resist an intrusion of armies but not an idea whose time has come. -Victor Hugo

3054. For certain is death for the born, and certain is birth for the dead. Therefore over the inevitable, thou shouldst not grieve. - Bhagavad Gita

3055. Nothing is as soft as water, yet who can withstand the raging flood? -Lao Ma

3056. Everything a human being wants can be divided into four components: love, adventure, power, and fame. -Johann Wolfgang von Goethe

3057. Success is where preparation and opportunity meet. -Bobby Unser

3058. Love is the great miracle cure. Loving ourselves works miracles in our lives. -Louise Hay

3059. I met a fool in the forest, a motley fool. -William Shakespeare

3060. Delay is the deadliest form of denial. -C. Northcote Parkinson

3061. I have had dreams and I have had nightmares, but I have conquered my nightmares because of my dreams. -Jonas Salk

3062. The world is round; it has no point. -Adrienne E. Gusoff

3063. America is the country where you buy a lifetime supply of aspirin for one dollar and use it up in two weeks. -John Barrymore

3064. People forget how fast you did a job, but they remember how well you did it. -Howard W. Newton

3065. Only those who dare to fail greatly can ever achieve greatly. -Robert Francis Kennedy

3066. If you must play, decide upon three things at the start: the rules of the game, the stakes, and the quitting time. -Chinese Proverb

3067. The only thing that's been a worse flop than the organization of non-violence has been the organization of violence. -Joan Baez

3068. I guess we'd be living in a boring perfect world if everybody wished everybody else well. -Jennifer Aniston

3069. No race can prosper till it learns that there is as much dignity in tilling a field as in writing a poem. -Booker T. Washington

3070. What luck for rulers that men do not think. -Adolf Hitler

3071. It's easy to halve the potato where there's love. -Irish Proverb

3072. Prejudice is the child of ignorance. -William Hazlitt

3073. The reward for work well done is the opportunity to do more. -Dr. Jonas Salk

3074. Joy comes from using your potential. -Will Schultz

3075. To bear failure with courage is the best proof of character that anyone can give. -W. Somerset Maugham

3076. An unpopular rule is never long maintained. -Seneca

3077. This great misfortune - to be incapable of solitude. -Jean de La Bruyere

3078. Look for the good, not the evil in the conduct of members of the family. -Jewish Proverb

3079. There are lots of people who cannot think seriously without injuring their minds. - John Jay Chapman

3080. There is only one universal passion: fear. -George Bernard Shaw

3081. One who walks in another's tracks leaves no footprints. -Proverb

3082. You can have it all. You just can't have it all at once. -Oprah Winfrey

3083. A great country worthy of the name does not have any friends. - Charles De Gaulle

3084. With the new day comes new strength and new thoughts. - Eleanor Roosevelt

3085. Your temper is the only thing you can lose and still have.

3086. If you don't know where you're going, how do you expect to get there?

3087. Values are tapes we play on the Walkman of the mind any tune we choose so long as it does not disturb others. -Jonathan Sacks

3088. Peace cannot be achieved through violence; it can only be attained through understanding. -Ralph Waldo Emerson

3089. Fight for your opinions but do not believe that they contain the whole truth or the only truth. -Charles A. Dana

3090. I only work to enjoy when I am not working.

3091. Everyone should carefully observe which way his heart draws him, and then choose that way with all his strength. -Hasidic saying

3092. I can think of nothing less pleasurable than a life devoted to pleasure. -John D. Rockefeller

3093. It is seldom easy to do what's right or right to do what's easy.

3094. We're all capable of mistakes but I do not care to enlighten you on the mistakes we may or may not have made. -Dan Quayle

3095. Most of us are pretty good at keeping promises to others and pretty bad at keeping promises to ourselves. -Lawrence LeShan

3096. The only Zen you find on the tops of mountains is the Zen you bring up there. -Robert M. Pirsig

3097. An invasion of armies may be resisted, but not an idea whose time has come. -Victor Hugo

3098. I have never met a man so ignorant that I couldn't learn something from him. -Galileo Galilei

3099. Prayer does not cause faith to work, faith causes prayer to work. -Gloria Copeland

3100. Freedom of expression is the matrix, the indispensable condition of nearly every other form of freedom. -Benjamin Cardozo

3101. There is no elevator to success. You have to take the stairs. - Author unknown

3102. It is better to light one small candle than to curse the darkness. -Confucius

3103. Age is a matter of feeling...not of years. -George William Curtis

3104. It was never what I wanted to buy that held my heart's hope. It was what I wanted to be. -Lois McMaster Bujold

3105. Success is getting up just one more time than you fall down.

3106. It is always the ones who talk loudest who do the least.

3107. They (corporations) cannot commit treason, nor be outlawed, nor excommunicated, for they have no souls. - Lord Edward Coke

3108. Gambling: The sure way of getting nothing for something.

3109. Regimen is superior to medicine. -Voltaire

3110. Some of the waiters discuss the menu with you as if they were sharing wisdom picked up in the Himalayas. -Seymour Britchky

3111. Do not meddle in the affairs of wizards for they are subtle and quick to anger. -J. R. R. Tolkien

3112. Susan Johnson Whoever has the greatest command of the language holds the power.

3113. A friend may well be reckoned the masterpiece of nature. - Ralph Waldo Emerson

3114. When you come to a roadblock take a detour. -Mary Kay Ash

3115. Insanity in individuals is something rare, but in groups, parties, nations, and epochs it is the rule. -Friedrich Nietzsche

3116. Two men look out through the same bars One sees the mud and one the stars. -Frederick Langbridge

3117. Never let your persistence and passion turn into stubbornness and ignorance. -Anthony D'Angelo

3118.   Love, truth, and pardon error. -Voltaire

3119.   There are many fine ideals which are not realizable and yet we do not refrain from teaching them. -Peretz Smolenskin

3120.   To live your life to the fullest, you've got to be a master of economics...after all, time's demand is always far exceeding its supply.

3121.   The true civilization is where every man gives to every other every right that he claims for himself. -Robert G. Ingersoll

3122.   If you go into what I call a bubble boom every bubble bursts. -Margaret Hilda Thatcher

3123.   Intuition will tell the thinking mind where to look next. -Dr. Jonas Salk

3124.   I'm not afraid of storms, for I'm learning to sail my ship. -Louisa May Alcott

3125.   If its sanity you are after, there is no recipe like laughter. -Henry Elliot

3126.   My view is that one should not break up a winning combination. -Richard Milhous Nixon

3127.   Nothing is a waste of time if you use the experience wisely. -Rodin

3128.   It matters not what goal you seek Its secret here reposes: You've got to dig from week to week To get Results or Roses.—Edgar Guest

3129.   I do not know whether I was then a man dreaming I was a butterfly, or whether I am now a butterfly dreaming I am a man. -Chuang-Tzu

3130.   Each happiness of yesterday is a memory for tomorrow. -George W. Douglas

3131.   The speed of the leader determines the rate of the pack. -Wayne Lukas

3132.   Not that the story need be long but it will take a long while to make it short. -Henry David Thoreau

3133.   Life is just one damned thing after another. -Elbert Hubbard

3134.   Drop the question what tomorrow may bring and count as profit every day that fate allows you. -Horace

3135.   There are some defeats more triumphant than victories. -Michel de Montaigne

3136.   Good people are good because they've come to wisdom through failure. We get very little wisdom from success you know. -William Saroyan

3137.   Opportunity often comes disguised in the form of misfortune, or temporary defeat. -Napoleon Hill

3138.   The chief value of money lies in the fact that one lives in a world in which it is overestimated. -H. L. Mencken

3139.   It is only as we develop others that we permanently succeed. -Harvey S. Firestone

3140.   The quality of your life is the quality of your communication with yourself as well as with others. -Anthony Robbins

3141.   Love is shown in your deeds, not in your words. - George De Benneville

3142.   If you would be loved, love, and be loveable. -Benjamin Franklin

3143.   Education is a progressive discovery of our own ignorance. -Will Durant

3144.   I really wonder what gives us the right to wreck this poor planet of ours. -Kurt Vonnegut Jr.

3145.   You can do what you have to do, and sometimes you can do it even better than you think you can. -Jimmy Carter

3146.   The Creator has not given you a longing to do what you have no ability to do. -Orison Swett Marden

3147.   Let us be of good cheer, however, remembering that the misfortunes hardest to bear are those which never come. -James Russell Lowell

3148.   Decide what you want, decide what you are willing to exchange for it. Establish your priorities and go to work. -H. L. Hunt

3149.   If life were easy, then it would be boring. -Charles Beck

3150.   Do what you fear and fear disappears. -David Joseph Schwartz

3151.   It is when we forget ourselves that we do things that are most likely to be remembered.

3152.   Silence is a friend who will never betray. -Confucius

3153. A person will sometimes devote all his life to the development of one part of his body; the wishbone. -Robert Frost

3154. Woe to the man whose heart has not learned while young to hope, to love - and to put its trust in life. - Joseph Conrad

3155. It takes as much energy to wish as it does to plan. -Eleanor Roosevelt

3156. Quite frankly, teachers are the only profession that teach our children. -Dan Quayle

3157. There's a little truth in all jive, and a little jive in all truth. - Leonard Barnes

3158. I try to lose weight, but it keeps finding me.

3159. To play it safe is not to play. -Robert Altman

3160. Don't wake me for the end of the world unless it has very good special effects. -Roger Zelazny

3161. One fails forward toward success. -Charles Kettering

3162. I despise the pleasure of pleasing people that I despise. -Mary Wortley Montagu

3163. Integrity is the cornerstone of trust.

3164. You spend all your life trying to do something they put people in asylums for. -Jane Fonda

3165. Our passions are like convulsion fits which though they make us stronger for a time leave us the weaker ever after. -Alexander Pope

3166. He has conferred on the practice of vacillation the aura of statesmanship. - Kenneth Baker

3167. To let a fool kiss you is stupid. To let a kiss fool you is worse.

3168. Americans never quit. -General Douglas MacArthur

3169. An effective way to deal with predators is to taste terrible. - Unknown

3170. Charity in necessary things, unity in doubtful things, liberty in all things. -Richard Baxter

3171. There's no business like show business. -Irving Berlin

3172. No hatred is so bitter as that of near relations. -Cornelius Tacitus

3173.   Little minds attain and are subdued by misfortunes; but great minds rise above them. -Washington Irving

3174.   The first proof of a person's incapacity to achieve is their endeavoring to fix the stigma of failure on others. -B. R. Hayden

3175.   Where will you be sitting in eternity - smoking or non-smoking?

3176.   We are what we pretend to be so we must be careful what we pretend to be. -Kurt Vonnegut Jr.

3177.   Expecting the world to treat you fairly because you are good is like expecting the bull not to charge because you are a vegetarian.

3178.   Change begets change. -Charles Dickens

3179.   All kids need is a little help, a little hope and somebody who believes in them. -Earvin Johnson

3180.   It was when Lucifer first congratulated himself upon his angelic behavior that he became the tool of evil. -Dag Hammarskjöld

3181.   I love all beauteous things I seek and adore them God hath no better praise And man in his hasty days is honored for them. -Robert Bridges

3182.   He who has great power should use it lightly. - Seneca

3183.   To each his own. -Cicero

3184.   The urge to gamble is so universal, and its practice so pleasurable that I assume it must be evil. -Heywood Broun

3185.   Don't anthropomorphize computers - they hate it. - Anonymous

3186.   To find a friend, one must close one eye; to keep him, two. - Norman Douglas

3187.   Always bear in mind that your own resolution to succeed is more important than any other one thing. -Abraham Lincoln

3188.   Success in marriage is more than finding the right person. It's becoming the right person.

3189.   Your worth consists in what you are and not in what you have. - Thomas Alva Edison

3190.   No Jesus - No Love. Know Jesus - Know Love.

3191. He who is afraid of asking is ashamed of learning. -Danish Proverb

3192. In my day we didn't have self-esteem we had self-respect and no more of it than we had earned. -Jane Haddam

3193. Today is the tomorrow you worried about yesterday. -Unknown

3194. A year from now you may wish you had started today. -Karen Lamb

3195. The only difference between a rut and a grave... is in their dimensions. -Ellen Glasgow

3196. Four snakes gliding up and down a hollow for no purpose that I could see - not to eat not for love but only gliding. -Ralph Waldo Emerson

3197. The herd instinct among forecasters makes sheep look like independent thinkers. - Edgar R. Fiedler

3198. It is only with the heart that one can see rightly. What is essential is invisible to the eye. -Antoine de Saint Exupery

3199. But when you start disagreeing with the answers you've got a problem. -R. E. Phillips

3200. Ah, but a man's reach should exceed his grasp, or what's a heaven for? -Robert Browning

3201. Even a mosquito doesn't get a slap on the back until it starts to work. -Anonymous

3202. The cold absolute truth is much more preferred than a kind and uncertain lie. -Gabe Suico

3203. You can't be truly rude until you understand good manners. - Rita Mae Brown

3204. Ultimately, the only power to which man should aspire is that which he exercises over himself. -Elie Wiesel

3205. Nothing is more unpleasant that a virtuous person with a mean mind. -Walter Bagehot

3206. For peace of mind we need to resign as general manager of the universe. -Larry Eisenberg

3207. A successful marriage requires falling in love many times, always with the same person. -Mignon McLaughlin

3208. The bitterness of poor quality remains long after low pricing is forgotten! -Leon M. Cautillo

3209. If you love the life you live, you will live a life of love. -Unknown Author

3210. One of the first duties of the physician is to educate the masses not to take medicine. -William Osler

3211. Nothing recedes like success. -Walter Winchell

3212. Originality is the art of concealing your source. -Franklin P. Jones

3213. Without tenderness a man is uninteresting. -Marlene Dietrich

3214. When someone asks me what I think, I tell them: "I think all of the meat around a pig's ass is pork." -Tim Early

3215. To acquire knowledge one must study but to acquire wisdom one must observe. -Marilyn vos Savant

3216. The artist alone sees spirits. But after he has told of their appearing to him everybody sees them. -Johann Wolfgang von Goethe

3217. Weeping may endure for a night but joy cometh in the morning. -George Weiss

3218. Assumptions are the termites of relationships. -Henry Winkler

3219. My definition of an expert in any field is a person who knows enough about what's really going to be scared. -P. J. Plauger

3220. As I was going up the stair, I met a man who wasn't there. He wasn't there again today. I wish I wish he'd stay away. -Hughes Mearns

3221. A good teacher protects his pupils from his own influence. -Bruce Lee

3222. In the night of death, hope sees a star, and listening love can hear the rustle of a wing. -Robert Ingersoll

3223. People seldom refuse help if one offers it in the right way. -C. Benson

3224. We can do no great things; only small things with great love. -Wolfgang Amadeus Mozart

3225. I must govern the clock, not be governed by it. -Golda Meir

3226. The more things change the more they are the same. -Alphonse Karr

3227. For a man to achieve all that is demanded of him he must regard himself as greater than he is. -Johann von Goethe

3228. Respect a man; he will do the more. -James Howell

3229. We occasionally stumble over the truth, but most of us pick ourselves up and hurry on as if nothing happened.

3230. I think we have more machinery of government than is necessary too many parasites living on the labor of the industrious. -Francis Bacon

3231. To see what is right and not do it, is want of courage. -Confucius

3232. I remember my mother's prayers and they have always followed me. They have clung to me all my life. -Abraham Lincoln

3233. When science discovers the center of the universe a lot of people will be disappointed to find they are not it. - Bernard Baily

3234. What's a man's age? He must hurry more that's all. Cram in a day what his youth took a year to hold. -Robert Browning

3235. All philosophy lies in two words: Sustain and Abstain. -Epictetus

3236. Only those who risk going too far can possibly find out how far they can go. -T. S. Eliot

3237. The bedfellows politics made are never strange. It only seems that way to those who have not watched the courtship. -Marcel Archard

3238. Respect is mutual, if you don't respect others viewpoints, chances are they won't acknowledge yours.

3239. Aristotle was once asked what those who tell lies gain by it. Said he that when they speak truth they are not believed. -Laertius Diogenes

3240. It is easier to forgive an enemy than to forgive a friend. -William Blake

3241. The game is up. -William Shakespeare

3242. Love is a great beautifier. -Louisa May Alcott

3243. The only man who never makes a mistake is the man who never does anything. -Theodore Roosevelt

3244. War will cease when men refuse to fight. -F. Hansen

3245. Circumstances do not make a man, they reveal him. -Dr. Wayne W. Dyer

3246. You have three choices in any situation; the sooner you choose, the less stress you'll feel: change, accept or leave.

3247. What you are is God's gift to you. What you make of yourself is your gift back to God. -Kelly Jeppesen

3248. Success isn't permanent and failure isn't fatal. -Mike Ditka

3249. Character, in the long run, is the decisive factor in the life of an individual and of nations alike. -Theodore Roosevelt

3250. Tis not every question that deserves an answer. -Thomas Fuller

3251. There is nothing more agreeable in life than to make peace with the establishment and nothing more corrupting. -A.J.P. Taylor

3252. A man ought to read just as inclination leads him for what he reads as a task will do him little good. -Samuel Johnson

3253. The cost of living is going up and the chance of living is going down. -Flip Wilson

3254. Man is most nearly himself when he achieves the seriousness of a child at play. -Heraclitus

3255. I love my government not least for the extent to which it leaves me alone. -John Updike

3256. From a fallen tree all make kindling. -Danish proverb

3257. I don't feel obliged to believe that the same God who has endowed us with sense, reason, and intellect has intended us to forgo their use.

3258. The most important thing is to be whatever you are without shame. -Rod Steiger

3259. The most pathetic person in the world is someone who has sight but has no vision. -Helen Keller

3260. It sometimes seems that we have only to love a thing greatly to get it. -Robert Collier

3261. Never break your putter and your driver in the same round or you're dead. -Tommy Bolt

3262. Do not let what you cannot do interfere with what you can do. -John Wooden

3263. Do not speak of repulsive matters at table. -Amy Vanderbilt

3264. Man has responsibility not power. -Tuscarora Proverb

3265. You shall judge a man by his foes as well as by his friends. -Joseph Conrad

3266. We have to fight them daily like fleas, those many small worries about the morrow, for they sap our energies. -Etty Hillesum

3267. All that is human must retrograde if it does not advance. -Edward Gibbon

3268. Friendship consists in forgetting what one gives, and remembering what one receives. -Alexandre Dumas

3269. One thing you will probably remember well is any time you forgive and forget. -Franklin P. Jones

3270. Let every fox take care of his own tail. -Italian Proverb

3271. When grace is joined with wrinkles it is adorable. There is an unspeakable dawn in happy old age. -Victor Hugo

3272. You must not only aim right, but draw the bow with all your might. -Henry David Thoreau

3273. Once the toothpaste is out of the tube, it's hard to get it back in. -H.R. Haldeman

3274. To carry a grudge is like being stung to death by one bee. -William H. Walton

3275. Americans will put up with anything provided it doesn't block traffic. -Arnold Bennett

3276. Good judgement is the result of experience ... Experience is the result of bad judgement. -Fred Brooks

3277. It is impossible to overestimate the immense need that humans have to be listened to, understood, and taken seriously.

3278. They always say time changes things but you actually have to change them yourself. -Andy Warhol

3279. Life is not measured by the number of breaths we take, but by the moments that take our breath away. -Nicola A. Sills

3280. Nothing sets a person so much out of the devil's reach as humility. -Jonathan Edwards

3281. We must all suffer one of two things: the pain of discipline or the pain of regret or disappointment. -E. James Rohn

3282. History teaches us that when a barbarian race confronts a sleeping culture, the barbarian always wins. -Arnold J. Toynbee

3283. Miracles are not contrary to nature, but only contrary to what we know about nature. -St. Augustine

3284. Character is not made in a crisis it is only exhibited. -Robert Freeman

3285. Love has reasons that reason knows nothing of.

3286. The fate of love is that it always seems too little or too much. -Anonymous

3287. A wise man sees as much as he ought not as much as he can. -Michel Eyquem de Montaigne

3288. Neurotics build castles in the air psychotics live in them. My mother cleans them. -Rita Rudner

3289. Your children know you love them by your presence, not your presents.

3290. Life is what you have while you are waiting to have one.

3291. Fall seven times, stand up eight. -Japanese Proverb

3292. Keep your feet on the ground and your thoughts at lofty heights. -Pilgrims

3293. My Grandmother is over eighty and still doesn't need glasses. Drinks right out of the bottle. -Henny Youngman

3294. Ford used to have a better idea; now they don't have a clue. -Steve Kravitz

3295. I believe we are on an irreversible trend toward more freedom and democracy - but that could change. -Dan Quayle

3296. Nothing can be done at once hastily and prudently. -Publilius Syrus

3297. One does evil enough when one does nothing good. -German proverb

3298. We are never so happy or unhappy as we think. -La Rochefoucauld

3299. Honesty pays dividends both in dollars and in peace of mind. -B. C. Forbes

3300. One is left with the horrible feeling now that war settles nothing that to win a war is as disastrous as to lose one. -Agatha Christie

3301. Jesus is coming! Look Busy.

3302. The best way to help poor people is to not be one of them. -Bob Harrington

3303. No object is mysterious. The mystery is in your eye. -Elizabeth Bowen

3304. In every real man, a child is hidden that wants to play. -Friedrich Wilhelm Nietzsche

3305. What does reason demand of a man? A very easy thing - to live in accord with his nature. -Seneca

3306. Determination, patience and courage are the only things needed to improve any situation. -Unknown Author

3307. It is the great north wind that made the Vikings. -Scandinavian Proverb

3308. Since we cannot get what we like let us like what we can get. -Danish proverb

3309. Nature abhors a vacuum and if I can only walk with sufficient carelessness I am sure to be filled. -Henry David Thoreau

3310. His Unique Selling Position was to make the world work for 100% of humanity. . -Buckminster Fuller

3311. The lesson is what you read in the fine print. The experience is what you get when you don't.

3312. We are that which activates the body. -Pilgrims

3313. He who has been bitten by a snake fears a piece of string. -Persian Proverb

3314. We cease loving ourselves if no one loves us. -Germaine de Staël

3315. Nobody will believe in you unless you believe in yourself. - Liberace

3316. Can atheists get insurance for acts of God?

3317. You see things and you say Why But I dream things that never were and I say Why not? -George Bernard Shaw

3318. You have within you, right now, everything you need to deal with whatever the world can throw at you. -Brian Tracy

3319. As for life, it is a battle and a sojourning in a strange land, but the fame that comes after is oblivion. -Marcus Aurelius

3320. Nothing is easy to the unwilling. -Nikki Giovanni

3321. A handful of patience is worth more than a bushel of brains. - Dutch Proverb

3322. Rash indeed is he who reckons on the morrow or haply on days beyond it for tomorrow is not until today is past. -Sophocles

3323. Those who love deeply never grow old they may die of old age but they die young. -Sir Arthur Wing Pinero

3324. A cause a day keeps reality away. -Jim Fraser

3325. Most people who succeed in the face of seemingly impossible conditions are people who simply don't know how to quit. -Dr. Robert Schuller

3326. Change is difficult but often essential to survival. -Les Brown

3327. Men are not prisoners of fate but only prisoners of their own mind. -Franklin Delano Roosevelt

3328. Time is the wisest counsellor. -Pericles

3329. An enemy can partly ruin a man but it takes a good-natured injudicious friend to complete the thing and make it perfect. -Mark Twain

3330. Genius is the ability to put into effect what is on your mind. -F. Scott

3331. Don't sacrifice your political convictions for the convenience of the hour. -Edward M. Kennedy

3332. Most managers were trained to be the thing they most despise, bureaucrats. -Alvin Toffler

3333. The price works so well so efficiently that we are not aware of it most of the time. -Milton Friedman

3334. Expenditure rises to meet income. -C. Northcote Parkinson

3335. My father hated radio and could not wait for television to be invented so he could hate that too. -Peter De Vries

3336. A second ago is gone, and a second from now might be. Now is all you've got. Go for it! -Lyn St. James

3337. Never complain and never explain. -Benjamin Disraeli

3338. Today if you are not confused you are just not thinking clearly. -U. Peter

3339. A smile is a curve that sets things straight.

3340. Change everything except your loves. -Francois Marie Arouet Voltaire

3341. It is not enough to be busy; the question is what are we busy about. -Henry David Thoreau

3342. All the windows of my heart I open to the day. -John Greenleaf Whittier

3343. Time is equal to life; therefore, waste your time and waste of your life, or master your time and master your life. -Alan Lakein

3344. I have loved many the more and the few - I have loved many that I might love you. -Grace Fallow Norton

3345. I am the toughest golfer mentally. -Tiger Woods

3346. What happens is not as important as how you react to what happens. -Thaddeus Golas

3347. What is reality anyway Just a collective hunch. -Jane Wagner

3348. Anyone who has a child today should train him to be either a physicist or a ballet dancer. Then he'll escape. -Wystan Hugh Auden

3349. All the beautiful sentiments in the world weigh less than a single lovely action. -James Russell Lowell

3350. If you would not be known to do anything, never do it. -Ralph Waldo Emerson

3351. The willow knows what the storm does not; the power to endure harm outlives the power to inflict it.

3352. Be humble, if thou would'st attain to Wisdom. Be humbler still, when Wisdom thou hast mastered. -Helena Petrova Blavatsky

3353. The people are not to be disarmed of their weapons. They are left in full possession of them. -Zachariah Johnson

3354. An inch of time cannot be bought by an inch of gold. -Chinese proverb

3355. Success is counted sweetest by those who ne'er succeed. -Emily Dickinson

3356. A billion here, a billion there, pretty soon it adds up to real money. -Senator Everett Dirksen

3357. I would rather be able to appreciate things I cannot have than to have things I am not able to appreciate. -Elbert Hubbard

3358. Your intellect may be confused but your emotions will never lie to you. -Roger

3359. Women complain about premenstrual syndrome, but I think of it as the only time of the month that I can be myself

3360. Praise can be your most valuable asset as long as you don't aim it at yourself.

3361. This body is not a home but an inn and that only briefly. -Seneca

3362. Life is full of misery loneliness and suffering - and it's all over much too soon. -Woody Allen

3363. Facts are stupid things. -Ronald Reagan

3364. We need to learn to set our course by the stars, not by the lights of every passing ship. -Omar Nelson Bradley

3365. No amount of experimentation can ever prove me right a single experiment can prove me wrong. -Albert Einstein

3366. Success is not to be pursued; it is to be attracted by the person you become. -Jim Rohn

3367. Never go to excess but let moderation be your guide. -Cicero

3368. True nobility is in being superior to your previous self. -Hindustani Proverb

3369. Our happiness depends on wisdom all the way. -Sophocles

3370. The world needs anger. The world often continues to allow evil because it isn't angry enough. - Bede Jarrett

3371. You are the bows from which your children as living arrows are sent forth. -Kahlil Gibran

3372. We are each of us angels with only one wing. And we can only fly by embracing each other. -Comte DeBussy-Rabutin

3373. Shyness has a strange element of narcissism - a belief that how we look, how we perform is truly important to other people. -Andre Dubus

3374. One path alone leads to a life of peace-- The path of virtue. - Juvenal

3375. It was all so different before everything changed.

3376. He who will not economize will have to agonize. -Confucius

3377. Fear is the tax that conscience pays to guilt. -Howard Aiken

3378. Joy is not in things; it is in us. -Richard Wagner

3379. You can employ men and hire hands to work for you, but you must win their hearts to have them work with you. -Tiorio

3380. Let no man undervalue the price of a virtuous woman's counsel. - George Chapman

3381. Learn to relax. Your body is precious, as it houses your mind and spirit. Inner peace begins with a relaxed body. -Norman Vincent Peale

3382. A deadline is negative inspiration. Still, it's better than no inspiration at all. -Rita Mae Brown

3383. Cheerfulness in most cheerful people is the rich and satisfying result of strenuous discipline. -Edwin Percy Whipple

3384. Let us consider the reason of the case. For nothing is law that is not reason. -John Powell

3385. Men seek but one thing in life - their pleasure. -W. Somerset Maugham

3386. Everyone should carefully observe which way his heart draws him and then choose that way with all his strength. -Hasidic Saying

3387. Education's purpose is to replace an empty mind with an open one. -Malcolm Forbes

3388. Wide-sounding Zeus takes away half a man's worth on the day when slavery comes upon him. -Homer

3389. A woman is like a tea bag - you can't tell how strong she is until you put her in hot water. -Nancy Davis Reagan

3390. If you laugh a lot, when you get older your wrinkles will be in the right places. -Andrew Mason

3391. I finally figured out the only reason to be alive is to enjoy it. -Rita Mae Brown

3392. While there's life, there's hope! -Roman saying

3393. The ship is safer in the harbor, but it is not meant for that.

3394. Nobody loves me, but my mother, and she could be jivin' too. -B. B. King

3395. A teacher who is attempting to teach without inspiring the pupil with a desire to learn is hammering on a cold iron. -Horace Mann

3396. If you love it, let it go. If it returns to you, cherish it. If not, it was never truly yours. -Proverb

3397. He that climbs the tall tree has won right to the fruit. -Sir Walter Scott

3398. Enjoy when you can and endure when you must. -Johann Wolfgang von Goethe

3399. The best way to predict the future is to invent it. -Alan Kay

3400. It is necessary to try to surpass oneself always this occupation ought to last as long as life. -Queen Christina

3401. I've learned that you should never say no to a gift from a child. -Andy Rooney

3402. I believe that man will not merely endure; he will prevail. -William Faulkner

3403. The greatest happiness of life is the conviction that we are loved; loved for ourselves, or rather, loved in spite of ourselves.

3404. Be who you are and say what you feel because those who mind don't matter and those who matter don't mind. -Dr. Seuss

3405. There is a coherent plan in the universe, though I don't know what it's a plan for. -Fred Hoyle

3406. Too much sanity may be madness. And maddest of all to see life as it is and not as it should be. -Miguel de Cervantes

3407. To reach a great height a person needs to have great depth. -Anonymous

3408. People who have heard me sing, say I don't. -Mark Twain

3409. When you shoot an arrow of truth, dip its point in honey. -An old Arab proverb

3410. Never do anything that you aren't prepared to face the true consequences of. -Dr. Laura Schlessinger

3411. I take a simple view of life keep your eyes open and get on with it. -Sir Laurence Kerr Olivier

3412. Doublethink means the power of holding two contradictory beliefs in one's mind simultaneously and accepting both of them. -George Orwell

3413. There are always survivors at a massacre. Among the victors if nowhere else. -Lois McMaster Bujold

3414. Life without a friend is death without a witness. -Eugene Benge

3415. Reputation is what other people know about you. Honor is what you know about yourself. -Lois McMaster Bujold

3416. A careless word may kindle strife. A cruel word may wreck a life. A timely word may level stress. A loving word may heal and bless.

3417. A child will perform from their mind for their coach/teacher, but for a parent they perform from their heart.

3418. Great minds think independently not alike. -Unknown

3419. My best friend and I can do anything or nothing and have the best time.

3420. May no portent of evil be attached to the words I say. -Anonymous

3421. Don't condescend to unskilled labor. Try it for half a day first. -Brooks Atkinson

3422. Enjoy your own life without comparing it with that of another. -Marquis de Condorcet

3423. To greed all nature is insufficient. -Seneca

3424.   If thou are a master be sometimes blind if a servant sometimes deaf. -Thomas Fuller

3425.   Zeal without humanity is like a ship without a rudder, liable to be stranded at any moment. - Owen Felltham

3426.   When you hear a kind word spoken about a friend, tell her so.

3427.   The butterfly counts not months but moments, and has time enough. -Rabindranath Tagore

3428.   People want the front of the bus; back of the church, and center of attention.

3429.   Knowledge is that which is acquired by learning. Wisdom is knowing what to do with it?

3430.   The truth of the matter is that you always know the right thing to do. The hard part is doing it. -Norman Schwarzkopf

3431.   Try not to become a man of success but rather try to become a man of value.

3432.   We own almost all our knowledge not to those who have agreed but to those who have differed. - Charles Caleb Colton

3433.   All work and no play makes Jack a dull boy. -James Howell

3434.   Evil will always triumph because good is dumb. -Rick Moranis

3435.   Home is the place where when you have to go there, they have to take you in. -Robert Frost

3436.   Tis an ill wind that blows no minds. -Malaclypse the Younger

3437.   Do what's right. Do it right. Do it right now. -Malcolm Stevenson Forbes

3438.   The last of the human freedoms is to choose one's attitudes. - Victor Frankl

3439.   The curiosity to know things has been given to man as a scourge. - Apocrypha

3440.   Memories important, yesterdays were once todays. Treasure and notice today. -Gloria Gaither

3441.   The man we call a specialist today was formerly called a man with a one-track mind. -Endre Balogh

3442.   The first principle of success is desire - knowing what you want. Desire is the planting of your seed. -Robert Collier

3443. The great gift of human beings is that we have the power of empathy. -Meryl Streep

3444. There's never a new fashion but it's old. -Chaucer

3445. Genuine goodness is threatening to those at the opposite end of the moral spectrum. -Charles Spencer

3446. Coming generations will learn equality from poverty and love from woes. -Kahlil Gibran

3447. Art can only be truly Art by presenting an adequate outward symbol of some fact in the interior life. -Margaret Fuller

3448. When they send for you, you go in alive, you come out dead, and it's your best friend that does it. -Donnie Brasco Lefty

3449. A good rest is half the work. -Yugoslav Proverb.

3450. There is a budding morrow in midnight. -John Keats

3451. The point of living and of being an optimist is to be foolish enough to believe the best is yet to come. -Peter Ustinov

3452. You don't lose if you get knocked down, you lose if you stay down.

3453. It is true we have won all our wars but we have paid for them. We don't want victories anymore. -Golda Meir

3454. Great minds must be ready not only to take opportunities, but to make them. -C. C. Colton

3455. You have to lead people gently toward what they already know is right. -Philip

3456. Anyone can hold the helm when the sea is calm. -Publilius Syrus

3457. Love cannot survive if you just give it scraps of yourself scraps of your time scraps of your thoughts. -Mary O'Hara

3458. Never refuse any advance of friendship for if nine out of ten bring you nothing one alone may repay you. -Madame de Tencin

3459. When you have eliminated the impossible whatever remains, however improbable, must be the truth. -Conan Doyle

3460. Always and never are two words you should always remember never to use. -Wendell Johnson

3461. Tough girl, I'm almost single, my husband's on death row. - Coming to America

3462. When the character of a man is not clear to you, look at his friends. -Japanese Proverb

3463. Ask a question and you're a fool for three minutes; do not ask a question and you're a fool for the rest of your life. -Chinese proverb

3464. Man does not live by words alone, despite the fact that sometimes he has to eat them. -Broderick Crawford

3465. Our way is not soft grass it's a mountain path with lots of rocks. But it goes upward forward toward the sun. -Ruth Westheimer

3466. The discovery of a new dish does more for human happiness than the discovery of a new star. -Anthelme Brillat-Savarin

3467. The elevator to success is out of order. You'll have to use the stairs... one step at a time. - Joe Girard

3468. Good judgment comes from bad experience, and a lot of that comes from bad judgment.

3469. The act of writing is the act of discovering what you believe. - David Hare

3470. There is only one religion, though there are a hundred versions of it. -George Bernard Shaw

3471. Did Noah include termites on the ark?

3472. I've learned that simple walks with my father, around the block on summer nights when I was a child, did wonders for me as an adult. - Andy Rooney

3473. Difficulties increase the nearer we approach our goal. -Johann von Goethe

3474. We could accomplish a lot more if we'd get rid of our ifs and and's; and get off our butts.

3475. Genuine change is never a function of dominance, or even education, but of empathy and common ground. -Alan Briskin

3476. No one is so generous as he who has nothing to give. -French Proverb

3477. How different the new order would be if we could consult the veteran instead of the politician. -Henry Miller

3478. Whoever loves becomes humble. Those who love have so to speak pawned a part of their narcissism. -Sigmund Freud

3479. You don't understand. I could have had class. I could have been a contender. -Budd Schulberg

3480. There is a difference between ignorance and stupidity. Ignorance can be cured by learning and reading. Stupidity isn't willing to be cured.

3481. Men do not die from overwork. They die from dissipation and worry. -Charles Evans Hughes

3482. That's the fourth extra base hit for the Padres - two doubles and a triple. -Jerry Coleman

3483. You can't choose the ways in which you'll be tested. -Robert J. Sawyer

3484. When you have eliminated the impossible whatever remains however improbable must be the truth. -Sherlock Holmes

3485. Think of yourself as an incandescent power illuminated and perhaps forever talked to by God and his messengers. -Brenda Ueland

3486. The first time I see a jogger smiling, I'll consider it. -Joan Rivers

3487. If history repeats itself and the unexpected always happens how incapable must Man be of learning from experience. -George Bernard Shaw

3488. While there's life, there's hope. -Terence

3489. Where you start is not as important as where you finish. -Zig Ziglar

3490. Being defeated is often a temporary condition. Giving up is what makes it permanent. -Marilyn vos Savant

3491. Are you green and growing or ripe and rotting? -Ray Kroc

3492. I always turn to the sports pages first which records people's accomplishments. The front page has nothing but man's failures. -Earl Warren

3493. Other people may not have high expectations of me but I have high expectations for myself. -Shannon Miller

3494. Change when it comes cracks everything open. -Dorothy Allison

3495. If A equals success then the formula is A equals X plus Y plus Z. X is work. Y is play. Z is keep your mouth shut. -Albert Einstein

3496. The problem with any unwritten law is that you don't know where to go to erase it. -Glaser and Way

3497. Know how to listen and you will profit even from those who talk badly. -Plutarch

3498. It is a mistake to try to look too far ahead. The chain of destiny can only be grasped one link at a time. -Sir Winston Churchill

3499. We cannot live only for ourselves. A thousand fibers connect us with our fellow men. -Herman Melville

3500. If youth but had the knowledge and old age the strength. - French Proverb

3501. I both love and do not love and am mad and not mad. - Anacreon

3502. Before borrowing money from a friend, it's best to decide which you need most. -Joe Moore

3503. Do not condemn the judgement of another because it differs from your own. You may both be wrong. -Dandemis

3504. The trouble isn't that there are too many fools but that the lightning isn't distributed right. -Mark Twain

3505. The way I see it if you want the rainbow you gotta put up the rain. -Dolly Parton

3506. The deep joy we take in the company of people with whom we have just recently fallen in love is undisguisable. -John Cheever

3507. Of my friends I am the only one I have left. -Terence

3508. Sports are 90% inspiration and 10% perspiration. -Johnny Miller

3509. The mediocre teacher tells. The good teacher explains. The superior teacher demonstrates. The great teacher inspires. -William A. Ward

3510. All my games were political games. I was like Joan of Arc perpetually being burned at the stake. -Indira Nehru Gandhi

3511. With someone holding nothing but trumps it is impossible to play cards. - Proverb

3512.   It takes two to speak truth - One to speak and another to hear. -Henry David Thoreau

3513.   Men in no way approach so nearly to the gods as in doing good to men. -Marcus Tullius Cicero

3514.   The stars are constantly shining but often we do not see them until the dark hours. -Earl Riney

3515.   The more man becomes irradiated with the Divinity of Christ the more not the less truly he is man. -Phillips Brooks

3516.   Work expands to fill the time available for its completion. -Cyril Northcote Parkinson

3517.   For not many men the proverb saith can love a friend whom fortune prospereth unenvying. -Aeschylus

3518.   We are never more fully alive more completely ourselves or more deeply engrossed in anything than when we are playing. -Charles Schaefer

3519.   You can sort of be married, you can sort of be divorced, you can sort of be living together, but you can't sort of have a baby. -David Shire

3520.   Those who do not find time for exercise will have to find time for illness.

3521.   To err from the right path is common to mankind. -Sophocles

3522.   We shall draw from the heart of suffering itself the means of inspiration and survival. -Sir Winston Churchill

3523.   Good clothes open all doors. - Thomas Fuller

3524.   I am indeed rich since my income is superior to my expense and my expense is equal to my wishes. -Kahlil Gibran

3525.   You are forgiven for your happiness and your successes only if you generously consent to share them. -Albert Camus

3526.   Unless a man undertakes more than he possibly can do, he will never do all that he can. -Henry Drummond

3527.   Eternity is a mere moment just long enough for a joke. - Hermann Hesse

3528.   There is only one way to come into this world there are too many ways to leave it. -Donald Harington

3529. Happiness is something that comes into our lives through doors we don't even remember leaving open. -Rose Lane

3530. I keep my ideals, because in spite of everything I still believe that people are really good at heart. -Anne Frank

3531. It is worse still to be ignorant of your ignorance. -Saint Jerome

3532. Character develops itself in the stream of life. -Johann Wolfgang von Goethe

3533. A thing long expected takes the form of the unexpected when at last it comes. -Mark Twain

3534. No person will make a great business who wants to do it all himself or get all the credit. -Andrew Carnegie

3535. Success is a state of mind. If you want success, start thinking of yourself as a success. -Dr. Joyce Brothers

3536. A faithful friend is a strong defense and he that hath found such an one hath found a treasure. -Sirach 6:14

3537. Success is doing what you want to do, when you want, where you want, with whom you want, as much as you want. -Anthony Robbins

3538. You always admire what you really don't understand. -Eleanor Roosevelt

3539. Formula for success-- Under promise and over deliver. -Thomas Peters

3540. It is nice to be important, but it's more important to be nice.

3541. The easiest way to find something lost around the house is to buy a replacement.

3542. The more I live, the more I think that humor is the saving sense. -Jacob August Riis

3543. The covetous man is ever in want. -Horace

3544. Whatever women do they must do twice as well as men to be thought half as good. Luckily this is not difficult. -Charlotte Whitton

3545. Love is the triumph of imagination over intelligence. -H.L. Mencken

3546.   Tragedy is when I cut my finger. Comedy is when you walk into an open sewer and die. -Mel Brooks

3547.   A moment on the lips, an eternity on the hips.

3548.   Advice is least heeded when most needed. -English Proverb

3549.   Success is not access to excess. -Unknown Author

3550.   Why is "abbreviation" such a long word?

3551.   If you would be known and not know vegetate in a village If you would know and not be known live in a city. -Charles Caleb Colton

3552.   Every trial endured and weathered in the right spirit makes a soul nobler and stronger than it was before. -James Buckham

3553.   A good storyteller is a person who has a good memory and hopes other people haven't. -Irvin Shrewsbury Cobb

3554.   Wonder is the beginning of wisdom. -Anonymous, Greek Proverb

3555.   The difference between a mountain and a molehill is your perspective. -Al Neuharth

3556.   The trouble with the world is that the stupid are cocksure and the intelligent full of doubt. -Bertrand Russell

3557.   I tried marijuana once. I did not inhale. -William J. Clinton

3558.   Fear of death has been the greatest ally of tyranny past and present. -Sydney Hook

3559.   He who knows others is learned. He who knows himself is wise. -Lao Tzu, 604-531 BC

3560.   To the sick, while there is life there is hope. -Marcus T. Cicero

3561.   A man who strains himself on the stage is bound, if he is any good, to strain all the people sitting in the stalls. - Bertolt Brecht

3562.   Our feelings are our most genuine paths to knowledge. -Audre Lorde

3563.   The good or ill of a man lies within his own will. -Epictetus

3564.   There is something about poverty that smells like death. -Zora Neale Hurston

3565.   You know what charm is a way of getting the answer yes without having asked any clear question. -Albert Camus

3566.   Failing to plan is a plan to fail. -Effie Jones

3567. Cessation of work is not accompanied by cessation of expenses. - Cato The Elder

3568. An atheist is a man who has no invisible means of support. - John Buchan

3569. Building castles in the air and making yourself a laughing-stock. -Miguel de Cervantes

3570. The easiest kind of relationship for me is with ten thousand people. The hardest is with one. -Joan Baez

3571. A kiss is a lovely trick designed by nature to stop speech when words become superfluous. -Ingrid Bergman

3572. Celebrate what you want to see more of. -Thomas J. Peters

3573. It's choice - not chance - that determines your destiny. -Jean Nidetch

3574. Anger is never without an argument, but seldom with a good one. - George Saville

3575. When your bow is broken and your last arrow spent then shoot, shoot with your whole heart. -Roger Zelazny

3576. We should be too big to take offense and too noble to give it. - Abraham Lincoln

3577. Speak the truth, do not yield to anger, give if thou art asked for little: by these three steps thou wilt go near the gods. -The Dhammapada

3578. For all their strength, men were sometimes like little children. - Lawana Blackwell

3579. I am prepared to meet my Maker. Whether my Maker is prepared for the great ordeal of meeting me is another matter. -Sir Winston Churchill

3580. Whenever you see a successful business, someone once made a courageous decision. -Peter Drucker

3581. In time we hate that which we often fear. -William Shakespeare

3582. After all, all he did was string together a lot of old well-known quotations. -H.L. Mencken

3583. Even knowledge has to be in the fashion, and where it is not, it is wise to affect ignorance. - Baltasar Gracian

3584. The wise man has long ears and a short tongue. -German proverb

3585. What we have to do is to be forever curiously testing new opinions and courting new impressions. -Walter Pater

3586. The worst is not so long as we can say, "This is the worst." -William Shakespeare

3587. A precedent embalms a principle. -Benjamin Disraeli

3588. You can only be young once. But you can always be immature. -Dave Barry

3589. Stride and strut goeth before a fall; tried and true goeth before a raise.

3590. Before you can break out of prison, you must realize that you are locked up.

3591. Law is order and good law is good order. -Aristotle

3592. Deliberate with caution but act with decision and yield with graciousness or oppose with firmness. -Charles Caleb Colton

3593. It is hard to face the problem, when the problem is your face.

3594. Don't cry because it's over smile because it happened. -Unknown

3595. Isn't it interesting that the same people who laugh at science fiction listen to weather forecasts and economists? -Kelvin III Throop

3596. The best things in life aren't things. -Art Buchwald

3597. Often the surest way to convey misinformation is to tell the strict truth. -Mark Twain

3598. Mediocrity is self-inflicted. Genius is self-bestowed. -Walter Russell

3599. Most people want to serve God - but only in an advisory capacity.

3600. The cure for writer's cramp is writer's block. -Inigo DeLeon

3601. Success is dependent upon the glands - sweat glands. -Zig Ziglar

3602. The graveyards are full of indispensable men. -Charles De Gaulle

3603. In soft regions are born soft men. -Herodotus

3604. Curiosity is as much the parent of attention as attention is of memory. -Richard Whately

3605. We must use time wisely and forever realize that the time is always ripe to do right. -Nelson Mandela

3606. Carpe per diem - seize the check. - Robin Williams

3607. Truthfulness is the main element of character. -Brian Tracy

3608. Nothing in the world is more haughty than a man of moderate capacity when once raised to power. - Baron Wessenberg

3609. Sports serve society by providing vivid examples of excellence. - George Will

3610. Nonsense is so good only because common sense is so limited. - George Santayana

3611. All sunshine makes a desert. -Arabic Proverb

3612. Faith - is the pierless bridge supporting what we see unto the scene that we do not. -Emily Elizabeth Dickinson

3613. I am a galley slave to pen and ink. -Honore de Balzac

3614. Why do we look in our handkerchiefs after blowing our nose?

3615. Those who wish to appear wise among fools among the wise seem foolish. -Quintilian

3616. What one fool can do another can. -Ancient Simian Proverb

3617. Thought is a dangerous thing; it makes one see that the popular notions of society are wrong. - Jon R. Sime

3618. An ounce of blood is worth more than a pound of friendship. - Danish proverb

3619. The great object is that every man be armed. Everyone who is able may have a gun. -Patrick Henry

3620. You can only perceive real beauty in a person as they get older. - Anouk Aimee

3621. If your only measure of value is color then you shall never appreciate the transparence of diamonds. -Ameer Sadet Mahdy

3622. If someone says can't, that shows you what to do. -John Cage

3623. If there be any truer measure of a man than by what he does it must be by what he gives. -Robert South

3624. Vote early and vote often. -Al Capone

3625. When people are free to do as they please, they usually imitate each other. -Eric Hoffer

3626. What we're all striving for is authenticity, a spirit-to-spirit connection. -Oprah Winfrey

3627. Lady, you bereft me of all words. Only my blood speaks to you in my veins, and there is such confusion in my powers.-William Shakespeare

3628. Daddy, what does FORMATTING DRIVE C mean?

3629. To see what is right and not to do it is want of courage or of principle. -Confucius

3630. Tradition is a guide and not a jailer. -W. Somerset Maugham

3631. Let a fool hold his tongue and he will pass for a sage. -Publilius Syrus

3632. Angels fly because they take themselves lightly. -G.K. Chesterton

3633. Know how to ask. There is nothing more difficult for some people nor for others easier. -Baltasar Gracian

3634. Nobody plans to fail, they just fail to plan.

3635. Three may keep a secret if two of them are dead. -Benjamin Franklin

3636. What oxygen is to the lungs such is hope to the meaning of life. -Emil Brunner

3637. We challenge each other to be funnier and smarter. -Annie Gottlieb

3638. As gold which he cannot spend will make no man rich so knowledge which he cannot apply will make no man wise. -Samuel Johnson

3639. I don't pretend we have all the answers. But the questions are certainly worth thinking about. -Arthur C. Clarke

3640. If you want a thing well done, do it yourself. -Charles Haddon Spurgeon

3641. Hold yourself responsible for a higher standard than anybody else expects of you, never excuse yourself. -Henry Ward Beecher

3642. To get out of a difficulty, one usually must go through it.

3643. The sweetest of all sounds is praise. -Xenophon

3644. Success is the sum of small efforts, repeated day in and day out... - Robert Collier

3645. Adult: A person who has stopped growing at both ends and is now growing in the middle.

3646. The reason there are so few female politicians is that it is too much trouble to put makeup on two faces. -Maureen Murphy

3647. Love tells us many things that are not so. -Ukranian Proverb

3648. An archaeologist is the best husband any woman can have; the older she gets the more interested he is in her. -Agatha Christie

3649. It's a job that's never started that takes the longest to finish. -J. R. R. Tolkien

3650. The telephone is the greatest nuisance among conveniences the greatest convenience among nuisances. -Robert Staughton Lynd

3651. Whenever A annoys or injures B on the pretense of saving or improving X A is a scoundrel.-Henry Louis Mencken

3652. It is more difficult and it calls for higher energies of soul to live a martyr than to die one. -Horace Mann

3653. When a fellow says it ain't the money but the principle of the thing, it's the money. -Artemus Ward

3654. Greater is he who acts from love than he who acts from fear. - Simeon Ben Eleazar

3655. Every man's life lies within the present; for the past is spent and done with, and the future is uncertain. -Marcus Aurelius

3656. Things are more like they are now than they ever were before. - Dwight D. Eisenhower

3657. Truth sits upon the lips of dying men. -Matthew Arnold

3658. Success always occurs in private, and failure in full view.

3659. Love and kindness are never wasted. They always make a difference. -Barbara de Angelis

3660. The loveliest of faces are to be seen by moonlight when one sees half with the eye and half with the fancy. -Persian Proverb

3661. Jesus paid a debt he didn't owe because we had a debt we couldn't pay.

3662. History repeats itself, but each time the price goes up.

3663. There are no extraordinary men...just extraordinary circumstances that ordinary men are forced to deal with. -William Bull Halsey

3664. Falsehood often lurks upon the tongue of him who by self-praise seeks to enhance his value in the eyes of others. -Arnold Bennett

3665. By the time a man realizes that his father was right, he has a son who thinks he's wrong.

3666. Talent is only the starting point. -Irving Berlin

3667. A dreamer lives forever and a toiler dies in a day. -John Boyle O'Reilly

3668. Men are what their mothers made them. -Ralph Waldo Emerson

3669. With you, I should love to live with you be ready to die. -Horace

3670. The attempt and not the deed confounds us. -William Shakespeare

3671. Upon our children - how they are taught - rests the fate - or fortune - of tomorrow's world. -B. C. Forbes

3672. Life is a promise; fulfill it. -Mother Teresa

3673. In the morning be first up and in the evening last to go to bed for they that sleep catch no fish. -English Proverb

3674. Enjoy yourself. It's later than you think. -Chinese Proverb

3675. The very ink with which history is written is merely fluid prejudice. -Mark Twain

3676. Whoever acquires knowledge and does not practice it resembles him who ploughs his land and leaves it unsown. -Gulistan, 1258

3677. Nothing great will ever be achieved without great men, and men are great only if they are determined to be so. -Charles De Gaulle

3678. It is only with the heart that one can see rightly what is essential is invisible to the eye. -Antoine De Saint-Exupery

3679. There is no cure for birth and death save to enjoy the interval. -George Santayana

3680. If you could kick the person responsible for most of your troubles in the backside, you wouldn't be able to sit down for two weeks.

3681. There is no such thing as an underestimate of average intelligence. -Henry Adams

3682. If you have both feet planted on level ground, then the university has failed you. -Robert F. Goheen

3683. Money is a good servant but a poor master. -Dominique Bouhours

3684. To every complex problem there is an easy answer; and it is wrong!

3685. Morale is when your hands and feet keep on working when your head says it can't be done. -Benjamin Morrell

3686. He knows not his own strength that hath not met adversity. -Ben Jonson

3687. Why fools are endowed by nature with voices so much louder than sensible people possess is a mystery. It is a fact emphasized throughout history.

3688. You are today where your thoughts have brought you; you will be tomorrow where your thoughts take you. - James Allen

3689. Why is it that no matter what color of bubble bath you use the bubbles are always clear?

3690. Man needs for his happiness not only the enjoyment of this or that but hope and enterprise and change. -Bertrand Russell

3691. Tonight-to you the great silent majority of my fellow Americans-I ask for your support. (On his Vietnam War policy). -Richard Milhous Nixon

3692. UGLINESS, n. A gift of the gods to certain women, entailing virtue without humility. - Elayne Boosler

3693. It's the Brady Act taking manpower and crime-fighting capability off the streets. -Dennis Martin

3694. Love is the essence of God. -Ralph Waldo Emerson

3695. You give but little when you give of your possessions. It is when you give of yourself that you truly give. -Kahlil Gibran

3696. Everything I did in my life that was worthwhile I caught hell for. -Earl Warren

3697. You can tell more about a person by what he says about others than you can by what others say about him. -Leo Aikman

3698. Leaders help others to succeed. -Erin Templet

3699. Let not the sun go down upon your wrath. -Ephesians: Bible, New Testament

3700. Anybody who thinks talk is cheap never argued with a traffic cop.

3701. Youth would be an ideal state if it came a little later in life. -Herbert Henry Asquith

3702. The smallest deed is better than the grandest intention. -Roger Baldwin

3703. Some weasel took the cork out of my lunch. -W. C. Fields

3704. Flowers will not grow but die if they don't get rained on every once in a while.

3705. The minute you start talking about what you're going to do if you lose, you have lost. -George Shultz

3706. Patience is the best remedy for every trouble. -Titus Maccius Plautus

3707. If grass can grow through cement love can find you at every time in your life. -Cher

3708. If virtue precede us every step will be safe. -Seneca

3709. In America anybody can be president. That's one of the risks you take. -Adlai Ewing Stevenson

3710. A wise person escapes temptation and leaves no forwarding address.

3711. No news at a.m. is good. -Lady Bird Johnson

3712. A man travels the world over in search of what he needs and returns home to find it. -George Moore

3713. Where there is great love, there are always miracles. -Willa Cather

3714. Language exerts hidden power like a moon on the tides. -Rita Mae Brown

3715. I realize that I'm generalizing here, but as is often the case when I generalize, I don't care. -Dave Barry

3716. Do today what you usually can't do and save the frequent and usual things for tomorrow. -Cristina Rose Schumacher

3717. Sit quietly, doing nothing, spring comes, and the grass grows by itself. -A Zen Saying

3718. Every difficulty slurred over will be a ghost to disturb your repose later on. -Rabindranath Tagore

3719. There is no way of keeping profits up but by keeping wages down. - David Ricardo

3720. One's religion is whatever he is most interested in and yours is Success. -Joseph Addison

3721. Friends are born, not made. -Henry Adams

3722. To be able to look back upon one's life in satisfaction is to live twice. -Kahlil Gibran

3723. We are never so defenseless against suffering as when we love. - Sigmund Freud

3724. If you can keep your head when all about you are losing theirs, it's just possible you haven't grasped the situation. -Jean Kerr

3725. A true friend reaches for your hand and touches your heart.

3726. Unlike presidential administrations problems rarely have terminal dates. -Dwight D. Eisenhower

3727. Do what you fear most, and you control fear. -Tom Hopkins

3728. Two human loves make one divine. -Elizabeth Barrett Browning

3729. You should pray for a sound mind in a sound body. -Juvenal

3730. There is no more vulnerable human combination than an undergraduate. -John Sloan Dickey

3731. Ordinary riches can be stolen: real riches cannot. In your soul are infinitely precious things that cannot be taken from you. -Oscar Wilde

3732. The weak can never forgive. Forgiveness is the attribute of the strong. -Mohandas Gandhi

3733. Our thoughts take the wildest flight; even at the moment when they should arrange themselves in thoughtful order. -Lord Byron

3734. Most people would rather be certain they're miserable than risk being happy. -Robert Anthony

3735. It is better to have enough ideas for some of them to be wrong, than to be always right by having no ideas at all. -Edward de Bono

3736. We're all stumbling towards the light with varying degrees of grace at any given moment. -Bo Lozoff

3737. We composers are at least as significant as the stars who make million or million. You just don't see us. -Michael Kamen

3738. One half of the world cannot understand the pleasures of the other. -Jane Austen

3739. I am so glad God sees the whole video tape of my life, and not just a snapshot of where I am now.

3740. If you can't describe what you are doing as a process, you don't know what you're doing. -W. Edwards Deming

3741. You can fool too many of the people too much of the time. -James Grover Thurber

3742. Respect is love in plain clothes. - Frankie Byrne

3743. I believe in the forgiveness of sin and the redemption of ignorance. -Adlai E. Jr. Stevenson

3744. Dream big and dare to fail. -Norman D. Vaughan

3745. Deeds not stones are the true monuments of the great.

3746. Nothing changes your opinion of a friend so surely as success - yours or his. -Franklin P. Jones

3747. The greatest obstacle to discovery is not ignorance-it is the illusion of knowledge. -Daniel J Boorstin

3748. To die is to go into the Collective Unconscious to lose oneself in order to be transformed into form pure form. -Hermann Hesse

3749. He that wrestles with us strengthens our nerves and sharpens our skill. Our antagonist in our helper. -Edmund Burke

3750. We crucify ourselves between two thieves- regret for yesterday and fear of tomorrow.

3751. People say that life is the thing, but I prefer reading. -Logan Pearsall Smith

3752. If you can't stand the heat, get out of the kitchen. -Harry S Truman

3753. What's been great about the human race gives you a sense of how great you might get, how far you can reach. -Jerry Garcia

3754. It is better to have loved and lost than never to have lost at all. -Samuel Butler

3755. The wheel of fortune turns round incessantly, and who can say to himself, I shall today be uppermost.—Confucius

3756. While intelligent people can often simplify the complex, a fool is more likely to complicate the simple. -Gerald W. Grummet

3757. Faith! he must make his stories shorter or change his comrades once a quarter.—Jonathan Swift

3758. Never wrestle with a pig. You both get all dirty, and the pig likes it.

3759. The moment we choose to love we begin to move towards freedom... -bell hooks

3760. Study the past if you would define the future. -Confucius

3761. Vision without action is a daydream. Action without vision is a nightmare. -Japanese Proverb

3762. A friend is a person with whom I may be sincere. Before him I may think aloud. -Ralph Waldo Emerson

3763. Happiness is not a reward-it is a consequence. Suffering is not a punishment-it is a result. -Robert Green Ingersoll

3764. If our democracy is to flourish, it must have criticism; if our government is to function, it must have dissent. -Henry Commager

3765. Jealousy is all the fun you think they had. -Erica Jong

3766. For the truly faithful, no miracle is necessary. For those who doubt, no miracle is sufficient. -Nancy Gibbs

3767. The greatest discovery of my generation is that a human being can alter his life by altering his attitudes of mind. -William James

3768. We should often be ashamed of our finest actions if the world understood our motives. -François de La Rochefoucauld

3769.   Sometimes the child in one behaves a certain way and the rest of oneself follows behind slowly shaking its head. -Niels Henrik David Bohr

3770.   Marriage is like vitamins; we supplement each other's minimum daily requirements. -Kathy Mohnke

3771.   An expert is a man that has made all mistakes possible in a narrow field of expertise. -Albert Einstein

3772.   The most important thing in communication is to hear what isn't being said. -Peter Drucker

3773.   Youth cannot know how age thinks and feels. But old men are guilty if they forget what it was to be young. -J. K. Rowling

3774.   Absence of proof is not proof of absence. -Michael Crichton

3775.   Ability may get you to the top but it takes character to keep you there. -John Wooden

3776.   You see but you do not observe. - Arthur Conan Doyle

3777.   If you are not in fashion you are nobody. -Lord Chesterfield

3778.   Your theory is crazy but it's not crazy enough to be true. -Niels Bohr

3779.   The flower is the poetry of reproduction. It is an example of the eternal seductiveness of life. -Jean Giraudoux

3780.   Diamonds are nothing more than chunks of coal that stuck to their jobs. -Malcolm Stevenson Forbes

3781.   Better to light a candle than to curse the darkness. -Chinese proverb

3782.   What is listed as the hair color on a driver's license of a bald headed man?

3783.   Live out of your imagination, not your history. -Stephen Covey

3784.   For fast acting relief, try slowing down. -Lily Tomlin

3785.   We must learn to live together as brothers or perish together as fools. -Martin Luther King Jr.

3786.   Keep your conscious mind focused on what you want and your subconscious mind will unerringly guide you to it. -Unknown

3787.   You do not lead by hitting people over the head - that's assault, not leadership. -Dwight D. Eisenhower

3788.   If you can learn from hard knocks, you can also learn from soft touches. - Mannequin: My Life as a Model. - Carolyn Kenmore

3789.   If you are not part of the solution, you are part of the precipitate.

3790.   When it's third and ten you can take the milk drinkers and I'll take the whiskey drinkers every time. -Max McGee

3791.   When you cannot get a compliment any other way, pay yourself one. -Mark Twain

3792.   A book is a version of the world. If you do not like it, ignore it or offer your own version in return. -Salman Rushdie

3793.   Have the courage to be ignorant of a great number of things in order to avoid the calamity of being ignorant of everything. -Sydney Smith

3794.   He has the right to criticize who has the heart to help. - Abraham Lincoln

3795.   In the arithmetic of love, one plus one equals everything and two minus one equals nothing. -Mignon McLaughlin

3796.   The cure for boredom is curiosity. There is no cure for curiosity. -Dorothy Parker

3797.   Praising what is lost makes the remembrance dear. -William Shakespeare

3798.   Oh Sleep! It is a gentle thing, beloved from pole to pole. - Samuel Taylor Coleridge

3799.   About the most originality that any writer can hope to achieve honestly is to steal with good judgment. -Josh Billings

3800.   Blowing out another's candle will not make yours shine brighter.

3801.   Be fully in the moment. Open yourself to the powerful energies dancing around you. -Ernest Hemingway

3802.   Truly to tell lies is not honorable, but when the truth entails tremendous ruin, to speak dishonorably is pardonable. -Sophocles

3803.   The only way to get rid of responsibilities is to discharge them. - Walter S. Robertson

3804.   There are three kinds of lies: Lies, damned lies, and statistics. -Benjamin Disraeli

3805.   Reason has always existed but not always in a reasonable form. -Karl Marx

3806.   Never fight an inanimate object. -P. J. O'Rourke

3807.   Responsibility is the price of freedom. -Elbert Hubbard

3808.   Truth persuades by teaching but does not teach by persuading. -Quintus Septimius Tertullianus

3809.   Daring ideas are like chessmen moved forward. They may be beaten but they may start a winning game. -Johann von Goethe

3810.   What are the chances of a guy like you and a girl like me... ending up together -Dumb & Dumber, Lloyd

3811.   I would rather be right and die than be wrong and kill. -Holly Lisle

3812.   Dream no small dreams. They have no power to stir the souls of men. -Victor Hugo

3813.   What a waste it is to lose one's mind. Or not to have a mind is being very wasteful. How true that is. -Dan Quayle

3814.   You never know till you try to reach them how accessible men are, but you must approach each man by the right door. -Henry Ward Beecher

3815.   A sad Texan once prayed, "Lord, I wish you would make it rain - not so much for me, I've seen it - but for my 7-year-old."

3816.   A wise man sees as much as he should, not as much as he can.

3817.   Choose your friends carefully. Your enemies will choose you. -Yasser Arafat

3818.   The longest journey is the journey inward. -Dag Hammarskjöld

3819.   Attitudes are more important than facts. -Karl A. Menninger

3820.   One often learns more from ten days of agony than from ten years of contentment. -Merle Shain

3821.   A kiss makes the heart young again and wipes out the years -Rupert Brooke

3822.   Just go out there and do what you've got to do. -Martina Navratilova

3823. Keeping score of old scores and scars, getting even, and one-upping always make you less than you are. -Malcolm Forbes

3824. A kind and compassionate act is often its own reward. - William John Bennett

3825. Never advise anyone to go to war or to marry. -Danish proverb

3826. He who knows he has enough is rich. -Lao-Tzu

3827. A dream is just a dream. A goal is a dream with a plan and a deadline. -Harvey Macka

3828. The harder I work, the luckier I get. -Sam Goldwyn

3829. Discretion is the salt and fancy the sugar of life the one preserves the other sweetens it. -John Christian Bovee

3830. The world is moving so fast these days that the man who says it can't be done is generally interrupted by someone doing it. -Elbert Hubbard

3831. The only 15 letter word that can be spelled without repeating a letter is uncopyrightable.

3832. In men of the highest character and noblest genius there is to be found an insatiable desire for honor command power and glory. - Cicero

3833. If Pete Rose brings the Reds in first they ought to bronze him and put him in cement. -Jerry Coleman

3834. Illegal aliens have always been a problem in the United States. Ask any Indian. -Robert Orben

3835. An intellectual is a person who has discovered something more interesting than sex. -Aldous Huxley

3836. Man's mind stretched to a new idea never goes back to its original dimensions. -Sri da Avabhas

3837. Every time an artist dies part of the vision of mankind passes with him. -Franklin Delano Roosevelt

3838. Computers are unreliable, but humans are even more unreliable.

3839. Man is the measure of all things. -Protagoras

3840. The language of friendship is not words but meanings. -Henry David Thoreau

3841. To change and to change for the better are two different things. -German proverb

3842. Always borrow money from a pessimist, he doesn't expect to be paid back. -Unknown Author

3843. Chickens: The only animals you eat before they are born and after they are dead.

3844. He that is soon angry dealeth foolishly: and a man of wicked devices is hated. -Proverbs 14:17

3845. A verbal contract isn't worth the paper it's written on.

3846. The man for whom law exists - the man of forms the Conservative is a tame man. -Henry David Thoreau

3847. If the brain were so simple we could understand it, we would be so simple we couldn't. -Lyall Watson

3848. There is no conversation more boring than the one where everybody agrees. -Michel de Montaigne

3849. We are all strong enough to endure the misfortunes of others. -Jean de La Rochefoucauld

3850. Beauty itself is but the sensible image of the infinite. - George Bancroft

3851. The greatest possession we have costs nothing, it's known as love. -Brian Jett

3852. Plan for the future because that's where you are going to spend the rest of your life. -Mark Twain

3853. If you're going to do something tonight that you'll be sorry for tomorrow morning....sleep late. -Henny Youngman

3854. Joy is a net of love by which you can catch souls. -Mother Theresa

3855. Seek first to understand and then to be understood. -Stephen Covey

3856. The noble Lord (Stanley) was the Prince Rupert to the Parliamentary army — his valor did not always serve his own cause.—Benjamin Disraeli

3857. Beware the anger of the dove. [Fr., Craignez la colere de la colombe.] - Proverb

3858.　If we do not change our direction, we are likely to end up where we are headed. -Chinese Proverb

3859.　The last suit that you wear, you don't need any pockets. -Wayne Dyer

3860.　I am neither an optimist nor pessimist, but a possibilist. -Max Lerner

3861.　A problem is a chance for you to do your best. -Duke Ellington

3862.　Our greatest glory consists not in never failing but in rising every time we fall. -Vincent Van Gogh

3863.　It's in the hole. -CaddyShack, Carl Spackler

3864.　Of course I know how to copy disks. Where's the Xerox machine?

3865.　Intellectual passion dries out sensuality. -Leonardo da Vinci

3866.　A little one shall become a thousand and a small one a strong nation. -Isaiah 60:22

3867.　Daring ideas are like chessmen moved forward. They may be beaten but they may start a winning game. -Johann Wolfgang von Goethe

3868.　Honest criticism is hard to take, particularly from a relative, a friend, an acquaintance, or a stranger. -Franklin P. Jones

3869.　I don't believe people are looking for the meaning of life as much as they are looking for the experience of being alive. -Joseph Campbell

3870.　Men are equal; it is not birth, but virtue that makes the difference. -Voltaire

3871.　Names are changed more readily than doctrines and doctrines more readily than ceremonies. -Thomas Love Peacock

3872.　It is as hard to take success as it is failure. -Louise Nevelson

3873.　The more deeply the path is etched, the more it is used, and the more it is used, the more deeply it etched. -Jo Coudert

3874.　Some people lose all respect for the lion unless he devours them instantly. There is no pleasing some people. -Will Cuppy

3875.　Love is an act of endless forgiveness - a tender look which becomes a habit. -Peter Ustinov

3876. He who dies with the most toys, is, nonetheless, still dead.

3877. There is nothing like returning to a place that remains unchanged to find the ways in which you yourself have altered. - Nelson Mandela

3878. The freedom of all is essential to my freedom. -Mikhail Bakunin

3879. Eloquence is a painting of the thoughts. -Blaise Pascal

3880. A broken bone can heal but the wound a word opens can fester forever. -Jessamyn West

3881. Thou shouldst not have been old till thou hadst been wise. - William Shakespeare

3882. The only paradise is paradise lost. -Marcel Proust

3883. You can observe a lot by watching. -Yogi Berra

3884. Don't compute and drive; the life you save may be your own.

3885. Service to others is the rent you pay for your room here on earth. -Muhammad Ali

3886. I pray without ceasing now. My personal prayer is: Make me an instrument which only truth can speak. -Pilgrims

3887. Humor is just another defense against the universe. -Mel Brooks

3888. A man does not die of love or his liver or even of old age; he dies of being a man. -Percival Arland Ussher

3889. Oregano is the spice of life. -Henry J. Tillman

3890. I always keep a supply of stimulant handy in case I see a snake - which I also keep handy. -W. C. Fields

3891. There is no legal obligation to perform impossibilities. -Publius Celsus

3892. We don't want a thing because we have found a reason for it- we find a reason for it because we want it.

3893. Strive for perfection in everything you do. Take the best that exists and make it better. When it does not exist, design it.

3894. Wealth is enjoying what we already have, not getting more of what we think will make us happy. -Peter McWilliams

3895. It's not that some people have willpower and some don't. It's that some people are ready to change and others are not. -James Gordon

3896. Sr. In this country men seem to live for action as long as they can and sink into apathy when they retire. -Charles Francis Adams

3897. Change in all things is sweet. -Aristotle

3898. England expects that every man will do his duty. -Lord Nelson

3899. Self-reliance is the only road to true freedom, and being one's own person is its ultimate reward. - Patricia Sampson

3900. To read means to borrow to create out of one's readings is paying off one's debts. -Georg Christoph Lichtenberg

3901. Be as you wish to seem. -Socrates

3902. To each man is reserved a work which he alone can do. -Susan Blow

3903. When I thought I couldn't go on, I forced myself to keep going. My success is based on persistence, not luck. -Norman Lear

3904. The more we do, the more we can do; the more busy we are, the more leisure we have. -William Hazlitt

3905. Strong lives are motivated by dynamic purposes. -Kenneth Hildebrand

3906. They that can give up essential liberty to obtain a little temporary safety deserve neither liberty nor safety. -Benjamin Franklin

3907. The fact that you are willing to say, "I do not understand, and it is fine," is the greatest understanding you could exhibit. -Wayne Dyer

3908. The church is looking for better methods. God is looking for better men.

3909. The truth shall make you free. -The Bible, John 8

3910. Vision is the art of seeing things invisible to others. -Jonathan Swift

3911. Don't let it end like this. Tell them I said something. -Pancho Villa

3912. He who does without the praise of the crowd will not deny himself an opportunity to be his own adherent. -Karl Kraus

3913. No act of kindness, no matter how small, is ever wasted. -Aesop

3914. The word politics is derived from the word poly, meaning many, and the word ticks, meaning blood sucking parasites. -Larry Hardiman

3915. The same refinement which brings us new pleasures exposes us to new pains. -Edward Bulwer-Lytton

3916. I know how men in exile feed on dreams of hope. -Aeschylus

3917. Mirrors should reflect a little before throwing back images. -Jean Cocteau

3918. As soon as you trust yourself you will know how to live. -Johann Wolfgang von Goethe

3919. Brilliance is typically the act of an individual but incredible stupidity can usually be traced to an organization. -Jon Bentley

3920. We believe that the applause of silence is the only kind that counts. -Alfred Jarry

3921. When neither their property nor their honor is touched, the majority of men live content. -Niccolo Machiavelli

3922. Violence commands both literature and life and violence is always crude and distorted. -Ellen Glasgow

3923. It is well that war is so terrible or we should grow too fond of it. -Robert E. Lee

3924. He used to say that it was better to have one friend of great value than many friends who were good for nothing. -Laertius Diogenes

3925. Real success is finding your lifework in the work that you love. -David McCullough

3926. Forgive your enemies but never forget their names. -John F. Kennedy

3927. The creative impulses of man are always at war with the possessive impulses. -Van Wyck Brooks

3928. The height of your accomplishments will equal the depth of your convictions. -William F. Scolavino

3929. What we fight against defines us as clearly as all we embrace.

3930.   You can come to understand your purpose in life by slowing down and feeling your heart's desires. -Marcia Wieder

3931.   You can't take it with you when you go. -Proverb

3932.   The first principle is that you must not fool yourself - and you are the easiest person to fool. -Richard Feynman

3933.   And that's the world in a nutshell: an appropriate receptacle. - Stan Dunn

3934.   Whom did it benefit? -Longinus Cassius

3935.   The ability to learn faster than your competitors may be the only sustainable competitive advantage. -Peter Senge

3936.   It is surprising what a man can do when he has to and how little most men will do when they don't have to. -Walter Linn

3937.   It is more noble to give yourself completely to one individual than to labor diligently for the salvation of the masses. -Dag Hammarskjöld

3938.   Love is a snowmobile racing across the tundra and then suddenly it flips over, pinning you underneath. At night, the ice weasels come. - John Harrigan

3939.   Don't let the computer bugs bite!

3940.   Hollywood grew to be the most flourishing factory of popular mythology since the Greeks. -Alistair Cooke

3941.   Victory attained by violence is tantamount to a defeat for it is momentary. -Mahatma Gandhi

3942.   Optimism is essential to achievement and it is also the foundation of courage and true progress. -Nicholas Murray Butler

3943.   I have found you an argument I am not obliged to find you an understanding. -James Boswell

3944.   Before you can see the light, you have to deal with the darkness. -Dan Millman

3945.   If a free society cannot help the many who are poor, it cannot save the few who are rich. -John F. Kennedy

3946.   Success seems to be connected with action. Successful men keep moving. They make mistakes but they don't quit. -Conrad Hilton

3947.	Laziness may appear attractive but work gives satisfaction. - Anne Frank

3948.	Trees though they are cut and lopped, grow up again quickly, but if men are destroyed it is not easy to get them again.- Pericles

3949.	The greater danger for most of us is not that our aim is too high and we miss it, but that it is too low and we hit it. -Michelangelo

3950.	Defeat should never be a source of discouragement but rather a fresh stimulus. -Robert South

3951.	Sometimes I know that there is intelligent life on other planets because they haven't tried to contact us.

3952.	Life is a unique combination of want to and how to and we need to give equal attention to both. -Jim Rohn

3953.	I consider being ill as one of the great pleasures of life provided one is not too ill. -Samuel Butler

3954.	It is the first of all problems for a man to find out what kind of work he is to do in this universe. -Thomas Carlyle

3955.	Of all the varieties of virtues liberalism is the most beloved. - Aristotle

3956.	You don't have to fear defeat if you believe it may reveal powers that you didn't know you possessed. -Napoleon Hill

3957.	Why do we act like we know what someone's talking about when we have no idea?

3958.	If you don't like something, change it. If you can't change it, change your attitude. Don't complain. -Maya Angelou

3959.	A great many people think they are thinking when they are really rearranging their prejudices. -Edward R. Murrow

3960.	There is no disinfectant like success. -Daniel J. Boorstin

3961.	The trouble with the rat race is that even when you win, you're still a rat. -Jane Wagner

3962.	Wars have never hurt anybody except the people who die. - Salvador Dali

3963.	Be humble if thou wouldst attain to Wisdom. Be humbler still when Wisdom thou hast mastered. -H. Hahn Blavatsky

3964. I am bound to furnish my antagonists with arguments, but not with comprehension. - Lord Byron (George Gordon Noel Byron)

3965. You may not be in a class by yourself but it sure doesn't take long to call the roll. -Bum Philips

3966. When I look at the world I'm pessimistic but when I look at people I am optimistic. -Carl R. Rogers

3967. Never cut a tree down in the wintertime. Never make a negative decision in the low time. -Dr. Robert Schuller

3968. Self-education is, I firmly believe, the only kind of education there is. -Isaac Asimov

3969. Some people are bitter, some sour, others are sweet. Who you hang out with depends on your taste.

3970. Great works are performed not by strength, but by perseverance. -Samuel Johnson

3971. Heaven means to be one with God. -Confucius

3972. The price of being the best is having to be the best. -Terry Pratchett

3973. Sometimes I would rather that people take away years from my life than take away a moment. -Pearl Bailey

3974. Yes'm, old friends is always best, 'less you can catch a new one that's fit to make an old one out of.- Sarah Orne Jewett

3975. You have to expect things of yourself before you can do them. - Michael Jordan

3976. If we are to judge of love by the consequences, it more nearly resembles hatred than friendship. -La Rochefoucauld

3977. Oh give thanks to the Lord for He is good; His love and His kindness go on forever. -Chronicles TLB, The Bible

3978. When a man finds no peace within himself, it is useless to seek it elsewhere.-François de La Rochefoucauld

3979. Love is a medicine for the sickness of the world, a prescription often given, too rarely taken. -Dr. Karl Menninger

3980. We shall find peace. We shall hear angels we shall see the sky sparkling with diamonds. -Anton Pavlovich Chekhov

3981.   Find something you love to do and you'll never have to work a day in your life. -Harvey Mackay

3982.   Talk sense to a fool and he calls you foolish. -Epicurus

3983.   Nothing happens to anybody which he is not fitted by nature to bear. -Marcus Aurelius

3984.   I love California; I practically grew up in Phoenix. -Dan Quayle

3985.   One needs to be slow to form convictions, but once formed they must be defended against the heaviest odds. -Mahatma Gandhi

3986.   Necessity is the mother of invention. -Anon.

3987.   Optimism is a kind of heart stimulant - the digitalis of failure. -Elbert Hubbard

3988.   What is yours is mine and all mine is yours. -Titus Maccius Plautus

3989.   For the things we have to learn before we can do them we learn by doing them. -Aristotle

3990.   Football is not a contact sport it's a collision sport - dancing is a contact sport. -Vince Lombardi

3991.   I only regret that I have but one life to give for my country. -Nathan Hale

3992.   The enthusiasm of a woman's love is even beyond the biographers. -Jane Austen

3993.   A conference is a gathering of important people who singly can do nothing but together can decide that nothing can be done. -Fred Allen

3994.   We take greater pains to persuade others that we are happy than in endeavoring to think so ourselves. -Confucius

3995.   To govern is always to choose among disadvantages. -Charles De Gaulle

3996.   Be able to be alone. Lose not the advantage of solitude and the society of thyself. -Sir Thomas Browne

3997.   Absence lessens the minor passions and increases the great ones as the wind douses a candle and kindles a fire. -La Rochefoucauld

3998.   A mirror reflects a man's face but what he is really like is shown by the kind of friends he chooses. -Proverbs, Bible

3999.   If you can't convince them, confuse them. -Harry S. Truman

4000.   I greet you as the shapers of American society. -Lyndon B. Johnson

4001.   Always endeavor to really be what you would wish to appear. - Granville Sharp

4002.   Work relieves us from three great evils, boredom, vice, and want. -French Proverb

4003.   Men should be what they seem. -William Shakespeare

4004.   If you want your children to improve, let them overhear the nice things you say about them to others. -Haim Ginott

4005.   Choose a job you love, and you will never have to work a day in your life. -Unknown Author

4006.   An optimist thinks this is the best of all worlds. A pessimist fears the same may be true. -Doug Larson

4007.   Be true to your work, your word, and your friend. - Henry David Thoreau

4008.   Your body is precious. It is our vehicle for awakening. Treat it with care. -Buddha

4009.   In love the paradox occurs that two beings become one and yet remain two. -Erich Fromm

4010.   It is quality rather than quantity that matters. -Seneca

4011.   Save time ... see it my way.

4012.   We are who we choose to be... now CHOOSE. -Spider-Man, Green Goblin

4013.   As a small businessperson, you have no greater leverage than the truth. - John Greenleaf Whittier

4014.   A day out-of-doors, someone I loved to talk with a good book, and some simple food and music - that would be rest. - Eleanor Roosevelt

4015.   Where I am I don't know I'll never know in the silence you don't know you must go on I can't go on I'll go on. -Samuel Beckett

4016.   To err is human; to admit it, superhuman. -Doug Larson, United Feature Syndicate

4017.   The hand that rocks the cradle is the hand that rules the world. -W.R. Wallace

4018.   A rumor without a leg to stand on will get around some other way. - John Tudor

4019.   There are people whom one loves immediately and forever. Even to know they are alive in the world with one is quite enough. -Nancy Spain

4020.   The way to gain a good reputation is to endeavor to be what you desire to appear. -Socrates

4021.   Work is not man's punishment. It is his reward and his strength and his pleasure. -George Sand

4022.   Coming together is a beginning; staying together is progress; working together is success. -Henry Ford

4023.   We can't control the wind, but we have the power to adjust the sails.

4024.   Two kinds of gratitude: The sudden kind we feel for what we take; the larger kind we feel for what we give. -Edwin Arlington Robinson

4025.   If you want things to be different, perhaps the answer is to become different yourself. -Norman Vincent Peale

4026.   The secret to creativity is knowing how to hide your sources. - Albert Einstein

4027.   The sole advantage of power is that you can do more good. - Baltasar Gracian

4028.   I'll be like Scarlett O'Hara. I'll think about it tomorrow. - Ronald Reagan

4029.   Always listen to experts. They'll tell you what can't be done and why. Then do it. -Robert A. Heinlein

4030.   Let us love, not in word or speech, but in truth and action. - The Bible, 1 John 3

4031.   Tact is the art of making guests feel at home when that's really where you wish they were. - George E. Bergman

4032.   Johnny Grubb slides into second with a standup double. -Jerry Coleman

4033. Anger: an acid that can do more harm to the vessel in which it is stored than to anything on which it is poured. - Seneca

4034. I shut my eyes in order to see. -Paul Gauguin

4035. A man is not where he lives but where he loves. -Latin Proverb

4036. Do not talk a little on many subjects but much on a few. - Pythagoras

4037. Happiness is not pleasure, it's victory. -Zig Ziglar

4038. Work joyfully and peacefully, knowing that right thoughts and right efforts will inevitable bring about right results. -James Allen

4039. I never know how much of what I say is true. -Bette Midler

4040. This world we live in is but thickened light. -Ralph Waldo Emerson

4041. Winning is important to me but what brings me real joy is the experience of being fully engaged in whatever I'm doing. -Phil Jackson

4042. Listen or thy tongue will keep thee deaf. -American Indian Proverb

4043. Men often applaud an imitation and hiss the real thing. -Aesop

4044. In order to succeed, we must first believe that we can. -Michael Korda

4045. You always succeed in producing a result. -Anthony Robbins

4046. Belief consists in accepting the affirmations of the soul unbelief in denying them. -Ralph Waldo Emerson

4047. The ex-left-hander Dave Roberts will be going for Houston. - Jerry Coleman

4048. Laugh at yourself first before anyone else can. -Elsa Maxwell

4049. It is better to offer no excuse than a bad one. -George Washington

4050. The Statue of Liberty is not that monument's name. It is Liberty Enlightening the World. -Deane Jordan

4051. All cruelty springs from weakness. -Seneca

4052. The man who rolls up his sleeves seldom loses his shirt. - Thomas Cowan

4053.   What we imagine is order is merely the prevailing form of chaos. -Kerry Thornley

4054.   It is easy to sit up and take notice. What is difficult is getting up and taking action. - Al Batt

4055.   You never saw a fish on the wall with its mouth shut. -Sally Berger

4056.   It's not the events of our lives that shape us, but our beliefs as to what those events mean. -Anthony Robbins

4057.   Change yourself and your work will seem different. -Norman Vincent Peale

4058.   Every man wishes to be wise and they who cannot be wise are almost always cunning. -Samuel Johnson

4059.   You wake me up early in the morning to tell me I am right Please wait until I am wrong. -Johann von Neumann

4060.   If you play it safe in life you've decided that you don't want to grow any more. -Shirley Mount Hufstedler

4061.   The human mind always makes progress, but it is a progress in spirals. -Germaine De Stael

4062.   There ought to be so many who are excellent, there are so few. - Janet Erskine Stuart

4063.   Everyone takes the limits of his own vision for the limits of the world. -Arthur Schopenhauer

4064.   Love takes off masks that we fear we cannot live without and know we cannot live within. -James Baldwin

4065.   Objects, as they exist in time, the clean eye and camera give us. Not falsified by seeing. -Jim Morrison

4066.   You can tell what a man is by what he does when he hasn't anything to do. -Anonymous

4067.   Change your thoughts and you change your world. -Norman Vincent Peale

4068.   There is in the worst of fortune the best of chances for a happy change. -Euripides

4069.   Love is something eternal; the aspect may change, but not the essence. -Vincent Van Gogh

4070.   RAM disk is NOT an installation procedure.

4071.   Civilization is a transient sickness. -Robinson Jeffers

4072.   No one travelling on a business trip would be missed if he failed to arrive. -Thorstein Veblen

4073.   Prosperity is a great teacher; adversity a greater. -William Hazlitt

4074.   When people agree with me, I always feel that I must be wrong. -Oscar Wilde

4075.   Only the spoon knows what is stirring in the pot. -Sicilian Proverb

4076.   A human being must have occupation if he or she is not to become a nuisance to the world. -Dorothy L. Sayers

4077.   The two basic processes of education are knowing and valuing. -Robert J. Havighurst

4078.   Someone's opinion of you does not have to become your reality. -Les Brown

4079.   When we get too caught up in the busyness of the world we lose connection with one another- and ourselves. -Jack Kornfield

4080.   Fortune favors the brave. -Virgil

4081.   One person with a belief is equal to a force of who have only interests. -John Stuart Mill

4082.   A mistake is simply another way of doing things. - Katharine Graham

4083.   An educational system isn't worth a great deal if it teaches young people how to make a living but doesn't teach them how to make a life.

4084.   The pursuit even of the best things ought to be calm and tranquil. -Marcus Tullius Cicero

4085.   Thou canst not touch the freedom of my mind. -John Milton

4086.   I bid him look into the lives of men as though into a mirror, and from others to take an example for himself. -Terence

4087.   Most of the things worth doing in the world had been declared impossible before they were done. -Louis. D. Brandeis

4088.   Destiny waits alike for the free man as well as for him enslaved by another's might. -Aeschylus

4089.   Call on God but row away from the rocks. -Indian Proverb

4090.   It is now possible for a flight attendant to get a pilot pregnant. -Richard J. Ferris

4091.   Turn the despair of being alone into the wonder of being alone with God.

4092.   Egotist: a person more interested in himself than in me. -Ambrose Gwinett Bierce

4093.   Character builds slowly, but it can be torn down with incredible swiftness. - Faith Baldwin

4094.   What is the difference between a Peeping Tom and someone who just got out of the bath? One is rude and nosy, and the other's nude and rosy.

4095.   It is what we do easily and what we like to do that we do well. -Orison Swett Marden

4096.   I took a speed reading course and read War and Peace in twenty minutes. It involves Russia. -Woody Allen

4097.   Money frees you from doing things you dislike. Since I dislike doing nearly everything, money is handy. -Groucho Marx

4098.   What you are will show in what you do. -Thomas Alva Edison

4099.   A man can't ride your back unless it's bent. -Martin Luther King Jr.

4100.   What I give form to in daylight is only one per cent of what I have seen in darkness. -M. C. Escher

4101.   Poverty within is as dangerous as poverty without. -Rowan Swan

4102.   What do you despise? By this are you truly known. -Frank Herbert

4103.   What is this world that is hastening me toward I know not what viewing me with contempt? -Kahlil Gibran

4104.   Happiness is enhanced by others but does not depend upon others.

4105.   The primary sign of a well-ordered mind is a man's ability to remain in one place and linger in his own company. -Seneca

4106.   Sincerity and truth are the basis of every virtue. -Confucius

4107.   Success is the progressive realization of a worthy goal or ideal. -Earl Nightingale

4108.   In the modern world the intelligence of public opinion is the one indispensable condition for social progress. -Charles W. Eliot

4109.   A great obstacle to happiness is to anticipate too great a happiness. -Bernard le Bovier de Fontenelle

4110.   Sure, luck means a lot in football. Not having a good quarterback is bad luck. -Don Schula

4111.   Education is the ability to think clearly, act well in the world of work and to appreciate life. -Brigham Young

4112.   Anything you lose automatically doubles in value. -Mignon McLaughin

4113.   If my hands are fully occupied in holding on to something, I can neither give nor receive. -Dorothee Solle

4114.   Respect for ourselves guides our morals; respect for others guides our manners. -Laurence Sterne

4115.   Where there is no vision, people perish. -Proverbs

4116.   We need to make a world in which fewer children are born and in which we take better care of them. -George Wald

4117.   Under conditions of tyranny it is far easier to act than to think. -Hannah Arendt

4118.   Ah this is obviously some strange usage of the word safe that I wasn't previously aware of. -Douglas Adams

4119.   Having seen and felt the end, you have willed the means to the realization of the end. -Thomas Troward

4120.   He has hay on his horns. [Lat., Foenum habet in cornu.] -Horace (Quintus Horatius Flaccus)

4121.   Ignorance of certain subjects is a great part of wisdom. -Hugo De Groot

4122.   You don't lead by pointing and telling people some place to go. You lead by going to that place and making a case. -Ken Kesey

4123.   One man's word is no man's word; we should quietly hear both sides. -Johann Wolfgang von Goethe

4124.   I never dared to be radical when young for fear it would make me conservative when old. -Robert Frost

4125.   Some people succeed because they are destined to but most people succeed because they are determined to.- Unknown

4126.   Failure is the opportunity to begin again more intelligently. -Henry Ford

4127.   The probability that we may fail in the struggle ought not to deter us from the support of a cause we believe to be just.- Abraham Lincoln

4128.   In the truest sense, freedom cannot be bestowed; it must be achieved. -Franklin D. Roosevelt

4129.   You can't have a light without a dark to stick it in.- Arlo Guthrie

4130.   Sometimes I think we'd be better off blind.- Lily Yeamans

4131.   If you wish your merit to be known, acknowledge that of other people. -Oriental Proverb

4132.   Samuel Johnson The world is not yet exhausted let me see something tomorrow which I never saw before.

4133.   Only when we give joyfully, without hesitation or thought of gain, can we truly know what love means. -Leo Buscaglia

4134.   Civilization is a progress from an indefinite incoherent homogeneity toward a definite coherent heterogeneity. -Herbert Spencer

4135.   Familiarity breeds contempt while rarity wins admiration. -Apuleius

4136.   I have never seen a more lucid, better, balanced, mad, mind than mine. -Vladimir Vladimirovich Nabokov

4137.   I need to know the price of a gallon of milk and a dozen eggs. I need to know right now. -Lamar Alexander

4138.   People laugh because I'm different, I laugh because they're all the same.

4139.   It's easier to go down a hill than up it but the view is much better at the top. -Henry Ward Beecher

4140.   A man running for office puts me in mind of a dog that's lost - he smells everybody he meets and wags himself all over. -Josh Billings

4141.   I dream my painting and then paint my dream. -Vincent Van Gogh

4142.   Rock and roll is the hamburger that ate the world. -Peter York

4143.   The pursuit of perfection, then, is the pursuit of sweetness and light. -Matthew Arnold

4144.   A suspicious mind always looks on the black side of things. - Publilius Syrus

4145.   The issue of race could benefit from a period of benign neglect. -Daniel Patrick Moynihan

4146.   I have noticed that nothing I have never said ever did me any harm. -Gandhi

4147.   Each body has its art... -Gwendolyn Brooks

4148.   Be more splendid, more extraordinary. Use every moment to fill yourself up. -Oprah Winfrey

4149.   Two paradoxes are better than one; they may even suggest a solution. -Edward Teller

4150.   If I had my life to live over, I would have burned the pink candle sculpted like a rose before it melted in storage. -Erma Bombeck

4151.   I may be crazy but it keeps me from going insane. -Waylon Jennings

4152.   Work joyfully and peacefully knowing that right thoughts and right efforts inevitably bring about right results. -James Allen

4153.   What difference is there between us, save a restless dream that follows my soul but fears to come near you. -Kahlil Gibran

4154.   Let us be grateful to people who make us happy they are the charming gardeners who make our souls blossom. -Jacques Prévert

4155.   Perhaps in time the so-called Dark Ages will be thought of as including our own. -Georg Christoph Lichtenberg

4156.   The law is a rule to the fool, but a guide to the wise.

4157.   While I see many hoof marks going in, I see none coming out. It is easier to get into the enemy's toils than out again. -Aesop

4158.   You can't help the poor man by destroying the rich.

4159.　Antiques are things one generation buys, the next generation gets rid of, and the following generation buys at auction at amazing prices.

4160.　No man is fit to command another that cannot command himself. -William Penn

4161.　To achieve, you need thought. You have to know what you are doing and that's real power. -Ayn Rand

4162.　Fear is static - that prevents me from hearing my intuition. - Hugh Prather

4163.　No one can give you authority. But if you act like you have it others will believe you do. -Karin Ireland

4164.　Happiness lies in the joy of achievement and the thrill of creative effort. -Franklin D Roosevelt

4165.　The greatest wealth is to live content with little. -Plato

4166.　An expert is a person who avoids small error as he sweeps on to the grand fallacy. -Benjamin Stolberg

4167.　The sufferings that fate inflicts on us should be borne with patience what enemies inflict with manly courage. -Thucydides

4168.　The only way to overcome is to hang in. Even I'm starting to believe that. -Dan O'Brien

4169.　We face the question whether a still higher standard of living is worth its costs in things natural wild and free. -Aldo Leopold

4170.　God made Truth with many doors to welcome every believer who knocks on them. -Kahlil Gibran

4171.　User error: replace user and press any key to continue.

4172.　Many people quit looking for work when they find a job.

4173.　Things which matter most must never be at the mercy of things which matter least. -Johann Wolfgang von Goethe

4174.　Laughter is the sun that drives winter from the human face. - Victor Hugo

4175.　The last dejected effort often becomes the winning stroke. -W.J. Cameron

4176.　A rising tide lifts all boats. -John Fitzgerald Kennedy

4177.   The worst bankruptcy in the world is the person who has lost his enthusiasm. -H. W. Arnold

4178.   If there is anything that keeps the mind open to angel visits and repels the ministry of evil it is pure human love. -N. P. Willis

4179.   The harder I work, the luckier I get.-Samuel Goldwyn

4180.   People need hard times and oppression to develop psychic muscles. - Frank Herbert

4181.   We perceive when love begins and when it declines by our embarrassment when alone together. -Jean de la Bruyere

4182.   Love from one being to another can only be that two solitudes come nearer, recognize, and protect and comfort each other. -Han Suyin

4183.   He who consistently plans each day will journey successfully through all of life's years. -Drew Eric Whitman

4184.   Character is what you know you are, not what others think you have. - Marva Collins

4185.   Wise sayings often fall on barren ground; but a kind word is never thrown away. -Sir Arthur Helps

4186.   Be of use, but don't be used.

4187.   Only actions give life strength only moderation gives it a charm. -Jean Paul Richter

4188.   I don't know if God exists but it would be better for His reputation if He didn't. -Jules Renard

4189.   Where you're going is more important than where you stand.

4190.   The trodden path is the safest. - Legal Maxim

4191.   Summer vacation is a time when parents realize that teachers are grossly underpaid.

4192.   No man is happy who does not think himself so. -Publilius Syrus

4193.   They talk most who have the least to say. -Matthew Prior

4194.   Wisdom is oft-times nearer when we stoop Than when we soar.—William Wordsworth

4195.   People who want the most approval get the least and people who need approval the least get the most. -Wayne Dyer

4196. I used to want to pack as much as I could into my life, but now I realize it's more about quality of life than quantity. -Sharon Stone

4197. Better be ignorant of a matter than half know it. -Publilius Syrus

4198. I regret that I have but one life to give for my country. -Nathan Hale

4199. Technology means the systematic application of scientific or other organized knowledge to practical tasks.

4200. The winning team has a dedication. It will have a core of veteran players who set the standards. They will not accept defeat. -Merlin Olsen

4201. You only live once - but if you work it right once is enough. - Joe E. Lewis

4202. The worst sin - perhaps the only sin - passion can commit is to be joyless. -Dorothy L. Sayers

4203. Nothing is so bitter that a calm mind cannot find comfort in it. -Seneca

4204. All reactionaries are paper tigers. -Mao Zedong

4205. The last thing we decide in writing a book is what to put first. - Blaise Pascal

4206. One of the advantages of being disorderly is that one is constantly making exciting discoveries. -A. Milne

4207. Those are my principles and if you don't like them... well I have others. -Groucho Marx

4208. Two things a man should never be angry at: what he can help, and what he cannot help. - Thomas Fuller

4209. Good humor is one of the best articles of dress one can wear in society. -William Makepeace Thackeray

4210. The only abnormality is the incapacity to love. -Anais Nin

4211. Listen to life it is the wisest teacher of all. -Unknown

4212. Deep Thoughts: It takes a big man to cry but it takes a bigger man to laugh at that man. -Jack Handey

4213. Never, never rest contented with any circle of ideas, but always be certain that a wider one is still possible. -Richard Jefferies

4214.   The bird a nest, the spider a web, man friendship. -William Blake

4215.   Ask not what tomorrow may bring, but count as blessing every day that fate allows you. -Horace

4216.   Pleasure of love lasts but a moment Pain of love lasts a lifetime. -Bette Davis

4217.   A good head and a good heart are always a formidable combination. -Nelson Mandela

4218.   The years teach much which the days never knew. -Ralph Waldo Emerson

4219.   Those who do not know how to weep with their whole heart, don't know how to laugh either. -Golda Meir

4220.   No passion so effectually robs the mind of its powers of acting and reasoning as fear. -Edmund Burke

4221.   Most new books are forgotten within a year especially by those who borrow them. -Evan Esar

4222.   If you want to understand democracy spend less time in the library with Plato and more time in the buses with people. -Simeon Strunsky

4223.   The best way to predict your future is to create it. -Stephen Covey

4224.   Bad guy can't win. It's a morality tale. One way or the other, He's gotta go down. -Swordfish Stan

4225.   It is in men as in soils where sometimes there is a vein of gold which the owner knows not of. -Jonathan Swift

4226.   We have to realize that we are as deeply afraid to live and to love as we are to die. -Ronald David Laing

4227.   By the time a man realizes that maybe his father was right he usually has a son who thinks he's wrong. -Charles Wadsworth

4228.   Grief teaches the steadiest minds to waver. -Sophocles

4229.   Death is not the worst; rather, in vain To wish for death, and not to compass it. -Sophocles

4230.   Never be a cynic even a gentle one. Never help out a sneer even at the devil. -Vachel Lindsay

4231. The surest way to be late is to have plenty of time. -Leo Kennedy

4232. Admonish thy friends in secret praise them openly. - Publilius Syrus

4233. There's a monster outside my room can I have a glass of water. - Signs Bo

4234. One good thing about forgetting is that you can no longer worry about whatever it was you forgot.

4235. The best education consists in immunizing people against systematic attempts at education. -Paul Karl Feyerabend

4236. What I like in a good author is not what he says but what he whispers. -Logan Pearsall Smith

4237. He who establishes his argument by noise and command shows that his reason is weak. - Michel Eyquem De Montaigne

4238. Hold a true friend with both hands. -Nigerian Proverb

4239. We fear death yet we long for slumber and beautiful dreams. - Kahlil Gibran

4240. I live in the crowds of jollity not so much to enjoy company as to shun myself. -Samuel Johnson

4241. Go often to the house of thy friend for weeds soon choke up the unused path. -Scandinavian Proverb

4242. I prefer the company of peasants because they have not been educated sufficiently to reason incorrectly. -Michel de Montaigne

4243. Silence is the most perfect expression of scorn. -George Bernard Shaw

4244. He who does not know how to be silent will not know how to speak. -Ausonius

4245. Nothing of course begins at the time you think it did. -Lillian Hellman

4246. Imagination will often carry us to worlds that never were. But without it we go nowhere. -Carl Sagan

4247. Of all the things which wisdom provides to make us entirely happy much the greatest is the possession of friendship. -Epicurus

4248. We know what a person thinks not when he tells us what he thinks but by his actions. -Isaac Bashevis Singer

4249. Man is what he believes. -Anton Chekhov

4250. Nothing counts so much as family the rest are just strangers. (as Nicholas Earpp in Wyatt Earp) -Gene Hackman

4251. What old people say you cannot do you try and find that you can. Old deeds for old people and new deeds for new. -Henry David Thoreau

4252. The best throw of the dice is to throw them away. -English proverb

4253. Food is an important part of a balanced diet. -Fran Lebowitz

4254. Reputation is what men and women think of us; character is what God and angels know of us. -Thomas Paine

4255. A young man is embarrassed to question an older one. -Homer

4256. Gentlemen it is better to have died as a small boy than to fumble this football. -John Heisman

4257. It is even harder for the average ape to believe that he has descended from man. -H.L. Mencken

4258. Where facts are few experts are many. -Donald R. Gannon

4259. I believe that every right implies a responsibility; every opportunity an obligation; every possession, a duty. -John D. Rockefeller

4260. If this is coffee please bring me some tea; but if this is tea please bring me some coffee. -Abraham Lincoln

4261. There is a time for departure even when there's no certain place to go. -Tennessee Williams

4262. Your work is to discover your work and then with all your heart to give yourself to it. -Buddha

4263. We were a silent hidden thought in the folds of oblivion and we have become a voice that causes the heavens to tremble. -Kahlil Gibran

4264. The greatest healing therapy is friendship and love. -Hubert Humphrey

4265. Only little boys and old men sneer at love. -Louis Auchincloss

4266.   Perhaps too much of everything is as bad as too little. -Edna Ferber

4267.   One's first step in wisdom is to question everything - and one's last is to come to terms with everything. -Georg Christoph Lichtenberg

4268.   If you would not step into the harlot's house, do not go by the harlot's door. -Thomas Secker

4269.   Music is Love in search of a word. -Sidney Lanier

4270.   Now and then it's good to pause in our pursuit of happiness and just be happy. -Guillaume Apollinaire

4271.   It is an old habit with theologians to beat the living with the bones of the dead. -Robert G. Ingersoll

4272.   Love is a kind of military service. -Latin Proverb

4273.   All historians even the most scientific have bias if in no other sense than the determination not to have any. -Carl Lotus Becker

4274.   The shortest distance between two points is under construction. -Noelie Alito

4275.   There is no expedient to which a man will go to avoid the real labor of thinking. -Thomas Alva Edison

4276.   Any excuse will serve a tyrant. -Aesop

4277.   To lead the people, walk behind them. -Lao Tzu

4278.   Eloquence is in the assembly not merely in the speaker. - William Pitt

4279.   Miracles happen to those who believe in them. -Bernhard Berenson

4280.   No matter how much data you add to your laptop, it will not get heavier.

4281.   Start off every day with a smile and get it over with. -W. C. Fields

4282.   A word is dead when it is said some say. I say it just begins to live that day. -Emily Elizabeth Dickinson

4283.   A man who is good enough to shed his blood for his country is good enough to be given a square deal afterwards. -Theodore Roosevelt

4284.   Cheerfulness and contentment are great beautifiers and are famous preservers of youthful looks. -Charles Dickens

4285.   Why do strong arms fatigue themselves with frivolous dumbbells? To dig a vineyard is worthier exercise for men. -Marcus Valerius Martialis

4286.   Respect commands itself and it can neither be given nor withheld when it is due. - Eldridge Cleaver

4287.   Man's character is his fate. -Heraclitus

4288.   There is little friendship in the world and least of all between equals. -Francis Bacon

4289.   All that spirits desire spirits attain. -Kahlil Gibran

4290.   You cannot escape the responsibility of tomorrow by evading it today. -Abraham Lincoln

4291.   Marriage should be a duet - when one sings the other claps. - Joe Murray

4292.   I've learned that life is like a roll of toilet paper - the closer it gets to the end, the faster it goes. - Andy Rooney

4293.   Patience makes lighter what sorrow may not heal. -Horace

4294.   Press any key to continue or any other key to quit...

4295.   If we could read the secret history of our enemies, we should find in each man's life sorrow and suffering enough to disarm any hostility.

4296.   Most of the trouble in the world is caused by people wanting to be important. -T.S. Elliot

4297.   I can believe anything provided it is incredible. -Oscar Wilde

4298.   What is play to the cat is death to the mouse. -Danish proverb

4299.   The bank of friendship cannot exist for long without deposits.

4300.   There is no more lovely, friendly, and charming relationship communion or company than a good marriage. -David Ben-Gurion

4301.   To be truly happy is a question of how we begin and not of how we end of what we want and not of what we have. -Robert Louis Stevenson

4302.   The greatest thing in the world is for a man to know how to be himself. -Michel Eyquem de Montaigne

4303.	The act of giving is more important than the merit of the receiver. -Glenn Kittler

4304.	Motivation is what gets you started. Habit is what keeps you going. -Jim Ryun

4305.	Deep Thoughts: It's easy to sit and scoff at an old man's folly. But also check out his Adam's apple. -Jack Handey

4306.	Language is the dress of thought. -Samuel Johnson

4307.	Having children makes you no more a parent than having a piano makes you a pianist. -Michael Levine

4308.	Civilization is unbearable but it is less unbearable at the top. -Timothy Leary

4309.	Look beneath the surface; let not the several quality of a thing nor its worth escape thee. -Marcus Aurelius

4310.	There's nothing sooner dry than women's tears. -John Webster

4311.	When men are pure laws are useless when men are corrupt laws are broken. -Benjamin Disraeli

4312.	Once conform, once do what others do because they do it, and a kind of lethargy steals over all the finer senses of the soul. -Montaigne

4313.	Events in the past may be roughly divided into those which probably never happened and those which do not matter. -William Ralph Inge

4314.	The Constitution only gives people the right to pursue happiness. You have to catch it yourself. -Ben Franklin

4315.	You will never "win" an argument concerning religion.

4316.	Whatever you do, do with all your might. -Marcus Tullius Cicero

4317.	To endure is the first thing that a child ought to learn and that which he will have the most need to know. -Jean Jacques Rousseau

4318.	The man who does not work for the love of work but only for money is not likely to make money nor find much fun in life. -Charles Schwab

4319.	The individual will always be a minority. If a man is in a minority of one we lock him up. -Oliver Wendell Holmes

4320. I am watching the postman wee up against someone's tree

4321. The ways by which you may get money almost without exception lead downward - from Live Without Principle, Henry David Thoreau

4322. I am a great believer in luck. The harder I work the more of it I seem to have. -Coleman Cox

4323. Better to do something imperfectly than to do nothing flawlessly. -Dr. Robert Schuller

4324. A day without newspapers is like walking around without your pants on. -Jerry Coleman

4325. The mode in which the inevitable comes to pass is through effort. -Oliver Wendell Holmes

4326. I am beginning to learn that it is the sweet simple things of life which are the real ones after all. -Laura Ingalls Wilder

4327. There was never in the history of the world a great politician who was not hated by large numbers of inferior men. -Unknown

4328. We need peacemakers not peacekeepers. -Paul Liu

4329. Jawaharlal Nehru The policy of being too cautious is the greatest risk of all.

4330. There is nothing permanent except change. -Heraclitus

4331. We haven't got the power to destroy the planet - or to save it. But we might have the power to save ourselves. -Michael Crichton

4332. Misery no longer loves company. Nowadays it insists on it. -Russell Baker

4333. Wherever we are it is our friends that make our world. -Henry Drummond

4334. Other things may change us but we start and end with the family. -Anthony Brandt

4335. A life of leisure and a life of laziness are two different things. -Benjamin Franklin

4336. Courage is being scared to death... and saddling up anyway. -John Wayne

4337. The nearest way to glory is to strive to be what you wish to be thought to be. -Socrates

4338.　It takes seventy-two muscles to frown, but only thirteen to smile. -Unknown Author

4339.　No one can harm the man who does himself no wrong. -Saint John Chrysostom

4340.　To confine our attention to terrestrial matters would be to limit the human spirit. -Stephen William Hawking

4341.　We are always getting ready to live but never living. -Ralph Waldo Emerson

4342.　Business is a game, the greatest game in the world if you know how to play it. - Thomas J. Watson

4343.　That which you cannot give away, you don't possess; it possesses you.

4344.　Be not surprised if thou findest thyself in possession of unexpected wealth. Allah will provide an unexpected use for it. - James J. Roche

4345.　For Brutus is an honorable man. So are they all. All honorable men. -William Shakespeare

4346.　Look for a thing until you find it and you'll not lose your labor. -Chinese Proverb

4347.　Learning is ever in the freshness of its youth even for the old. -Aeschylus

4348.　People ask for criticism but they only want praise. -W. Somerset Maugham

4349.　Our opportunities to do good are our talents. -Cotton Mather

4350.　There is not great talent without great will power. -Honore de Balzac

4351.　Always the more beautiful answer who asks the more beautiful question. – e.e. cummings

4352.　Those who dream by day are cognizant of many things which escape those who dream only by night. -Edgar Allan Poe

4353.　Some natural skepticism as to the purity of all human motives came and sat upon my chest... -Roger Zelazny

4354.　Prosperity depends more on wanting what you have than having what you want. -Geoffrey F. Albert

4355. Why does night fall but never break and day break but never fall?

4356. The man who views the world at the same as he did at has wasted years of his life. -Muhammad Ali

4357. I am realistic - I expect miracles. -Wayne Dyer

4358. That which we are capable of feeling, we are capable of saying. - Cervantes

4359. For it was not into my ear you whispered, but into my heart. It was not my lips you kissed, but my soul. -Judy Garland

4360. The soul of man is immortal and imperishable. -Plato

4361. Art is long life short judgment difficult opportunity transient. - Johann von Goethe

4362. Self-discipline is that which next to virtue truly and essentially raises one man above another. -Joseph Addison

4363. No matter how slow the film, Spirit always stands still long enough for the photographer it has chosen. -Minor White

4364. A compromise is the art of dividing a cake in such a way that everyone believes he has the biggest piece. -Ludwig Erhard

4365. Forgiveness is the best remedy for any injury.

4366. There is something that is much more scarce something rarer than ability. It is the ability to recognize ability. -Robert Half

4367. The devil hath power To assume a pleasing shape. -William Shakespeare

4368. To love and win is the best thing. To love and lose, the next best. -William M. Thackeray

4369. One thought driven home is better than three left on base. - James Liter

4370. When you truly give up trying to be whole through others, you end up receiving what you always wanted from others. -Shakti Gawain

4371. Republicans have been accused of abandoning the poor. It's the other way around. They never vote for us. -J. Danforth Quayle

4372. My family pride is something inconceivable. I can't help it. I was born sneering. - W. S. Gilbert

4373.   He who is afraid to ask is ashamed of learning. -Danish proverb

4374.   A nail is driven out by another nail. Habit is overcome by habit. -Desiderius Erasmus

4375.   Virtue is its own reward. There's a pleasure in doing good which sufficiently pays itself. -Sir John Vanbrugh

4376.   Anger ventilated often hurries towards forgiveness; anger concealed often hardens into revenge. - Sir Henry Bulwer

4377.   If the #2 pencil is the most popular, why isn't it #1?

4378.   Life without a friend is death without a witness. -Danish proverb

4379.   The need to write comes from the need to make sense of one's life and discover one's usefulness. -John Cheever

4380.   No problem is insurmountable. With a little courage, teamwork and determination a person can overcome anything. -B. Dodge

4381.   If you can't bite don't show your teeth. -Yiddish Proverb

4382.   Time is the fire in which we burn. -Gene Roddenberry

4383.   I realize that patriotism is not enough. I must have no hatred or bitterness towards anyone. -Edith Cavell

4384.   It's easy to make a buck. It's a lot tougher to make a difference. -Tom Brokaw

4385.   Oh treacherous night thou lendest thy ready veil to every treason and teeming mischiefs beneath thy shade. -Aaron Hill

4386.   Ambition drove many men to become false to have one thought locked in the breast another ready on the tongue. -Sallust

4387.   A people that values its privileges above its principles soon loses both. -Dwight D. Eisenhower

4388.   Failure is nature's plan to prepare you for great responsibilities. - Napoleon Hill

4389.   We treat this world of ours as though we had a spare in the trunk.

4390.   There are no days in life so memorable as those which vibrated to some stroke of the imagination. -Lawrence George Durrell

4391.   Wealth - any income that is at least one hundred dollars more a year than the income of one's wife's sister's husband. -H. L. Mencken

4392. Brave men are all vertebrates they have their softness on the surface and their toughness in the middle. -G. K. Chesterton

4393. Do not accustom yourself to use big words for little matters. -Samuel Johnson

4394. I will love the light for it shows me the way. Yet, I will endure the darkness for it shows me the stars. -Og Mandino

4395. Half of being smart is knowing what you are dumb about. -Solomon Short

4396. I think we might be going a bridge too far. -Sir Frederick Browning

4397. Travel is only glamorous in retrospect. -Paul Theroux

4398. Giving opens the way for receiving. -Florence Shinn

4399. It is easy to have a balanced personality. Just forget your troubles as easily as you do your blessings.

4400. Can it be a mistake that "desserts" gives "stressed" spelled backwards?

4401. Ignorance is the night of the mind but a night without moon and star. -Confucius

4402. Confidence is the sexiest thing a woman can have. It's much sexier than any body part. -Aimee Mullins

4403. In business for yourself, not by yourself. -Ray Kroc

4404. Solitude is as needful to the imagination as society is wholesome for the character. -James Russell Lowell

4405. He knew the things that were and the things that would be and the things that had been before. -Homer

4406. The mind is slow to unlearn what it learnt early. -Seneca

4407. A superstition is a premature explanation that overstays its time. -George Iles

4408. Because you are someone special I send you my love today For you are very wonderful In each and every way

4409. Responsibility is what awaits outside the Eden of Creativity. -Nadine Gordimer

4410. Few men have the virtue to withstand the highest bidder. -George Washington

4411. After hearing two eyewitness accounts of the same accident, you begin to wonder about history.

4412. Character is what a person is in the dark. -Dwight Moody

4413. Character is what you are when no one is looking. -Unknown

4414. One never goes so far as when one doesn't know where one is going. -Johann Wolfgang von Goethe

4415. After all is said and done, more is said than done.

4416. It's your attitude not your aptitude that determines your altitude. -Zig Ziglar

4417. To disarm the people... was the best and most effectual way to enslave them. -George Mason

4418. Nobody has a perfect life. What you see on the screen is the best of the artist. -Rene Angelil

4419. You can never solve a problem on the level on which it was created. -Albert Einstein

4420. I think Little League is wonderful. It keeps the kids out of the house. -Lawrence Peter Berra

4421. Praise is like sunlight to the human spirit we cannot flower and grow without it. -Jesse Lair

4422. Boredom sets into boring minds.

4423. People are simply incapable of prolonged sustained goodness. -Andrew Schneider

4424. Truth is the daughter of time. -Aulus Gellius

4425. All things are cause for either laughter or weeping. -Seneca

4426. Oh come on. If you can't laugh at the walking dead who can you laugh at. -Unknown

4427. The wages of sin are unreported. -Unknown

4428. To think I'll of mankind and not to wish ill to them is perhaps the highest wisdom and virtue. -William Hazlitt

4429. When asked by an anthropologist what the Indians called America before the white man came an Indian said simply, "Ours." -Father Andrew SDC

4430. The greatest actions of love often got unnoticed.

4431.   No revenge is more honorable than the one not taken. -Danish proverb

4432.   The greatest remedy for anger is delay. -Seneca

4433.   A friend is as it were a second self. -Cicero

4434.   You have to have confidence in your ability and then be tough enough to follow through. -Rosalynn Carter

4435.   Respect a man, and he will do all the more. -John Wooden

4436.   Pleasure in the job put perfection in the work. -Aristotle

4437.   More appealing than knowledge itself is the feeling of knowledge. -Daniel J. Boorstin

4438.   He who despairs over an event is a coward but he who holds hope for the human condition is a fool. -Albert Camus

4439.   Businesses are successful because someone makes the sacrifices others are unwilling to. - Kim Ki-Jung

4440.   Making the simple complicated is commonplace; making the complicated simple awesomely simple - that's creativity. -Charles Mingu

4441.   Excellence means when a man or woman asks of himself more than others do. -Jose Ortega y Gasset

4442.   The dog was created especially for children. He is the God of frolic. -Henry Ward Beecher

4443.   Computer Museum Usenet is like Tetris for people who still know how to read.

4444.   Enthusiasm releases the drive to carry you over obstacles and adds significance to all you do. -Norman Vincent Peale

4445.   Failure is the path of least resistance. -Sir James Matthew Barrie

4446.   His ignorance covered the whole earth like a blanket and there was hardly a hole in it anywhere. -Mark Twain

4447.   When you encounter seemingly good advice that contradicts other seemingly good advice ignore them both. -Al Franken

4448.   Young people tell you what they are doing, old people what they have done and fools what they wish to do. -French

4449. Read over your compositions and wherever you meet with a passage which you think is particularly fine strike it out. -Samuel Johnson

4450. Knowledge and human power are synonymous. - Francis Bacon

4451. Best be yourself imperial plain and true. -Elizabeth Barrett Browning

4452. It's blood, sweat, sometimes tears. -Bob Hayes

4453. God gave burdens, also shoulders. -Yiddish Proverb

4454. The man who is not a socialist at twenty has no heart but if he is still a socialist at forty he has no head. -Aristide Briand

4455. Piety requires us to honor truth above our friends. -Aristotle

4456. My evil genius Procrastination has whispered me to tarry 'til a more convenient season. -Mary Todd Lincoln

4457. Men are wise in proportion not to their experience but to their capacity for experience. -James Boswell

4458. Fall not in love therefore it will stick to your face. -National Lampoon

4459. First secure an independent income then practice virtue. -Greek Proverb

4460. The accords were fig leaves of democratic procedure to hide the nakedness of Stalinist dictatorship. -George Frost Kennan

4461. It is much more secure to be feared than to be loved. -Niccolo Machiavelli

4462. The good and the wise lead quiet lives. -Euripides

4463. There is surely a piece of divinity in us something that was before the elements and owes no homage unto the sun. -Sir Thomas Browne

4464. We are an impossibility in an impossible universe. -Ray Bradbury

4465. Anyone who thinks the sky is the limit, has limited imagination. -Unknown Author

4466. Find your horse. Discover the direction the horse is going. Ride the horse in that direction. -Peter McWilliams

4467. The quality of expectations determines the quality of our action. -Andre Godin

4468. The past always looks better than it was. It's only pleasant because it isn't here. -Finley Peter Dunne

4469. We cannot control the evil tongues of others but a good life enables us to disregard them. -Cato the Elder

4470. Don't love the things you own, lest they own you.

4471. He is happiest be he king or peasant who finds peace in his home. -Johann Wolfgang von Goethe

4472. If you owe the bank $100 that's your problem. If you owe the bank $100 million, that's the bank's problem. - J. Paul Getty

4473. An eye for an eye leaves the whole world blind. -Mohandas Gandhi

4474. Life was made to be enjoyed as well as endured. -Unknown

4475. The results you achieve will be in direct proportion to the effort you apply. -Denis Waitley

4476. A penny will hide the biggest star in the Universe if you hold it close enough to your eye. -Samuel Grafton

4477. If you go out looking for friends, you're going to find they are very scarce. If you go out to be a friend, you'll find them everywhere. -Paul Newman

4478. Acting is a question of absorbing other people's personalities and adding some of your own experience.-Unknown

4479. It is well to give when asked but it is better to give unasked through understanding. -Kahlil Gibran

4480. That Jim Brown. He says he isn't Superman. What he really means is that Superman isn't Jimmy Brown. -Kahlil Gibran

4481. There's a period of life when we swallow a knowledge of ourselves and it becomes either good or sour inside. -Pearl Bailey

4482. Don't offer me advice. Give me money. -Danish proverb

4483. A husband is what is left of the lover after the nerve has been extracted. -Helen Rowland

4484. To do just the opposite is also a form of imitation. -Georg Christoph Lichtenberg

4485. Your own mind is a sacred enclosure into which nothing harmful can enter except by your permission. -Ralph Waldo Emerson

4486. The immature mind hops from one thing to another; the mature mind seeks to follow through. -Harry A. Overstreet

4487. My best friend is the one who brings out the best in me. -Henry Ford

4488. Without change, something sleeps inside us and seldom awakens. The sleeper must awaken. -Frank Herbert

4489. Everything you add to the truth subtracts from the truth. -Aleksandr Solzhenitsyn

4490. Americans adore me and will go on adoring me until I say something nice about them. -George Bernard Shaw

4491. The contented person is never poor. The discontented is never rich.

4492. A diamond is a chunk of coal that made good under pressure. -Unknown Author

4493. In science, as in love, too much concentration on technique can often lead to impotence. -P.L. Berger

4494. Experience is an expensive school, but a fool will learn from no other. -Japanese Proverb

4495. Transformation literally means going beyond your form. -Wayne Dyer

4496. Energy and persistence conquer all thing. -Benjamin Franklin

4497. Happiness is the real sense of fulfillment that comes from hard work. -Joseph Barbara

4498. Money will come to you when you are doing the right thing. -Michael Phillips

4499. Oppression can only survive through silence. -Carmen de Monteflores

4500. When you play, play hard. When you work, don't play at all. -Theodore Roosevelt

4501. A good memory is one trained to forget the trivial. -Clifton Fadiman

4502. If you would be pungent, be brief for it is with words as with sunbeams - the more they are condensed, the deeper they burn. - Robert Southey

4503. Something deeply hidden had to be behind things. -Albert Einstein

4504. A man too busy to take care of his health is like a mechanic too busy to take care of his tools. -Danish proverb

4505. A happy person is not a person in a certain set of circumstances, but rather a person with a certain set of attitudes. -Hugh Downs

4506. Assert your right to make a few mistakes. If people can't accept your imperfections that's their fault. -Dr. David M. Burns

4507. Laws are like sausages. It's better not to see them being made. - Otto von Bismarck

4508. Our favorite holding period is forever. - Warren Buffett

4509. Nothing emboldens sin so much as mercy. -William Shakespeare

4510. Exhaustion and exasperation are frequently the handmaidens of legislative decision. -Barber B. Conable Jr.

4511. Play is the beginning of knowledge. -George Dorsey

4512. The true teacher defends his pupils against his own personal influence. -Amos Bronson Alcott

4513. One should count each day a separate life. -Seneca

4514. One dies only once and then for such a long time. -Moliere

4515. Many would be cowards if they had courage enough. -Thomas Fuller

4516. The time you enjoy wasting is not wasted time. -Bertrand Russell

4517. Now cracks a noble heart. Good night sweet prince And flights of angels sing thee to thy rest. -William Shakespeare

4518. Whoever would overthrow the liberty of a nation must begin by subduing the freeness of speech. -Benjamin Franklin

4519. Although the world is full of suffering, it is full also of the overcoming of it. -Helen Keller

4520. Never assume for it makes an ASS out of U and ME. -Anon.

4521.   Time: the devourer of all things. -Ovid

4522.   Success is not measured by what one brings, but rather by what one leaves. -Unknown Author

4523.   You are getting old when you don't care where your spouse goes, just as long as you don't have to go along.

4524.   There is no agony like bearing an untold story inside of you. -Maya Angelou

4525.   A face without freckles is like a sky without stars.

4526.   Quieting the chattering mind promotes directed action.

4527.   A man can only do what he can do. But if he does that each day he can sleep at night and do it again the next day. -Albert Schweitzer

4528.   You can't try to do things you simply must do them. -Ray Douglas Bradbury

4529.   Conscience is the inner voice that warns us somebody may be looking. -H.L. Mencken

4530.   My spelling is Wobbly. It's good spelling but it Wobbles and the letters get in the wrong places. -Alan Alexander Milne

4531.   Thoughts are but dreams till their effects be tried. -William Shakespeare

4532.   The sun sets without thy assistance. -The Talmud

4533.   Post-Watergate morality, by which anything left private is taken as presumptive evidence of wrongdoing. -Charles Krauthammer

4534.   If all else fails, immortality can always be assured by spectacular error. -John Kenneth Galbraith

4535.   Realize that if you have time to whine and complain about something then you have the time to do something about it. -Anthony D'Angelo

4536.   The ascent from earth to heaven is not easy. -Seneca

4537.   Artichokes are like humans: you have to go through so much to get to the heart. -Kathy Good

4538.   Cheerfulness keeps up a kind of daylight in the mind and fills it with a steady and perpetual serenity. -Joseph Addison

4539.   It's not the load that breaks you down, it's the way you carry it. -Lena Horne

4540.   When your work speaks for itself, don't interrupt. -Henry J. Kaiser

4541.   Better a mouse in the pot than no meat at all. -Romanian Proverb

4542.   A goal is not always meant to be reached; it often serves simply as something to aim at. -Bruce Lee

4543.   What's another word for Thesaurus? -Steven Wright

4544.   Integrity has no need of rules. -Albert Camus

4545.   The reason why people do not obtain success is because it is disguised as hard work.

4546.   Give a man a fish and he will eat for a day. Teach a man to fish and he will eat for the rest of his life. -Chinese Proverb

4547.   Hope is the parent of faith. -Cyrus A. Bartol

4548.   When the time is right, you just got to do it. -Jack Simplot

4549.   Not he who has much is rich, but he who gives much. -Erich Fromm

4550.   Always seek out the seed of triumph in every adversity. -Og Mandino

4551.   Friendships are fragile things and require as much handling as any other fragile and precious thing. -Randolph Silliman Bourne

4552.   Think like a man of action, and act like a man of thought. -Henri Bergson

4553.   You add insult to injury. -Anonymous

4554.   Was she so loved because her eyes were so beautiful or were her eyes so beautiful because she was so loved? -Anzia Yenerska

4555.   One must ask children and birds how cherries and strawberries taste. -Johann von Goethe

4556.   If there is no wind, row. -Latin Proverb

4557.   Hope, in reality, is the worst of all evils because it prolongs the torments of man. -Susanna Moodie

4558.   If the phone doesn't ring, it's me. -Jimmy Buffett

4559.   As was his language so was his life. -Seneca

4560.   What is history but a fable agreed upon. -Napoleon Bonaparte

4561.   The greater part of happiness or misery depends on our dispositions not our circumstances. -Martha Washington

4562.   Chilo advised, "not to speak evil of the dead." -Laertius Diogenes

4563.   You will come across hope and despair in almost every situation. Only one of them wins each time.

4564.   There will come a time when you believe everything is finished. That will be the beginning. -Louis L'Amour

4565.   Nobody ever died of laughter. -Max Beerbohm

4566.   To be amused by what you read - that is the great spring of happy quotations. -C. E. Montague

4567.   Dear brightest star o'er Bethlehem, O let your precious light shine in with hope and peace toward men in every home tonight. -Swedish Carol

4568.   Art is an experience, not the formulation of a problem. -Lindsay Anderson

4569.   People who have no weaknesses are terrible there is no way of taking advantage of them. -Anatole France

4570.   It is light grief that can take counsel. -Anonymous

4571.   The inspiration of the almighty gives man understanding. -Bible

4572.   Depend on the rabbit's foot if you will, but remember it didn't work for the rabbit. -R. E. Shay

4573.   I don't think the intelligence reports are all that hot. Some days I get more out of the New York Times. -John Fitzgerald Kennedy

4574.   I've been trying for some time to develop a lifestyle that doesn't require my presence. -Gary Trudeau

4575.   Love is an attempt to change a piece of a dream world into reality. -Theodor Reik

4576.   Humor is always based on a modicum of truth. Have you ever heard a joke about a father-in-law? -Dick Clark

4577.   He who throws away a friend is as bad as he who throws away his life. -Sophocles

4578.   Any lady who is first lady likes being first lady. I don't care what they say they like it. -Richard Milhous Nixon

4579. To be without some of the things you want is an indispensable part of happiness. -Bertrand Russell

4580. Commitment in the face of conflict produces character. -Unknown

4581. Woe be to him that reads but one book. -George Herbert

4582. If you want to win anything-a race, yourself, your life-you have to go a little berserk. -George Sheehan

4583. What do we live for, if it is not to make life less difficult for each other? -George Eliot

4584. The longer one lives the more one realizes that nothing is a dish for every day. -Norman Douglas

4585. You cannot shake hands with a clenched fist. -Indira Gandhi

4586. Blaze with the fire that is never extinguished. -Luisa Sigea

4587. Work while you have the light. You are responsible for the talent that has been entrusted to you. -Henri-Frederic Amiel

4588. You gotta have a dream. If you don't have a dream, how you gonna make a dream come true? (South Pacific) -Oscar Hammerstein II

4589. Patience, persistence, and perspiration, make an unbeatable combination for success. -Napoleon Hill

4590. We win half the battle when we make up our minds to take the world as we find it including the thorns. -Orison Swett Marden

4591. Life is not fair, but life is not fair for everyone. That makes life fair.

4592. The longer the title, the less important the job. -George Stanley McGovern

4593. Friendship is the inexpressible comfort of feeling safe with a person having neither to weigh thoughts nor measure words. -George Eliot

4594. The soul that is within me no man can degrade. - Frederick Douglas

4595. We adore chaos because we love to produce order. -M. C. Escher

4596. Truth is more of a stranger than fiction. -Mark Twain

4597. I send no agent or medium offer no representative of value. - Walt Whitman

4598. A word of encouragement during a failure is worth more than an hour of praise after success.

4599. Those whom God wishes to destroy he first makes mad. - Euripides

4600. Where life is more terrible than death, it is then the truest valor to dare to live. -Sir Thomas Browne

4601. The important work of moving the world forward does not wait to be done by perfect men. -George Eliot

4602. I'm good enough. I'm smart enough, and doggone it, people like me. -Al Franken

4603. Failing to plan is planning to fail. -Allen Lakein

4604. I can't believe that God put us on this earth to be ordinary. - Lou Holtz

4605. The purpose of life is a life of purpose. -Robert Byrne

4606. My success has allowed me to strike out with a higher class of women. -Woody Allen

4607. Adversity has the effect of eliciting talents, which, in prosperous circumstances, would have lain dormant. -Horace

4608. Believe in life! Always human beings will progress to greater, broader, and fuller life.—W. E. B. Du Bois

4609. All doubt despair and fear become insignificant once the intention of life becomes love rather than dependence on love. -Sri da Avabhas

4610. Beware of over-great pleasure in being popular or even beloved. - Margaret Fuller

4611. Compassion will cure more sins than condemnation. -Henry Ward Beecher

4612. Skeptical scrutiny is the means in both science and religion by which deep insights can be winnowed from deep nonsense. -Carl Sagan

4613. Always get married early in the morning. That way if it doesn't work out you haven't wasted a whole day. -Mickey Rooney

4614.   I shot an arrow into the air and it stuck. -

4615.   Striving for excellence motivates you; striving for perfection is demoralizing. -Harriet Braiker

4616.   Not everything that is faced can be changed, but nothing can be changed until it is faced. -James Baldwin

4617.   Govern a great nation as you would cook a small fish. Do not overdo it. -

4618.   Let him who would move the world, first move himself. - Socrates

4619.   Politeness n. The most acceptable hypocrisy. -Ambrose Bierce

4620.   You can pretend to be serious you can't pretend to be witty. - Sacha Guitry

4621.   Adversity is the trial of principle. Without it, a man hardly knows whether he is honest or not. -Henry Fielding

4622.   None of us are responsible for all the things that happen to us but we are responsible for the way we act when they do happen. - Unknown

4623.   Show me a genuine case of platonic friendship and I shall show you two old or homely faces. -Austin O'Malley

4624.   If ye break faith with us who die, we shall not sleep though poppies grow in Flanders fields. -

4625.   My heart has joined the thousand, for my friend stopped running today. -Richard Adams

4626.   If you can find something everyone agrees on it's wrong. -Mo Udall

4627.   To cease smoking is the easiest thing I ever did. I ought to know I've done it a thousand times. -Mark Twain

4628.   Being angered is the greatest defeat to a human being. - Kazi Shams

4629.   The trouble is not that players have sex the night before a game. It's that they stay out all night looking for it. -Casey Stengel

4630.   If you plan on being anything less than you are capable of being, you will probably be unhappy all the days of your life. -Abraham Maslow

4631. Puritanism: The haunting fear that someone somewhere may be happy. -H.L. Mencken

4632. When I die, I hope to go to Heaven, whatever the Hell that is. -Ayn Rand

4633. If you wish good advice, consult an old man. -Romanian Proverb

4634. Life is a tale told by an idiot - full of sound and fury signifying nothing. -William Shakespeare

4635. Propaganda is the art of persuading others of what you don't believe yourself. -Ausonius

4636. Not only is there no God, but try getting a plumber on weekends. -Woody Allen

4637. What is defeat? Nothing but education. Nothing but the first step to something better. -Wendell Phillips

4638. Be more prompt to go to a friend in adversity than in prosperity. -Chilo

4639. Any sufficiently advanced technology is indistinguishable from magic. -Arthur C. Clarke

4640. A mind troubled by doubt cannot focus on the course to victory. -Arthur Golden

4641. Love rules without rules. -Italian Proverb

4642. A child's life is like a piece of paper on which every person leaves a mark. -Chinese Proverb

4643. Kent Abbott is in the on-deck circuit. -Jerry Coleman

4644. Music is essentially useless as life is. -George Santayana

4645. Swing away Merrill. Merrill... swing away. -Signs Graham

4646. Most men pursue pleasure with such breathless haste that they hurry past it. -Kierkegaard

4647. His conduct still right with his argument wrong. - Oliver Goldsmith

4648. He who speaks the truth must have one foot in the stirrup. -American Proverb

4649. Lady Conductor: She raised her baton.... and Beethoven answered. -John C Lehman, Jr.

4650.   If you want to make beautiful music you must play the black and the white notes together. -Richard Milhous Nixon

4651.   No problem can stand the assault of sustained thinking. -Francois Marie Arouet de Voltaire

4652.   He who cannot obey himself will be commanded. That is the nature of living creatures. -Friedrich Wilhelm Nietzsche

4653.   Think like a man of action, act like a man of thought.

4654.   If you can't be content with what you have received, be thankful for what you have escaped.

4655.   Patience accomplishes its object, while hurry speeds to its ruin. -Saadi, Persian poet

4656.   You may be deceived if you trust too much but you will live in torment if you don't trust enough. -Frank H. Crane

4657.   The man who didn't want his wife to work has been succeeded by the man who asks about her chances of getting a raise. -Earl Wilson

4658.   Courage is more than standing for a firm conviction. It includes the risk of questioning that conviction. -Julian Weber Gordon

4659.   You will never do anything in this world without courage. It is the greatest quality of the mind next to honor. -James Allen

4660.   Example is not the main thing in influencing others. It is the only thing. -Albert Schweitzer

4661.   I am here and you will know that I am the best and will hear me. -Leontyne Price

4662.   What comes from the heart, goes to the heart. -Samuel Taylor Coleridge

4663.   You sort of start thinking anything's possible if you've got enough nerve. -J. K. Rowling

4664.   Work joyfully and peacefully, knowing that right thoughts and right efforts will inevitably bring about right results. -James Allen

4665.   Whatever is to make us better and happy God has placed either openly before us or close to us. -Seneca

4666.   There's always somebody who is paid too much and taxed too little - and it's always somebody else. -Cullen Hightower

4667.   No man is a failure who has friends. -Clarence

4668.   Most of our so-called reasoning consists in finding arguments for going on believing as we already do. -James Harvey Robinson

4669.   Programming graphics in X is like finding the square root of PI using Roman numerals. -Henry Spencer

4670.   Opposition brings concord. Out of discord comes the fairest harmony. -Heraclitus

4671.   Follow your inclinations with due regard to the policeman round the corner. -W. Somerset Maugham

4672.   Be good and you will be lonesome. -Mark Twain

4673.   Work is man's most natural form of relaxation. -Dagobert D. Runes

4674.   Anything that is of value in life only multiplies when it is given. -Deepak Chopra

4675.   I detest life-insurance agents; they always argue that I shall someday die, which is not so. -Stephen Leacock

4676.   Trouble in marriage often starts when a man gets so busy earning his salt that he forgets his sugar.

4677.   A man's as old as he's feeling; a woman as old as she looks. -Mortimer Collins

4678.   The more original a discovery, the more obvious it seems afterwards. -Arthur Koestler

4679.   The peace of heaven is theirs that lift their swords, in such a just and charitable war. -William Shakespeare

4680.   O, it is excellent to have a giant's strength, but it is tyrannous to use it like a giant. -William Shakespeare

4681.   Education is what survives when what has been learnt has been forgotten. -B. F. Skinner

4682.   I try to make everyone's day just a little more surreal. -Bill Watterson

4683.   There is a remedy for all things but death, which will be sure to lay us out flat some time or other. -Miguel de Cervantes

4684.   Remember, you only have to succeed the last time. -Brian Tracy

4685.   I count him braver who conquers his desires than him who conquers his enemies for the hardest victory is the victory over self. -Aristotle

4686.   It is better to know some of the questions than all of the answers. -James Thurber

4687.   The smallest good deed is better than the grandest good intention. -Unknown

4688.   The biggest fool may come out with a bit of sense when you least expect it. -Eden Phillpotts

4689.   We steal if we touch tomorrow. It is God's. -Henry Ward Beecher

4690.   The art of advice is to make the recipient believe he thought the thought of it himself. -Frank Tyger

4691.   Let us be resolute in prosecuting our ends and mild in our methods of so doing. -Aquaviva

4692.   Every man has enough power left to carry out that of which he is convinced. -Johann Wolfgang Von Goethe

4693.   The more you know the less you understand. -Tao Le Ching

4694.   Did Adam and Eve have belly buttons?

4695.   Success is never certain. Failure is never final. -Robert Schuller

4696.   The human mind is our fundamental resource. -John Fitzgerald Kennedy

4697.   The common denominator for success is work. -John D. Rockefeller

4698.   I hear and I forget, I see and I remember, I do and I understand. -Chinese proverb

4699.   The poet judges not as a judge judges but as the sun falling around a helpless thing. -Walt Whitman

4700.   The young have aspirations that never come to pass the old have reminiscences of what never happened. -Saki

4701.   If you want to make peace you don't talk to your friends. You talk to your enemies. -Moshe Dayan

4702.   Promise yourself to be so strong that nothing can disturb your peace of mind. -Christian Larson

4703.   Three things it is best to avoid: a strange dog, a flood, and a man who thinks he is wise. -Welsh Proverb

4704.   Old age means realizing you will never own all the dogs you wanted to. -Joe Gores

4705.   Regret for wasted time is more wasted time. -Mason Cooley

4706.   If you see ten troubles coming down the road, you can be sure that nine will run into the ditch before they reach you. -Calvin Coolidge

4707.   The young man who has not wept is a savage and the old man who will not laugh is a fool. -George Santayana

4708.   Well done is better than well said. -Benjamin Franklin

4709.   Look up and not down. Look forward and not back. Look out and not in, and lend a hand. -Edward Everett Hale

4710.   The extreme limit of wisdom - that is what the public calls madness. -Jean Cocteau

4711.   The more laws the less justice. -Marcus Tullius Cicero

4712.   The high minded man must care more for the truth than for what people think. -Aristotle

4713.   The only thing dumber than a pitcher is two pitchers. -Ted Williams

4714.   Tell a man he is brave, and you help him to become so. -Thomas Carlyle

4715.   The whole world steps aside for the man who knows where he is going. -Unknown Author

4716.   Dust is a protective coating for fine furniture. -Mario Burata

4717.   My heart is wax molded as she pleases, but enduring as marble to retain. -Miguel de Cervantes

4718.   I've always been a sucker for attention. -Cuba Gooding Jr.

4719.   Moody Character is what you are in the dark. -Dwight Lyman

4720.   One of the hardest things in life is having words in your heart that you can't utter. -James Earl Jones

4721.   Silence is deep as Eternity speech is shallow as Time. -Thomas Carlyle

4722. The world began without man and it will complete itself without him. -Claude Levi-Strauss

4723. A tough lesson in life that one has to learn is that not everybody wishes you well. -Dan Rather

4724. The man who comes with a tale about others has himself an ax to grind. -Chinese Proverb

4725. People are coughing on the train, shall I put them down

4726. Hope and fear are inseparable. There is no hope without fear nor any fear without hope. -La Rochefoucauld

4727. You can judge your age by the amount of pain you feel when you come in contact with a new idea. -John Nuveen

4728. There is no witness so dreadful no accuser so terrible as the conscience that dwells in the heart of every man. -Polybius

4729. It is the wretchedness of being rich that you have to live with rich people. -Logan Pearsall Smith

4730. An expert is a man who has made all the mistakes which can be made in a narrow field. -Niels Henrik David Bohr

4731. My dog is worried about the economy because Alpo is up to $.99 a can. That's almost $7 in dog money. -Joe Weinstein

4732. Real generosity is doing something nice for someone who will never find it out. -Frank A. Clark

4733. The trouble with born-again Christians is that they are an even bigger pain the second time around. -Herb Caen

4734. The trouble with doing something right the first time is that nobody appreciates how difficult it was.

4735. The excellence of a gift lies in its appropriateness rather than in its value. -Charles Dudley Warner

4736. Knowledge rests not upon truth alone but upon error also. -Carl Gustav Jung

4737. Light is the task where many share the toil. -Homer

4738. You must remain focused on your journey to greatness. -Les Brown

4739. Anger and jealousy can no more bear to lose sight of their objects than love. - George Eliot

4740. Fear is never a reason for quitting; it is only an excuse. -Norman Vincent Peale

4741. Much speech is one thing well-timed speech is another. - Sophocles

4742. The greatest mistake you can make in life is to be continually fearing you will make one. -Elbert Hubbard

4743. A sobering thought what if at this very moment I am. -Jane Wagner

4744. It takes struggle, a goal and enthusiasm to make a champion. - Norman Vincent Peale

4745. The true meaning of life is to plant trees, under whose shade you do not expect to sit. -Nelson Henderson

4746. Bad or missing mouse driver. Spank the cat [Y/N]?

4747. There's no secret about success. Did you ever know a successful man who didn't tell you about it? -Kim Hubbard

4748. Never help a child with a task at which he feels he can succeed. -Maria Montessori

4749. If there is no enemy within, the enemy outside can do us no harm. -African proverb

4750. Always the more beautiful answer who asks the more beautiful question. —e.e. cummings

4751. This is an age in which one cannot find common sense without a search warrant. -George Will

4752. Self-denial is painful for a moment, but very agreeable in the end. - Jane Taylor

4753. When the mouth stumbles, it is worse than the foot. -West African Proverb

4754. Caring is a powerful business advantage. - Scott Johnson

4755. Friends are those rare people who ask how you are and then wait for the answer. -Unknown

4756. Don't expect mangoes when you plant papayas. - Mimfa A. Gibson

4757. I am extraordinarily patient, provided I get my own way in the end. -Margaret Thatcher

4758. What an artist the world is losing in me. -Nero Claudius Caesar

4759. Knowledge rests not upon truth alone, but upon error also. - Carl Jung

4760. You can't love anyone until you understand that you can't love everyone. -Real Live Preacher

4761. Never go to bed angry. Stay up and fight. - J. W. Eagan

4762. One of the greatest delusions in the world is the hope that the evils in this world are to be cured by legislation. -Thomas B. Reed

4763. Do not hire a man who does your work for money, but him who does it for love of it. -Henry David Thoreau

4764. In politics I am growing indifferent - I would like it if I could now return to my planting and books at home. -Voltaire

4765. Is it true that cannibals don't eat clowns because they taste funny?

4766. I have discovered that all human evil comes from this man's being unable to sit still in a room. -Blaise Pascal

4767. It is not raining. The sky leaks.

4768. Whoever refuses to remember the inhumanity is prone to new risks of infection. -Richard von Weizscker

4769. A loud voice cannot compete with a clear voice even if it's a whisper. -Barry Neil Kaufman

4770. I'd rather do something and fail than do nothing and succeed!

4771. Imagination is more important than knowledge. Knowledge is limited. Imagination encircles the world.

4772. Helen Keller There is plenty of courage among us for the abstract but not for the concrete. -Albert Einstein

4773. Think lovingly, speak lovingly, act lovingly, and every need shall be supplied. -James Allen

4774. The secret of being boring is to tell everything. -Francois Marie Arouet Voltaire

4775. Where there is great love, there are always wishes. - Willa Cather

4776. One of the penalties for refusing to participate in politics is that you end up being governed by your inferiors. -Plato

4777. This thing that we call failure is not the falling down but the staying down. -Mary Pickford

4778. You should not live one way in private, another in public. - Publilius Syrus

4779. All the sounds of the earth are like music. -Oscar Hammerstein

4780. Without words, without writing, and without books, there would be no history there could be no concept of humanity. - Hermann Hesse

4781. My doctor told me to stop having intimate dinners for four. Unless there are three other people. -Orson Welles

4782. All diplomacy is a continuation of war by other means. -Enlai Zhou

4783. It is not death that a man should fear, but he should fear never beginning to live. -Marcus Aurelius

4784. Learning is not attained by chance. It must be sought for with ardor and attended to with diligence. - Abigail Adams

4785. I cannot and will not cut my conscience to fit this year's fashions. -Lillian Hellman

4786. All prosperity begins in the mind and is dependent only on the full use of our creative imagination. -Ruth Ross

4787. Young leading cadres have risen up by helicopter. They should really rise step by step. -Deng Xiaoping

4788. One of the indictments of civilizations is that happiness and intelligence are so rarely found in the same person. -William Feather

4789. Information's pretty thin stuff unless mixed with experience. - Clarence Day

4790. Life we learn too late is in the living the tissue of every day and hour. -Stephen Butler Leacock

4791. Spoon feeding in the long run teaches us nothing but the shape of the spoon. -E. M. Forster

4792. Small to greater matters must give way. -William Shakespeare

4793. Take time to deliberate but when the time for action has arrived stop thinking and go in. -Napoleon Bonaparte

4794. The leader has to be practical and a realist yet must talk the language of the visionary and the idealist. -Eric Hoffer

4795. Nancy Reagan fell down and broke her hair. -Johnny Carson

4796. Lauder Keep right on to the end of the road. -Sir Harry MacLennan

4797. A prudent mind can see room for misgiving lest he who prospers would one day suffer reverse. -Sophocles

4798. It's never crowded along the extra mile. -Dr. Wayne Dyer

4799. The strongest man in the world is the man who stands alone. -Thomas Huxley

4800. Difference of religion breeds more quarrels than difference of politics. -Wendell Phillips

4801. Nothing is good or bad, but thinking makes it so. -William Shakespeare

4802. Right now I'm having amnesia and deja vu at the same time. I think I've forgotten this before.

4803. Science has promised us truth. It has never promised us either peace or happiness. -Gustave Le Bon

4804. Be happy. Be supportive. Be Naughty. Be just like the way you are, but don't get bored. -Unknown

4805. The shortest answer is doing. -English Proverb

4806. Strong beliefs win strong men, and then make them stronger. -Walter Bagehot

4807. A Shade upon the mind there passes as when on noon a cloud the mighty sun encloses. -Emily Elizabeth Dickinson

4808. It is strange how an earthquake 4,000 miles away seems less of a catastrophe than the first scratch on your new car.

4809. No person is important enough to make me angry. -Carlos Castaneda

4810. Incorrect assumptions lie at the root of every failure. Have the courage to test your assumption. -Brian Tracy

4811. No matter how smart you are, you spend much of your day being an idiot. -Scott Adams

4812. It is impossible to travel faster than the speed of light, and certainly not desirable, as one's hat keeps blowing off. -Woody Allen

4813. A subtle thought that is in error may yet give rise to fruitful inquiry that can establish truths of great value. -Isaac Asimov

4814. Would that the Roman people had a single neck to cut off their head. -Caligula

4815. I have no need of your God-damned sympathy. I only wish to be entertained by some of your grosser reminiscences. -Alexander Woollcott

4816. A hole is nothing at all, but you can break your neck in it.

4817. Science conducts us step by step through the whole range of creation until we arrive at length at God. -Marguerite de Valois

4818. Silence is argument carried on by other means. - Che Guevara

4819. If you have integrity, nothing else matters. -Alan Simpson

4820. A "Bay Area Bisexual" told me I didn't quite coincide with either of her desires. -Woody Allen

4821. A diplomat is a man who always remembers a woman's birthday but never remembers her age. -Robert Frost

4822. Don't stay in bed unless you can make money in bed. -George Burns

4823. When I dream, I am ageless. -Elizabeth Coatsworth

4824. Serious Sincere Systematic Service Surely Secures Supreme Success. -Unknown

4825. Do not always prove yourself to be the one in the right. The right will appear. You need only give it a chance. -C. H. Fowler

4826. In the business world everyone is paid in two coins: cash and experience. Take the experience first; the cash will come later. - Harold Green

4827. To array a man's will against his sickness is the supreme art of medicine. -Henry Ward Beecher

4828. Keep your mind on the things you want and off the things you don't want. -Hannah Whitall Smith

4829. The greatest pleasure in life is doing what people say you cannot do. -Walter Bagehot

4830.   The question is no longer between violence and non-violence it is between non-violence and non-existence. -Martin Luther King Jr.

4831.   The difference between a boss and a leader: a boss says, 'Go!' -a leader says, 'Let's go!'. - E. M. Kelly

4832.   It is in the thirties that we want friends. In the forties we know they won't save us any more than love did. -Euripides

4833.   There is a time for some things and a time for all things a time for great things and a time for small things. -Miguel de Cervantes

4834.   If you have a lemon, make lemonade. -Howard Gossage

4835.   Fortitude is the marshal of thought the armor of the will and the fort of reason. -Francis Bacon

4836.   You traverse the world in search of happiness which is within the reach of every man. A contented mind confers it on all. -Horace

4837.   Life is a bitch; get used to her or else she will make you pay for having her. -Mohammad Haroon

4838.   Save a little money each month, and at the end of the year you'll be surprised at how little you have. -Ernest Haskins

4839.   If you are not enjoying your work, you should either change your attitude, or change your job. -Leo Tolstoy

4840.   To live outside the law you must be honest. -Bob Dylan

4841.   If there is one eternal truth of politics, it is that there are always a dozen good reasons for doing nothing. -John le Carre

4842.   Let not the sands of time get in your lunch. -National Lampoon

4843.   The scientist is not a person who gives the right answers; he's one who asks the right questions. -Claude Levi-Strauss

4844.   In the factory we make cosmetics; in the store we sell hope. - Charles Revson

4845.   Not all those who know their minds know their hearts as well. - La Rochefoucauld

4846.   Words have a longer life than deeds. -Pindar

4847.   Those who want to learn listen; those who know it all interrupt.

4848.   Anger should never be an overnight guest. - Neal A. Maxwell

4849.   Traffic signals in New York are just rough guidelines. -David Letterman

4850.   Now I am become death, destroyer of worlds. -J. Robert
Oppenheimer

4851.   Morning people: "Early to bed and early to rise makes a man
healthy, wealthy, and wise."

4852.   Don't spoil what you have by desiring what you have not; but
remember that what you have now was once among the things you
only hoped for.

4853.   Imagination grows by exercise and contrary to common belief is
more powerful in the mature than in the young. -W. Somerset
Maugham

4854.   Where there is hatred, let me sow love. Where there is injury,
pardon. Where there is doubt, faith. -Saint Francis of Assisi

4855.   Make money, money by fair means if you can, if not, but any
means money. -Horace

4856.   Formal education will make you a living; self-education will
make you a fortune. -Jim Rohn

4857.   It is the chiefest point of happiness that a man is willing to be
what he is. -Desiderius Erasmus

4858.   True hope is swift and flies with swallow's wings Kings it makes
gods and meaner creatures kings. -William Shakespeare

4859.   We only part to meet again. -John Gay

4860.   It is a man's own mind not his enemy or foe that lures him to
evil ways. -Buddha

4861.   All men who have turned out worth anything have had the chief
hand in their own education. =Sir Walter Scott

4862.   Aerodynamically, the bumble bee shouldn't be able to fly, but
the bumblebee doesn't know it, so it goes on flying anyway. -Mary
Kay Ash

4863.   We learn from experience that men never learn anything from
experience. - Sioux Indian Prayer

4864.   Work as though you would live forever, and live as though you
would die today. -Og Mandino

4865.   There will come a time when you believe everything is finished.
That will be the beginning. -Louis L'Amour

4866. Correct me if I'm wrong, but hasn't the fine line between sanity and madness gotten finer? -George Price

4867. No snowflake in an avalanche ever feels responsible. -George Burns

4868. 7/5th of all people do not understand fractions.

4869. I think everyone should experience defeat at least once during their career. You learn a lot from it. -Lou Holtz

4870. You will find only what you bring in. -Yoda

4871. I can't seem to find the PM radio stations.

4872. All virtue is summed up in dealing justly. -Aristotle

4873. Look to be treated by others as you have treated others. - Publilius Syrus

4874. It is no use to blame the looking glass if your face is awry. - Nikolai Gogol

4875. Greatness lies not in being strong, but in the right use of strength. -Henry Ward Beecher

4876. Hollywood actors and actress are not better than you - They just act like they are. -Eric Pio

4877. You must first have a lot of patience to learn to have patience. - Ralph Marston

4878. A friend loveth at all times and a brother is born for adversity. - Proverbs 17:17

4879. The point is that nobody likes having salt rubbed into their wounds even if it is the salt of the earth. -Rebecca West

4880. Among my most prized possessions are the words that I have never spoken. -Orson Scott Card

4881. Nice guys finish last. -Leo Durocher

4882. I dialed one of those 900 numbers to get some financial advice. They advised me not to dial 900 numbers.

4883. Things have never been more like the way they are today in history. -Dwight D Eisenhower

4884. All is ephemeral - fame and the famous as well. -Marcus Aurelius

4885. A successful man makes more money than his woman can spend. A successful woman is one who can find such a man.

4886. The American people would not want to know of any misquotes that Dan Quayle may or may not make. -Dan Quayle

4887. All honor's wounds are self-inflicted. -Andrew Carnegie

4888. If you stand straight, do not fear a crooked shadow. -Chinese Proverb

4889. Swindon: What will history say? Burgoyne: History, sir, will tell lies as usual. -George Bernard Shaw

4890. The only real mistake is the one from which we learn nothing. -John Powell

4891. The best ideas come from jokes. Make your thinking as funny as possible. -David Ogilvie

4892. If I were two-faced, would I be wearing this one? - Antonio Machado

4893. Nothing shows a man's character more than what he laughs at. -Goethe

4894. Language is the blood of the soul into which thoughts run and out of which they grow. -Oliver Wendell Holmes

4895. Happiness isn't the easiest thing to find, but one place you're guaranteed to find it is in a friends smile. -Allison Poler

4896. Nobody can give you freedom. Nobody can give you equality or justice or anything. If you're a man you take it. -Malcolm X

4897. Reach high, for stars lie hidden in your soul. Dream deep, for every dream precedes the goal. -Ralph Vaull Starr

4898. Winning is a habit. Unfortunately, so is losing. -Vincent Lombardi

4899. A little wonton money which burned out the bottom of his purse. -Sir Thomas More

4900. Sometimes you have to play for a long time to be able to play like yourself. -Miles Davis

4901. He who wants a rose must respect the thorn. -Persian Proverb

4902. The average person thinks he isn't.

4903.	On the road from the City of Skepticism I had to pass through the Valley of Ambiguity. (Powers of Mind) -Adam Smith

4904.	Perplexity is the beginning of knowledge. -Kahlil Gibran

4905.	What do you call a man with no arms and no legs sitting on your front porch? - Matt

4906.	I'm as pure as the driven slush. -Tallulah Bankhead

4907.	Fish, to taste good, must swim three times: in water, in butter, and in wine.

4908.	We seem to believe it is possible to ward off death by following rules of good grooming. -Don Delillo

4909.	The pride of youth is in strength and beauty the pride of old age is in discretion. -Democritus

4910.	I have one yardstick by which I test every major problem-and that yardstick is, "Is it good for America?" -Dwight D. Eisenhower

4911.	People with goals succeed because they know where they are going... it's as simple as that. -Earl Nightingale

4912.	A theory can be proved by experiment, but no path leads from experiment to the birth of a theory. -Albert Einstein

4913.	There is no such thing in anyone's life as an unimportant day. -Alexander Woollcott

4914.	A positive attitude may not solve all your problems, but it will annoy enough people to make it worth the effort. -Herm Albright

4915.	Imagination is more important than knowledge. - Albert Einstein

4916.	Knowledge comes, but wisdom lingers. - Gwynn Thomas

4917.	The incompetent with nothing to do can still make a mess of it. -Laurence J. Peter

4918.	We are never nowhere. We are always now here.

4919.	Success is not forever, and failure is not fatal. -Coach Don Shula

4920.	Finley is going over to get a new piece of bat. -Jerry Coleman

4921.	Passion kept one fully in the present so that time became a series of mutually exclusive nows. -Sue Halpern

4922.   In his holy flirtation with the world, God occasionally drops a handkerchief. These handkerchiefs are called saints. -Frederick Buechner

4923.   If you are patient in one moment of anger, you will escape a hundred days of sorrow. - Chinese Proverb

4924.   Success is never final. -Sir Winston Leonard Spenser Churchill

4925.   Love one another and you will be happy. It's as simple and as difficult as that. - Harold Loukes

4926.   The innkeeper loves a drunkard, but not for a son-in-law. - Jewish Proverb

4927.   Men who are unhappy, like men who sleep badly, are always proud of the fact. -Bertrand Russell

4928.   The happiness of a man in this life does not consist in the absence but in the mastery of his passions. -Alfred Lord Tennyson

4929.   Coming together is a beginning; keeping together is progress; working together is success. -Henry Ford

4930.   That thou seest, man, become too thou must; God, if thou seest God, dust, if thou seest dust. -Brother Angelus

4931.   We must free ourselves of the hope that the sea will ever rest. We must learn to sail in high winds. - Hanmer Parsons Grant

4932.   The word of God will keep you from sin, or sin will keep you from the word of God.

4933.   Reputation is made in a moment: character is built in a lifetime.

4934.   Life is a wave which in no two consecutive moments of its existence is composed of the same particles. -John Tyndall

4935.   What you do speaks so loudly that I cannot hear what you say - Ralph Waldo Emerson

4936.   Death is as casual-and often as unexpected-as birth. It is as difficult to define grief as joy. Each is finite. Each will fade. -Jim

4937.   Red meat is NOT bad for you. Now blue-green meat - THAT'S bad for you -Tommy Smothers

4938.   Deep Thoughts: A quiz - If I am my brother's keeper, who am I? (Answer me.) -Jack Handey

4939.   Indeed, we do not really live unless we have friends surrounding us like a firm wall against the winds of the world. -Charles Hanson Towne

4940.   Prayer does not change God but changes him who prays. -Kierkegaard

4941.   In the 20th century, specialization has become the counterfeit of brilliance. -Richard Gordon

4942.   Love cures people - both the ones who give it and the ones who receive it. -Dr. Karl Menninger

4943.   A book is the only place in which you can examine a fragile thought without breaking it. -Edward P. Morgan

4944.   Every silver lining has a cloud. - Avon

4945.   It is the nature of thought to find its way into action. -Christian Nestell Bovee

4946.   Partake of some of life's sweet pleasures. And yes get comfortable with yourself. -Oprah Winfrey

4947.   It is in pardoning that we are pardoned. -Saint Francis of Assisi

4948.   I enjoy being a highly overpaid actor. -Roger Moore

4949.   Don't let people drive you crazy when it is within walking distance.

4950.   Happiness is a path, not a destination.

4951.   Experience keeps a dear school but fools will learn in no other. -Benjamin Franklin

4952.   Fear not a jest. If one throws salt at you, you will not be harmed unless you have sore places. -Latin Proverb

4953.   Tell me something my friend. You ever dance with the devil by the pale moonlight. -Batman, The Joker

4954.   The doors we open and close each day decide the lives we live. -Flora Whittemore

4955.   Every crowd has a silver lining. -Phineas Taylor Barnum

4956.   Every generation laughs at the old fashions, but follows religiously the new. -Henry David Thoreau

4957.   One kind word can warm three winter months. -Japanese Proverb

4958. Ladies of Fashion starve their happiness to feed their vanity, and their love to feed their pride. -Charles Caleb Colton

4959. The President has kept all of the promises he intended to keep. -George Stephanopoulos

4960. My favorite thing is to go where I've never been. -Diane Arbus

4961. If the wind stops, row! -Polish proverb

4962. Those who have suffered much become very bitter or very gentle. -Will Durant

4963. To talk to someone who does not listen is enough to tense the devil. -Pearl Bailey

4964. Flowers grow out of darker moments. -Corita Kent

4965. Book dedication: To myself, without whose inspired and tireless efforts this book would not have been possible. -Al Jaffee

4966. Doubts are the ants in the pants of faith. They keep it awake and moving. -Frederick Buechner

4967. He who has health has hope, and he who has hope has everything. -Arab Proverb

4968. The way of even the most justifiable revolution is prepared by personal impulses disguised into creeds. -Joseph Conrad

4969. The art of being wise is the art of knowing what to overlook. -William James

4970. The best way to make your dreams come true is to wake up. -Paul Valery

4971. What is worth having is worth waiting for.

4972. There are no great things only small things with great love. Happy are those. -Mother Theresa

4973. There is no religion higher than the truth. -H. Hahn Blavatsky

4974. Great opportunities to help others seldom come, but small ones surround us every day. - Sally Koch

4975. Faith is spiritualized imagination. -Henry Ward Beecher

4976. Be not angry that you cannot make others as you wish them to be, since you cannot make yourself as you wish to be. -Thomas a Kempis

4977. What is the hardest thing in the world? To think. -Ralph Waldo Emerson

4978. We can do no great things, only small things, with great love. -Mother Theresa

4979. Act the part and you will become the part. -William James

4980. Great works are performed, not by strength, but by perseverance. -Samuel Johnson

4981. You must learn from your past mistakes but not lean on your past successes. -Denis Watley

4982. The concept is interesting and well-formed, but in order to earn better than a C, the idea must be feasible. -Harry Morris Warner

4983. In much wisdom is much grief; and he that increaseth knowledge increaseth sorrow. - Ecclesiastes 1:18

4984. Certainly, travel is more than the seeing of sights; it is a change that goes on deep and permanent in the ideas of living. -Miriam Beard

4985. If I have seen further, it is by standing on the shoulders of giants. -Isaac Newton

4986. Remember there's no such thing as a small act of kindness. Every act creates a ripple with no logical end. -Scott Adams

4987. Don't just get something out of church, put something into it.

4988. Someone's sitting in the shade today because someone planted a tree a long time ago. -Warren Buffett

4989. I cannot afford to waste my time making money. -Jean Louis Rodolphe Agassiz

4990. To strive with difficulties and to conquer them is the highest human felicity. -Samuel Johnson

4991. If the grass on the other side of the fence appears greener...it must be all the fertilizer they are using! -Kevin Rodowicz

4992. You are wholly complete and your success in life will be in direct proportion to your ability to accept this truth about you. - Dr. Robert Anthony

4993. The only thing I can't stand is discomfort. -Gloria Steinem

4994. No mind is thoroughly well organized that is deficient in a sense of humor. -Samuel Taylor Coleridge

4995. Patience is the ability to idle your motor when you feel like stripping your gears.

4996. You can't wait for inspiration. You have to go after it with a club. -Jack London

4997. Every man over forty is a scoundrel. -George Bernard Shaw

4998. An ounce of action is worth a ton of theory. -Friedrich Engels

4999. The most dangerous strategy is to jump a chasm in two leaps. - Benjamin Disraeli

5000. Change is a part of every life. Resisting is often as futile as it is frustrating. -Unknown Author

5001. Dreaming permits each and every one of us to be quietly and safely insane every night of our lives.- William Dement

5002. Don't confuse fame with success. Madonna is one; Helen Keller is the other. -Erma Bombeck

5003. There are places and moments in which one is so completely alone that one sees the world entire.-Jules Renard

5004. Genius might be described as a supreme capacity for getting its possessors into trouble of all kinds.-Samuel Butler

5005. To control your cow, give it a bigger pasture. -Suzuki Roshi.

5006. The wonder of a single snowflake outweighs the wisdom of a million meteorologists.

5007. The last time I saw him he was walking down Lover's Lane holding his own hand. -Fred Allen

5008. A good friend is my nearest relation. -Thomas Fuller

5009. I love life because what more is there. -Anthony Hopkins

5010. Millions saw the apple fall but Newton was the one who asked why.-Bernard Mannes Baruch

5011. There are some remedies worse than the disease. -Publilius Syrus

5012. Life is not anything but an opportunity for something. -Johann von Goethe

5013. The past is certain the future obscure. -Thales

5014.	Do you realize if it weren't for Edison we'd be watching TV by candlelight?-Al Boliska

5015.	The best way not to have people in your way is to let them into your heart. -Alessandro Pronzato

5016.	In communities where men build ships for their own sons to fish or fight, from quality is never a problem.-J. Deville

5017.	I can take it... The tougher it gets the cooler I get... -Richard Milhous Nixon

5018.	It is always your next move. -Napoleon Hill

5019.	Nothing is a waste of time if you use the experience wisely. -Franois Auguste Ren Rodin

5020.	If you go as far as you can see, you will then see enough to go even farther. -John Wooden

5021.	There's nothing noble in being superior to your fellow men. True nobility is being superior to your former self. -Ernest Hemingway

5022.	I do not think much of a man who is not wiser today than he was yesterday. - Abraham Lincoln

5023.	If a little knowledge is dangerous, where is the man who has so much as to be out of danger? - Thomas Henry Huxley

5024.	A friend is one who knows who you are, understands where you have been, accepts what you become, and still gently invites you to grow.

5025.	Speak to the earth and it shall teach thee. -Biblical Proverb

5026.	Joy is not in things it is in us. -Richard Wagner

5027.	I love deadlines. I like the whooshing sound they make as they fly by. -Douglas Adams

5028.	Habit is habit and not to be flung out of the window by any man but coaxed downstairs a step at a time. -Mark Twain

5029.	My great concern is not whether you have failed, but whether you are content with your failure. -Abraham Lincoln

5030.	If you are not in fashion, you are nobody. - "Letter to his son", April 30, 1750. - Lord Chesterfield

5031.   A paperless office has about as much chance as a paperless bathroom.

5032.   The thing that is really hard and really amazing is giving up on being perfect and beginning the work of becoming yourself. -Anna Quindlen

5033.   Never look down on anybody unless you helping him up. -Jesse Jackson

5034.   Sports do not build character. They reveal it. -Heywood

5035.   Inspiration never arrived when you were searching for it. -Lisa Alther

5036.   It is not righteousness to outrage A brave man dead not even though you hate him. -Sophocles

5037.   Quality is presence of value, and not absence of mistake.

5038.   The secret source of humor itself is not joy but sorrow. There is no humor in heaven. -Mark Twain

5039.   I am not an Athenian or a Greek but a citizen of the world. -Socrates

5040.   I know what I can know, and am not troubled about what I cannot know. -Johann Fichte

5041.   A careless word may kindle strife.

5042.   Life consists not in holding good cards but in playing those you hold well. -Josh Billings

5043.   Age does not make us childish as some say it only finds us true children still. -Johann von Goethe

5044.   You have to know how to accept rejection and reject acceptance. -Ray Bradbury

5045.   Information can be treated like any other quantity and be subjected to the manipulation of a machine. -Stan Aogartem

5046.   The scars of others should teach us caution. -Saint Jerome

5047.   The best of men is he who blushes when you praise him and remains silent when you defame him. -Kahlil Gibran

5048.   It is the mark of an educated mind to be able to entertain a thought without accepting it. -Aristotle

5049.   Every invalid is a doctor. -Irish Proverb

5050. Jack: You seem somewhat familiar. Have I threatened you before? -Pirates of the Caribbean: The Curse of the Black Pearl

5051. The hare-brained chatter of irresponsible frivolity. -Benjamin Disraeli

5052. Help yourself, and Heaven will help you. -Jean De La Fontaine

5053. The words that enlighten the soul are more precious than jewels. -Hazrat Inayat Khan

5054. I take my children everywhere but they always find their way back home. -Robert Orben

5055. We are in danger of forgetting that we cannot do what God does, and that God will not do what we can do. -Oswald Chambers

5056. Let him that would move the world first move himself. -Socrates

5057. Love can't be proven until you both die loving each other. -Airon T. Reyes

5058. History is a better guide than good intentions. -Jeane J. Kirkpatrick

5059. Operationally, God is beginning to resemble not a ruler but the last fading smile of a cosmic Cheshire cat. -Sir Julian Huxley

5060. To change your life: start immediately; do it flamboyantly; no exceptions. -William James

5061. A child of five would understand this. Send someone to fetch a child of five. -Groucho Marx

5062. A closed mind is a good thing to lose.

5063. Having the right to do it, doesn't mean it is right to do it.

5064. What if everything is an illusion and nothing exists In that case I definitely overpaid for my carpet. -Woody Allen

5065. You've achieved success in your field when you don't know whether what you're doing is work or play. -Warren Beatty

5066. There are few sorrows, however poignant, in which a good income is of no avail. -Logan Pearsall Smith

5067. Kind words can be short and easy to speak, but their echoes are truly endless. -Mother Teresa

5068. The only disability in life is a bad attitude. -Scott Hamilton

5069. Take a chance! All life is a chance. The man who goes the furthest is generally the one who is willing to do and dare. -Dale Carnegie

5070. Everything is in a state of flux, including the status quo. -Robert Byrne

5071. Trouble is only opportunity in work clothes. -Henry J. Kaiser

5072. There are some things which men confess with ease and others with difficulty. -Epictetus

5073. Always forgive your enemies nothing annoys them so much. -Oscar Wilde

5074. You've got to be original because if you're like someone else, what do they need you for? -Bernadette Peters

5075. I hate it in friends when they come too late to help. -Euripides

5076. A sect or party is an elegant incognito devised to save a man from the vexation of thinking. -Ralph Waldo Emerson

5077. One of the symptoms of an approaching nervous breakdown is the belief that one's work is terribly important.

5078. You can't put the toothpaste back in the tube. -H.R. Haldeman

5079. We are all in the gutter but some of us are looking at the stars. -Oscar Wilde

5080. There never was a great soul that did not have some divine inspiration. -Marcus Tullius Cicero

5081. Lord save us all from old age and broken health and a hope tree that has lost the faculty of putting out blossoms. -Mark Twain

5082. The real problem is what to do with the problem-solvers after the problems are solved. -Gay Talese

5083. So much of what we call management consists in making it difficult for people to work. -Louis

5084. What is in the end to be thrown down, Begins by being first set on high. -Tao Saying

5085. Who depends on another man's table often dines late. -Italian Proverb

5086. Generally, we study too much and think too little. -Henry Latham Doherty

5087. I'm against a homogenized society because I want the cream to rise. -Robert Frost

5088. Never keep up with Joneses. Drag them down to your level. It's cheaper. -Quentin Crisp

5089. I had a terrible education. I attended a school for emotionally disturbed teachers. -Woody Allen

5090. Our live experiences fixed in aphorisms stiffen into cold epigrams. Our hearts blood as we write it turns to mere dull ink. -F. H. Bradley

5091. We come to love not by finding a perfect person but by learning to see an imperfect person perfectly.

5092. Absurdity. A statement or belief manifestly inconsistent with one's own opinion. -Ambrose Gwinett Bierce

5093. The surprises of thought are like those of love: they wear out. But here too you can carry on for a long time doing your conjugal duty.

5094. Wisdom is knowledge which has become a part of one's being. -Orison Swett Marden

5095. Small opportunities are often the beginning of great enterprises. -Demosthenes

5096. If you have never been hated by your child, you have never been a parent. -Bette Davis

5097. What a child doesn't receive, he can seldom later give. -P. D. James

5098. Has not peace honors and glories of her own unattended by the dangers of war? -Hermocrates of Syracuse

5099. To love what you do and feel that it matters - how could anything be more fun? -Katharine Graham

5100. A thick head can do as much damage as a hard heart. -H. W. Dodds

5101. I have often regretted my speech never my silence. -Publilius Syrus

5102. You are getting old when you get the same sensation from a rocking chair that you once got from a roller coaster.

5103. The power of man's virtue should not be measured by his special efforts, but by his ordinary doings. -Blaise Pascal

5104. Barring that natural expression of villainy which we all have, the man looked honest enough. -Mark Twain

5105. When love and skill work together, expect a masterpiece. -John Ruskin

5106. The best vision is insight. -Malcolm S. Forbes

5107. The only way of knowing a person is to love them without hope. -Walter Benjamin

5108. No form of Nature is inferior to Art for the arts merely imitate natural forms. -Marcus Aurelius

5109. I'm not worried about the bullet with my name on it... just the thousands out there marked Occupant. -Unknown

5110. We are not creatures of circumstance; we are creators of circumstance. -Benjamin Disraeli

5111. A woman seldom asks advice before she has bought her wedding clothes. -Joseph Addison

5112. Confidence is a very fragile thing. -Joe Montana

5113. The greatest advantage in gambling lies in not playing at all. -Girolamo Cardano

5114. You don't develop courage by being happy in your relationships every day. You develop it by surviving difficult times and challenging adversity

5115. Hard work doesn't guarantee success but improves its chances. -B. J. Gupta

5116. The strength of a nation derives from the integrity of the home. -Confucius

5117. Humanity is acquiring all the right technology for all the wrong reasons. -Richard Buckminster Fuller

5118. What pity is it that we can die but once to serve our country. -Joseph Addison

5119. Each man is led by his own liking. -Virgil

5120. Honesty is a good thing but it is not profitable to its possessor unless it is kept under control. -Don Marquis

5121.	A favorite has no friend! - Thomas Gray

5122.	The secret of getting ahead is getting started. -Sally Berger

5123.	High living and high thinking are poles apart. -B. J. Gupta

5124.	How can the cemetery raise its burial costs and blame it on the cost of living?

5125.	Lawyers spend a great deal of their time shoveling smoke. - Oliver Wendell Holmes

5126.	The only cure for contempt is countercontempt. -Henry Louis Mencken

5127.	A year spent in artificial intelligence is enough to make one believe in God.

5128.	If you make a living if you earn your own money you're free - however free one can be on this planet. -Theodore White

5129.	By the time you learn the rules of life, you're too old to play the game.

5130.	Comedy is the last refuge of the nonconformist mind. -Edward Albee

5131.	The artist is nothing without the gift, but the gift is nothing without work. -Emile Zola

5132.	Smile - it is the key that fits the lock of everybody's heart. - Anthony D'Angelo

5133.	To believe in one's dreams is to spend all of one's life asleep. - Yevgeny Aleksandrovich Yevtushenko

5134.	She got even in a way that was almost cruel. She forgave them. - Ralph McGill (on Eleanor Roosevelt)

5135.	The essence of worldliness is exclusion of God. - Henry Jacobsen

5136.	Nature to be commanded, must be obeyed. -Francis Bacon

5137.	Confidence is the feeling you have before you understand the situation.

5138.	He who has a thousand friends has not a friend to spare. While he who has one enemy shall meet him everywhere. -Ralph Waldo Emerson

5139.   Anger is momentary madness, so control your passion or it will control you. - Horace

5140.   Originality is nothing by judicious imitation. The most original writers borrowed one from another. -Francois Marie Arouet Voltaire

5141.   I think we have to make love on the front lawn like crazed weasels NOW!

5142.   Love is not blind - it sees more not less. But because it sees more it is willing to see less. -Julian Weber Gordon

5143.   The latest survey shows that 3 out of 4 people make up 75% of the population.

5144.   Prayer is the key to Heaven, but faith unlocks the door. -Mosie Lister

5145.   Look abroad through Nature's range; Nature's mighty law is change. -Robert Burns

5146.   Life is like playing a violin in public and learning the instrument as one goes on. -Samuel Butler

5147.   It takes a day to find a friend, a moment to lose them but a lifetime to forget them.

5148.   Only in America do we leave cars worth thousands of dollars in the driveway and leave useless things and junk in boxes in the garage.

5149.   Every time you smile at someone, it is an action of love a gift to that person, a beautiful thing. -Mother Theresa

5150.   This isn't right. This isn't even wrong. -Wolfgang Pauli

5151.   We're actors - we're the opposite of people. -Tom Stoppard

5152.   You can send a message around the world in 1/7 of a second; yet it may take several years to move a simple idea through a 1/4 inch of human skull.

5153.   Treat people as if they were what they should be, and you help them become what they are capable of becoming. -Johann Goethe

5154.   Deep Thoughts: Marta likes to talk about sensuality but I don't think she would know sensuality if it bit her on the ass. -Jack Handey

5155.   Energy is equal to desire and purpose. -Sheryl Adams

5156.   Self-denial is not a virtue it is only the effect of prudence on rascality. -George Bernard Shaw

5157. The education of the will is the object of our existence. -Ralph Waldo Emerson

5158. Dare to be wise. -Anonymous

5159. Gratitude is the most exquisite form of courtesy. -Jacques Maritain

5160. A plan is a list of actions arranged in whatever sequence is thought likely to achieve an objective. -John Argenti

5161. Realize that now, in this moment of time, you are creating. You are creating your next moment. That is what's real. -Sara Paddison

5162. A hundred men may make an encampment, but it takes a woman to make a home.

5163. The race is not always to the swift nor the battle to the strong. -Ecclesiastes, The Bible

5164. All mothers are working mothers.

5165. Look for your choices, pick the best one, then go with it. -Pat Riley

5166. Welcome to President Bush, Mrs. Bush, and my fellow astronauts. -Dan Quayle

5167. A man's mind, once stretched by a new idea, never goes back to its original dimensions. -Oliver Wendell Holmes

5168. Respect cannot be learned, purchased or acquired- it can only be earned.

5169. In arguing, too, the parson owned his skill, for even though vanquished he could argue still. - Oliver Goldsmith

5170. Set up as an ideal the facing of reality as honestly and as cheerfully as possible. -Dr. Karl Menninger

5171. Wrinkles should merely indicate where smiles have been. -Mark Twain

5172. Optometrist's office: If you don't see what you're looking for, you've come to the right place.

5173. A teacher affects eternity he can never tell where his influence stops. -Henry Adams

5174. The most wasted day of all is that on which we have not laughed. -Sebastien-Roch Nicolas de Chamfort

5175. Dreams are illustrations from the book your soul is writing about you. -Marsha Norman

5176. Do not ask for whom the bell tolls; it tolls for thee. -Ernest Hemingway

5177. The only successful substitute for brains is silence. -Unknown

5178. History is the record of an encounter between character and circumstances. -Donald Creighton

5179. There's folks 'ud stand on their heads and then say the fault was i' their boots. -George Eliot

5180. Nice to be here. At my age, it's nice to be anywhere. -George Burns

5181. When buying and selling are controlled by legislation, the first things to be bought and sold are legislators. -P. J. O'Rourke

5182. Nirvana, or lasting enlightenment, or true spiritual growth, can be achieved only through persistent exercise of real love. -M Scott Peck

5183. What we call the beginning is often the end. And to make an end is to make a beginning. The end is where we start from. -T. S. Eliot

5184. What the world needs is more geniuses with humility; there are so few of us left. -Oscar Levant

5185. If I had as much make-up on as he did, I'd have looked younger too. -Ronald Reagan

5186. That best portion of a good man's life His little nameless unremembered acts of kindness and of love. -William Wordsworth

5187. We find comfort among those who agree with us-growth among those who don't. -Frank Clark

5188. The business of preaching is to comfort the disturbed and to disturb the comfortable.

5189. Holding on to anger is like grasping a hot coal with the intent of throwing it at someone else you are the one who gets burned. -Buddha

5190. If you want children to keep their feet on the ground, put some responsibility on their shoulders. -Abigail Van Buren

5191.   There are varieties of shark not counting loan and pool. -L. M. Boyd

5192.   My father always used to say that when you die if you've got five real friends you've had a great life. -Elbert Hubbard

5193.   What happens to a man is less significant than what happens within him. -Louis L. Mann

5194.   The only reason for being a professional writer is that you can't help it. -Leo Rosten

5195.   Be not afraid of growing slowly be afraid only of standing still. -Chinese Proverb

5196.   You are looking as fresh as paint. -F. E. Smedley

5197.   It is a youthful failing to be unable to control one's impulses. -Seneca

5198.   Since you are like no other being ever created since the beginning of time you are incomparable. -Brenda Ueland

5199.   No one is rich enough to do without a neighbor. -Danish proverb

5200.   Your attitude is the librarian of your past, the speaker of your present, and the prophet of your future!

5201.   There is no such thing as a long piece of work except one that you dare not start. -Charles Baudelaire

5202.   When your outgo exceeds your income, your upkeep will be your downfall.

5203.   Change is inevitable. In a progressive country change is constant. -Benjamin Disraeli

5204.   The most violent element in society is ignorance. -Emma Goldman

5205.   Two friends, two bodies with one soul inspired. -Homer

5206.   There is an art of reading as well as an art of thinking and an art of writing. -Benjamin Disraeli

5207.   Start by doing what's necessary; then do what's possible; and suddenly you are doing the impossible. -St. Francis of Assisi

5208.   A business that makes nothing but money is a poor business. -Henry Ford

5209.   The English have no respect for their language and will not teach their children to speak it. -George Bernard Shaw

5210.   A friend is someone that won't begin to talk behind your back when you leave the room.

5211.   Drink wet cement and get really stoned.

5212.   The softest things in the world overcome the hardest things in the world. Through this I know the advantage of taking no action. -Lao Tzu

5213.   Patriotism is the willingness to kill and be killed for trivial reasons. -Bertrand Russell

5214.   Thought is the wind knowledge the sail and mankind the vessel. -Augustus Hare

5215.   If a writer wrote merely for his time, I would have to break my pen and throw it away. -Victor Hugo

5216.   The tip you leave now for lunch would have bought you one twenty years ago.

5217.   The young man knows the rules, but the old man knows the exceptions.

5218.   Whom the gods would destroy they first make mad. -Euripides

5219.   She is a friend of my mind... The pieces I am, she gather them and give them back to me in all the right order. -Toni Morrison

5220.   All wish to be learned but no one is willing to pay the price. -Juvenal

5221.   If you look good and dress well you don't need a purpose in life. -Robert Pante

5222.   What some call health, if purchased by perpetual anxiety about diet, isn't much better than tedious disease. -George Dennison Prentice

5223.   Writing is not necessarily something to be ashamed of, but do it in private and wash your hands afterwards. -Robert A. Heinlein

5224.   My tongue swore but my mind was still unpledged. -Euripides

5225.   Hollywood's a place where they'll pay you a thousand dollars for a kiss, and fifty cents for your soul. -Marilyn Monroe

5226.   In my case, adulthood itself was not an advance, although it was a useful waymark. -Nicholson Baker

5227.   America shudders at anything alien, and when it wants to shut its mind against any man's ideas, it calls him a foreigner. -Max Lerner

5228.   For every minute you are angry you lose sixty seconds of happiness. -Ralph Waldo Emerson

5229.   The art of being wise is the art of knowing what to overlook. -William James

5230.   Some minds are like concrete... all mixed up and permanently set.

5231.   If you do not wish to be prone to anger, do not feed the habit; give it nothing which may tend to its increase. -Epictetus

5232.   If a pig could give his mind to anything, he would not be a pig. -Charles Dickens

5233.   You can't find any true closeness in Hollywood because everybody does the fake closeness so well. -Carrie Fisher

5234.   Nothing is more damaging to a state than that cunning men pass for wise. -Francis Bacon

5235.   What we must decide is perhaps how we are valuable, rather than how valuable we are. -Edgar Friedenberg

5236.   Reality is a crutch for people who can't handle drugs. -Lily Tomlin

5237.   We can let circumstances rule us, or we can take charge and rule our lives from within. -Earl Nightingale

5238.   It is better to keep your mouth closed and let people think you are a fool than to open it and remove all doubt. -Mark Twain

5239.   Forgiveness is like the fragrance a flower gives after it's been stepped on.

5240.   Bright lights cast dark shadows when shone from only one direction. -David Kelley

5241.   I was working on the proof of one of my poems all the morning and took out a comma. In the afternoon I put it back again. -Oscar Wilde

5242.   Always do your best. What you plant now, you will harvest later. -Og Mandino

5243.   He who loses money loses much. He who loses a friend loses more. But he who loses faith loses all. -Henry H. Haskins

5244.   It is not length of life but depth of life. -Ralph Waldo Emerson

5245.   And the wind shall say, "Here were decent godless people. Their only monument the asphalt road. And a thousand lost golf balls." -T. S. Eliot

5246.   Death is hereditary.

5247.   For what is faith unless it is to believe what you do not see? -Augustine

5248.   Every path has its puddle. -English Proverb

5249.   Music expresses that which cannot be said and on which it is impossible to be silent. -Victor Hugo

5250.   My motto is that I enjoy life. I think there's a kind of simplicity to that way of thinking. -Jenna Elfman

5251.   When will people understand that words can cut as sharply as any blade, and that those cuts leave scars upon our souls? - Unknown

5252.   The next time the devil reminds you of your past, remind him of his future.

5253.   A user friendly computer first requires a friendly user.

5254.   The essence of all beautiful art, all great art, is gratitude. -Friedrich Nietzsche

5255.   A sound mind in a sound body is a short but full description of a happy state in this world. -John Locke

5256.   If you haven't got anything nice to say about anybody come sit next to me. -Alice Roosevelt Longworth

5257.   Pleasure in the job puts perfection in the work. -Aristotle

5258.   The tendency of an event to occur varies inversely with one's preparation for it. -David Searles

5259.   Beyond every effort put first lies an undiscovered opportunity. -Cassia Lewis

5260.   There is nobody so irritating as somebody with less intelligence and more sense than we have. -Don Herold

5261.   The very essence of leadership is that you have to have vision. You can't blow an uncertain trumpet. -Theodore Hesburgh

5262.   We promise according to our hopes and perform according to our fears. -François de La Rochefoucauld, French Classical Writer

5263.   True friendship is like sound health; the value of it is seldom known until it is lost.

5264.   Danish proverb Woe to the house where the hen crows and the rooster is still.

5265.   Don't find fault, find a remedy. (Henry Ford)

5266.   The most merciful thing in the world . . . is the inability of the human mind to correlate all its contents.- H. P. Lovecraft

5267.   It is better to have a permanent income than to be fascinating.- Oscar Wilde

5268.   We all walk in the dark and each of us must learn to turn on his or her own light.- Earl Nightingale

5269.   Since it architecture is music in space as it were a frozen music.- Friedrich von Schelling

5270.   When they call the roll in the Senate the Senators do not know whether to answer Present or Not guilty.- Theodore Roosevelt

5271.   In Israel in order to be a realist you must believe in miracles.- David Ben-Gurion

5272.   A week is a long time in politics. -Harold Wilson

5273.   Being president is like being a jackass in a hailstorm. There's nothing to do but to stand there and take it. -Lyndon B. Johnson

5274.   Very simple ideas lie within the reach only of complex minds. - Remy de Gourmont

5275.   Every individual has a place to fill in the world, and is important, in some respect, whether he chooses to be so or not. - Nathaniel Hawthorne

5276.   There is no security on this earth; there is only opportunity. - General Douglas MacArthur

5277.   We don't want to go back to tomorrow, we want to go forward. -Dan Quayle

5278. Action may not always be happiness, but there is no happiness without action.

5279. A nation that continues to produce soft-minded men purchases its own spiritual death on the installment plan. -Martin Luther King Jr.

5280. for whatever we lose (like a you or a me) it's always ourselves we find in the sea -e e cummings

5281. Love is a driver, bitter and fierce if you fight and resist him Easy-going enough once you acknowledge his power. -Ovid

5282. Never think that God's delays are God's denials. Hold on hold fast hold out. Patience is genius. -George-Louis Leclerc de Buffon

5283. He who has gone so we but cherish his memory abides with us, more potent, nay more present, than the living man. -Antoine De Saint-Exupery

5284. If you don't drive your business, you will be driven out of business. - B. C. Forbes

5285. My dear and old country here we are once again, together faced with a heavy trial. -Charles De Gaulle

5286. I'd walk through hell in a gasoline suit to play baseball. -Pete Rose

5287. To teach is to learn twice. -Joseph Joubert

5288. Nothing will come of nothing. -William Shakespeare

5289. There's a sucker born every minute. -P. T. Barnum

5290. It was a book to kill time for those who like it better dead. - Dame Rose Macaulay

5291. I was born an American; I will live an American; I shall die an American. -Daniel Webster

5292. Study men, not historians. -Harry S Truman

5293. All God wants of man is a peaceful heart. -Meister Eckhart

5294. There will always be a frontier where there is an open mind and a willing hand. -Charles F. Kettering

5295. Man can acquire accomplishments or he can become an animal, whichever he wants. God makes the animals, man makes himself. -G. C. Lichtenberg

5296. The difference between a good haircut and a bad haircut is about a week.

5297. Discontent is the first necessity of progress. -Thomas Alva Edison

5298. The surest way to make a monkey of a man is to quote him. - Robert Charles Benchley

5299. Little differences - like a letter in a word - make all the difference in the world.

5300. Do not trust all men, but trust men of worth - the former course is silly, the latter a mark of prudence. -Democritus

5301. The most powerful factors in the world are clear ideas in the minds of energetic men of good will. -J. Arthur Thomson

5302. I don't have a solution, but I admire the problem.

5303. You can always tell a real friend when you've made a fool of yourself; he doesn't feel you've done a permanent job. -Laurence J. Peter

5304. Half of the harm that is done in this world is due to people who want to feel important. -George Eliot

5305. Self-pity is our worst enemy and if we yield to it, we can never do anything wise in the world. -Helen Keller

5306. A good match blows fire...

5307. Fanaticism is the child of false zeal and of superstition; the father of intolerance and of persecution. -John William Fletcher

5308. First love is a kind of vaccination which saves a man from catching the complaint a second time. -Honore de Balzac

5309. Knowledge is power. -Francis Bacon

5310. Build a dream and the dream will build you. -Dr. Robert Schuller

5311. As I make my slow pilgrimage through the world, a certain sense of beautiful mystery seems to gather and grow. -C. Benson

5312. Only in quiet waters do things mirror themselves undistorted. Only in a quiet mind is adequate perception of the world. -Hans Margolius

5313.   Doubt is the vestibule through which all must pass before they can enter into the temple of wisdom. -Charles Caleb Colton

5314.   Anger is only one letter short of danger. -Eleanor Roosevelt

5315.   Familiarity breeds contempt - and children. -Mark Twain

5316.   I like to listen. I have learned a great deal from listening carefully. Most people never listen. -Ernest Hemingway

5317.   Never look down on anybody unless you're helping them up. - The Reverend Jesse Jackson, American Civil Rights Leader

5318.   Know thyself. -Thales

5319.   If you were born lucky, even your rooster will lay eggs. -Assyrian Proverb

5320.   Now and then an innocent man is sent to the legislature. -Kin Hubbard

5321.   Every fool knows that he cannot reach the stars but it never keeps a wise man from trying. -Ronnie B. Woods

5322.   Housework is something you do that nobody notices until you don't do it.

5323.   Hope is only the love of life. -Henri Frederic Amiel

5324.   No life without the sun, no Life without the Son.

5325.   The day a person becomes a cynic is the day he loses his youth. -Marvin D. Levy

5326.   The world hates change, yet it is the only thing that has brought progress. -Charles Franklin Kettering

5327.   Get happiness out of your work or you may never know what happiness is. -Elbert Hubbard

5328.   My one aim was to do a thing well and to excel if possible. - Josephine Demott Robinson

5329.   He who has a strong enough why can bear almost any how. - Friedrich Nietzsche

5330.   It is by chance we met, by choice we became friends. -Unknown

5331.   It takes all sorts to make a world. -Miguel Cervantes

5332.   The entire sum of existence is the magic of being needed by just one person. - Vi Putnam

5333. Digital Wisdom: Affirm brain on-line before opening mouth.com.

5334. The populace is like the sea, motionless in itself, but stirred by every wind even the lightest breeze. -Titus Livius

5335. Hard work never killed anyone, but why chance it?

5336. Every society honors its live conformists and its dead troublemakers. -Mignon McLaughlin

5337. Never drive faster than your guardian angel can fly.

5338. Of course there is no formula for success, except perhaps an unconditional acceptance of life and what it brings. -Arthur Rubinstein

5339. He who controls the past commands the future. He who commands the future conquers the past. -George Orwell

5340. A dreamer lives forever And a toiler dies in a day. -John Locke

5341. Motivation is what gets you started. Habit is what keeps you going. -Unknown

5342. I am never afraid of what I know. -Anna Sewell

5343. We would rather have one man or woman working with us than three merely working for us. - J. Dabney Day

5344. One cannot fix one's eyes on the commonest natural production without finding food for a rambling fancy. -Jane Austen

5345. I've got to keep breathing. It'll be my worst business mistake if I don't. -Sir Nathan Rothschild

5346. You will be as much value to others as you have been to yourself. -Marcus T. Cicero

5347. To me, old age is always years older than I am. -Bernard Baruch

5348. Nothing costs so much as what is bought by prayers. -Seneca

5349. A leading authority is anyone who has guessed right more than once.

5350. Sign at animal shelter: Children left unattended will be given a puppy or a kitten.

5351. I think it would be a good idea. -Mahatma Gandhi

5352. The sword of justice has no scabbard. -Antoine de Rivarol

5353. Great eagerness in the pursuit of wealth, pleasure, or honor, cannot exist without sin. -Desiderius Erasmus

5354. Our task is not to fix the blame for the past, but to fix the course for the future. -John Fitzgerald Kennedy

5355. I'm not saying my boyfriend is thick, but yesterday when we had a gas leak; he put a bucket under it.

5356. What lies behind us and what lies before us are tiny matters compared to what lies within us. -Unknown

5357. Man's way leads to a hopeless end! God's way leads to an endless hope!

5358. Defeat isn't bitter if you don't swallow it.

5359. In the province of the mind, what one believes to be true either is true or becomes true. -John Lilly

5360. Materialists and madmen never have doubts. -Gilbert Keith Chesterton

5361. The closer I'm bound in love to you, the closer I am to free. -Robert G. Ingersoll

5362. It's not the hours you put in your work that counts; it's the work you put in the hours. -Sam Ewig

5363. What is harder than rock or softer than water? Yet soft water hollows out hard rock. Persevere. -Ovid

5364. The world is content with setting right the surface of things. -John Henry Newman

5365. By courage, I repel adversity. -Anonymous

5366. If a thing goes without saying - let it. -Jacob Braude

5367. It is good to dream, but it is better to dream and work. Faith is mighty, but action with faith is mightier. -Thomas Robert Gaines

5368. In silence, man can most readily preserve his integrity. -Meister Eckhart

5369. When you are standing on the edge of a cliff a step forward is not progress. -Grandfather

5370. Without haste, but without rest. -Goethe

5371. Union gives strength. -Aesop

5372. No one can arrive from being talented alone. God gives talent; work transforms talent into genius. -Anna Pavlova

5373. Dignity consists not in possessing honors, but in the consciousness that we deserve them. -Aristotle

5374. When confronted with a Goliath-sized problem, which way do you respond: "He's too big to hit" or like David, "He's too big to miss"?

5375. American Indian Proverb: Every animal knows more than you do. Nez Perce

5376. Listen to life, and you will hear the voice of life crying, Be! -James Dillet Freeman

5377. Job dissatisfaction is the number one factor in whether you survive your first heart attack. -Anthony Robbins

5378. Peace cannot be achieved through violence, it can only be attained through understanding. - Albert Einstein

5379. Revenge is a kind of wild justice which the more man's nature runs to the more ought law to weed it out. -Francis Bacon

5380. If we are lucky, we can give in and rest without feeling guilty. We can stop doing and concentrate on being. -Kathleen Norris

5381. No rules for success will work if you don't. -Unknown Author

5382. Experience is what you get when you don't get what you want.

5383. Man is an animal which alone among the animals refuses to be satisfied by the fulfilment of animal desires. -Alexander Graham Bell

5384. The fewer the words the better the prayer. -Martin Luther

5385. I wish that all Americans would realize that American politics is world politics. -Theodore Roosevelt

5386. Hope for miracles but don't rely on one. -Yiddish Proverb

5387. My eyes are an ocean in which my dreams are reflected. -Anna M. Uhlich

5388. For myself I am an optimist - it does not seem to be much use being anything else. -Sir Winston Leonard Spenser Churchill

5389. If everybody thought before they spoke, the silence would be deafening. - George Barzan

5390. God does not care about our mathematical difficulties. He integrates empirically. -Albert Einstein

5391. Did you hear about the man who lost his whole left side? He's all right now.

5392. Some people think they are concentrating when they're merely worrying. -Bobby Jones

5393. Boys will be boys, and so will a lot of middle-aged men. -Kin Hubbard

5394. I am a great believer in luck, and I find the harder I work the more I have of it. -Thomas Jefferson

5395. If you love somebody, let them go, for if they return, they were always yours. And if they don't, they never were. -Kahlil Gibran

5396. The trouble is that everyone talks about reforming others and no one thinks about reforming himself. -Peter Alcantara

5397. My riches consist not in the extent of my possessions but in the fewness of my wants. -J. Brotherton

5398. Life does not cease to be funny when people die any more than it ceases to be serious when people laugh. -Antoine De Saint-Exupery

5399. The gem cannot be polished without friction, nor man perfected without trials. -Chinese proverb

5400. A doctor can bury his mistakes but an architect can only advise his client to plant vines. -Frank Lloyd Wright

5401. Free advice is worth the price. -Robert Half

5402. The best way to find yourself is to lose yourself in the service of others. -Mahatma Gandhi

5403. Disappointments should be cremated, not embalmed.

5404. The question is not whether we will die, but how we will live. -Joan Borysenko

5405. I think of a hero as someone who understands the degree of responsibility that comes with his freedom. -Bob Dylan

5406. The only truly affluent are those who do not want more than they have. -Erich Fromm

5407. Behind every great fortune there is a crime. -Honore de Balzac

5408.   What one knows is in youth of little moment they know enough who know how to learn. -Henry Adams

5409.   He who dies with the most toys is nonetheless still dead. -Anon.

5410.   It is good to vary in order that you may frustrate the curious especially those who envy you. -Baltasar Gracian

5411.   The harder you fall, the higher you bounce. -Anonymous

5412.   We are ready for any unforeseen event that may or may not occur. -Dan Quayle

5413.   The difference between a rebel and a patriot is whether who is in power.

5414.   I have changed my mind a dozen times. It seems to work better now.

5415.   Responsibilities gravitate to the person who can shoulder them. -Elbert Hubbard

5416.   There is no gathering the rose without being pricked by the thorns. -Vishnu Sarma

5417.   Mediocre idea that generates enthusiasm will go further than a great idea that inspires no one. -Mary Kay Ash

5418.   They can conquer who believe they can. -Virgil

5419.   Nothing happens unless first a dream. -Carl Sandburg

5420.   The average man who does not know what to do with his life wants another one which will last forever. -Anatole France

5421.   Nothing so conclusively proves a man's ability to lead others as what he does from day to day to lead himself. -Thomas John Watson Sr.

5422.   The unexamined life is not worth living. -Socrates

5423.   An anniversary says, Think of the dreams you have weathered together. They are intimate accomplishments. -Charles R. Swindoll

5424.   Calamity is the test of integrity. -Samuel Richardson

5425.   I value my garden more for being full of blackbirds than of cherries, and very frankly give them fruit for their songs. -Joseph Addison

5426.   The mind is just another muscle. -Ted Turner

5427. I believe in equality for everyone except reporters and photographers. -Mahatma Gandhi

5428. Love all love of other sights controls, and makes one little room an everywhere. -John Donne

5429. The entrepreneur always searches for change, responds to it, and exploits it as an opportunity. -Peter F. Drucker

5430. Progress lies not in enhancing what is but in advancing toward what will be. -Kahlil Gibran

5431. The pursuit of happiness is a most ridiculous phrase; if you pursue happiness, you'll never find it. -C. P. Snow

5432. In spite of the cost of living, it's still popular. -Laurence J. Peter

5433. An artist cannot fail; it is a success to be one. -Charles Horton Cooley

5434. That's the whole problem with science. You've got a bunch of empiricists trying to describe things of unimaginable wonder. -Bill Watterson

5435. It is curious that physical courage should be so common in the world and moral courage so rare. -Mark Twain

5436. There are times when forgetting can be just as important as remembering, and even more difficult.

5437. I ran the wrong kind of business, but I did it with integrity. - Sydney Biddle Barrows

5438. They are borne along by the violence of their rage, and think it is a waste of time to ask who are guilty. - Lucanus

5439. All political parties die at last of swallowing their own lies. - John Arbthnot

5440. He that dies a martyr proves that he was not a knave, but by no means that he was not a fool. -Charles Caleb Colton

5441. The aim of education is the knowledge not of fact, but of values. -William Ralph Inge

5442. Those who stand strong will stand forever. -Joshua D. Clark

5443. Good men must be affectionate men. Samuel Richardson

5444. If you want to be happy for a year, plant a garden; if you want to be happy for life, plant a tree. -English proverb

5445. A difference, to be a difference, must make a difference. -James Farr

5446. Porque el miedo sin ser Dios suele hacer algo de nada. (Fear can, though it is not God, create something from nothing.) -Caspar de Aguilar

5447. I don't know anything about music. In my line you don't have to. -Elvis Presley

5448. With coarse rice to eat, with water to drink, and my bended arm for a pillow-I have still joy in the midst of all these things. -Confucius

5449. Lots of folks confuse bad management with destiny. -Kin Hubbard

5450. If you haven't found something strange during the day, it hasn't been much of a day. -John A. Wheeler

5451. If you think nobody cares if you're alive, try missing a couple of payments.

5452. Develop the winning edge; small differences in your performance can lead to large differences in your results. -Brian Tracy

5453. Few people have any next, they live from hand to mouth without a plan, and are always at the end of their line. -Ralph Waldo Emerson

5454. Do not do to others what angers you if done to you by others. -Isocrates

5455. Must not all things at the last be swallowed up in death? -Plato

5456. A coward turns away but a brave man's choice is danger. -Euripides

5457. Not what we have But what we enjoy constitutes our abundance. -John Petit Senn

5458. In this world nothing is certain but death and taxes. -Benjamin Franklin

5459. I'm a great believer in luck, and I find that the harder I work, the more I have of it. -Thomas Jefferson

5460. Where there are friends there is wealth. -Titus Maccius Plautus

5461. There is only one happiness in life: to love and to be loved. - George Sand

5462. Woe to the man whose heart has not learned while young to hope to love - and to put its trust in life. -Joseph Conrad

5463. Grief can take care of itself, but to get the full value of a joy you must have somebody to divide it with. -Mark Twain

5464. All labor that uplifts humanity has dignity and importance and should be undertaken with painstaking excellence. -Martin Luther King Jr.

5465. Start slow and taper off. - Harry S. Truman

5466. The most important trip you may take in life is meeting people halfway. -Henry Boye

5467. When the time comes for friends to part, love will be the bride from heart to heart. -Unknown

5468. After one look at this planet, any visitor from outer space would say I want to see the manager. -William S. Burroughs

5469. Never, ever, ever, ever underestimate the power of "I'd like that."- John Mayer

5470. Avenge yourself; live long enough to be a problem to your children.

5471. Let everyone sweep in front of his own door and the whole world will be clean. -Johann Wolfgang Von Goethe

5472. Zeal is a volcano, the peak of which the grass of indecisiveness does not grow. -Kahlil Gibran

5473. Most games are lost, not won. -Casey Stengel

5474. No rest is worth anything except the rest that is earned. -Jean Paul

5475. Not for nothing is their motto TGIF - 'Thank God It's Friday.' They live for the weekends, when they can go do what they really want to do.

5476. A helping hand is no farther than at the end of your sleeve.

5477. A rumor without a leg to stand on will get around some other way. -John Tudor

5478. The greatest tragedy is when man gives up what he wants most for what he wants now!

5479. Dictators ride to and fro upon tigers which they dare not dismount. And the tigers are getting hungry. -Sir Winston Churchill

5480. The man who makes no mistakes does not usually make anything. -Edward Phelps

5481. By trying we can easily endure adversity. Another man's, I mean. -Mark Twain

5482. The greatest thing in the world is not so much where we are, but in what direction we are moving. -Oliver Wendell Holmes

5483. You never know what is enough unless you know what is more than enough. -James Agee

5484. When love is in excess, it brings a man nor honor nor any worthiness. -Euripides

5485. Everything on the earth has a purpose, every disease an herb to cure it, and every person a mission. - Mourning Dove

5486. If it helps to make people think a little bit more what those ideals are then I'll keep wearing this uniform. -Barbara Adams

5487. There is no respect for others without humility in one's self. - Henri Frederic Amiel

5488. And we are put on Earth a little space that we may learn to bear the beams of love. -William Blake.

5489. Just because you love someone doesn't mean you have to be involved with them. Love is not a bandage to cover wounds. -Hugh Elliott

5490. He who has a thousand friends has not a friend to spare, while he who has one enemy shall meet him everywhere. -Ali bin Abi Talib

5491. Get the facts or the facts will get you. And when you get them, get them right or they will get you wrong. -Thomas Fuller

5492. Buy a Pentium 586/200 so you can reboot faster.

5493. By all means marry; if you get a good wife, you'll be happy. If you get a bad one, you'll become a philosopher. -Socrates

5494. An economist is a man who states the obvious in terms of the incomprehensible. -Alfred A. Knopf

5495. All are lunatics, but he who can analyze his delusions is called a philosopher. -Ambrose Gwinett Bierce

5496. 640K ought to be enough for anybody.- Bill Gates

5497. I have noticed that the people who are late are often so much jollier than the people who have to wait for them. -Edward Verall Lucas

5498. It is easier to stay out than get out. -Mark Twain

5499. The man who trims himself to suit everybody will soon whittle himself away. -Charles Schwab

5500. I think we consider too much the good luck of the early bird and not enough the bad luck of the early worm. -Franklin Delano Roosevelt

5501. There are worse things than getting a call for the wrong number at AM. It could be the right number. -Doug Larson

5502. If your only goal is to become rich, you will never achieve it. - John D. Rockefeller

5503. Age does not make us childish, as some say it only finds us true children still. -Johann Wolfgang von Goethe

5504. You may delay but time will not. -Benjamin Franklin

5505. A homely face and no figure have aided many women heavenward. -Minna Antrim

5506. Like all weak men, he laid an exaggerated stress on not changing one's mind. -W. Somerset Maugham

5507. It is sad to grow old but nice to ripen. -Brigitte Bardot

5508. Men, like bullets, go farthest when they are smoothest. -Jean Paul Friedrich Richter

5509. The meeting of two personalities is like the contact of two chemical substances; if there is any reaction, both are transformed. - Carl Jung

5510. Advice is like castor oil, easy enough to give but dreadful uneasy to take. - Josh Billings

5511. You've never been lost until you've been lost at Mach 3. -Paul Crickmore

5512. Don't accept your dog's admiration as conclusive evidence that you are wonderful. -Ann Landers

5513. It's not the voting that's democracy; it's the counting. -Tom Stoppard

5514. Lane Olinghouse To err is human to refrain from laughing humane.

5515. It takes as much stress to be a success as it does to be a failure. -Emilio James Trujillo

5516. Success is never final and failure never fatal. It's courage that counts. -Jules Ellinger

5517. The minute you start talking about what you are going to do if you lose, you have lost. -George Schultz

5518. Tolerance implies no lack of commitment to one's own beliefs. Rather it condemns the oppression or persecution of others. -John F. Kennedy

5519. There are two primary choices in life; to accept conditions as they exist, or accept the responsibility for changing them. -Denis Waitley

5520. Talent hits the target which no one else can hit; genius hits the target which no one else can see.

5521. As a rule, software systems do not work well until they have been used and have failed repeatedly in real applications. -Dave Parnas

5522. The significant problems we face cannot be solved at the same level of thinking we were at when we created them. -Albert Einstein

5523. Accuracy of statement is one of the first elements of truth; inaccuracy is a near kin to falsehood. - Tryon Edwards

5524. Some people will never learn anything for this reason: because they understand everything too soon. -Alexander Pope

5525. Love begets love. Love knows no rules. This is the same for all. -Virgil

5526. What is man's chief enemy? Each man is his own. -Anacharsis Cloots

5527. Happiness is not a goal; it is a by-product. -Eleanor Roosevelt

5528. There is no wisdom without love. -N. Sri Ram

5529.   It isn't what they say about you it's what they whisper. -Errol Flynn

5530.   The challenge is not to manage time, but to manage ourselves. - Steven Covey

5531.   It is far more impressive when others discover your good qualities without your help.

5532.   To ask the laws of the universe to be annulled on behalf of a single petitioner confessedly unworthy. -Ambrose Bierce Pray

5533.   Dishonor will not trouble me once I am dead. -Euripides

5534.   The world of reality has its limits the world of imagination is boundless. -Jean Jacques Rousseau

5535.   The fundamental evil of the world arose from the fact that the good Lord has not created money enough. -Heinrich Heine

5536.   The first and last thing required of genius is the love of truth. - Johann Wolfgang von Goethe

5537.   Qaddafi counted on America to be passive. He counted wrong. - Ronald Reagan

5538.   Better than a thousand days of diligent study is one day with a great teacher. -Japanese Proverb

5539.   You either move toward something you love or away from something you fear. The first expands. The second constricts. -Tom Crum

5540.   Early to bed and early to rise, makes a man healthy, wealthy, and wise. -Benjamin Franklin

5541.   In order to shake a hypothesis, it is sometimes not necessary to do anything more than push it as far as it will go. - Denis Diderot

5542.   The way money goes so fast these days, they should paint racing stripes on it. -Mark Russell

5543.   I don't want to achieve immortality through my work... I want to achieve it through not dying. -Woody Allen

5544.   Standing in the middle of the road is very dangerous; you get knocked down by traffic from both sides. -Margaret Hilda Thatcher

5545.   Blossoms are scattered by the wind, and the wind cares nothing but the blossoms of the heart no wind can touch. -Yoshida Kenko

5546.   Peace and friendship with all mankind is our wisest policy, and I wish we may be permitted to pursue it. -Thomas Jefferson

5547.   In real love you want the other person's good. In romantic love, you want the other person. -Margaret Anderson

5548.   If you forget you have to struggle for improvement you go backward. -Geoffrey Hickson

5549.   It is a far, far better thing to have a firm anchor in nonsense than to put out on the troubled sea of thought. -John Kenneth Galbraith

5550.   The only real failure in life is the failure to try. -Anonymous

5551.   The harder the conflict, the more glorious the triumph. -Thomas Paine

5552.   They never fail who die in a great cause. -George Gordon Byron

5553.   For a good cause, wrongdoing is virtuous. -Publilius Syrus

5554.   Sign on a church bulletin board: You aren't too bad to come in. You aren't good enough to stay out.

5555.   Let us hope that we are all preceded in this world by a love story. -Don Snyder

5556.   Chocolate covered raisins, cherries, orange slices & strawberries all count as fruit, so eat as many as you want.

5557.   In Hollywood all the marriages are happy; it's trying to live together afterwards that causes all the problems. -Shelly Winters

5558.   The least initial deviation from the truth is multiplied later a thousand old. -Aristotle

5559.   Work to survive. Survive by consuming. Survive to consume. The hellish cycle is complete. -Raoul Vaneigem

5560.   If a cow can't eat it, I don't want to play on it. -Dick Allen

5561.   Suburbia is where the bulldozers have knocked down all the trees and the planners rename the roads after them. -Anon., US TV

5562.   We discovered that peace at any price is no peace at all. -Eve Denise Curie

5563.   Comfort zones are most often expanded through discomfort. -Peter McWilliams

5564.   By asking for the impossible, obtain the best possible. -Italian Proverb

5565.   Word is a shadow of a deed. -Democritus

5566.   Stupidity is NOT a handicap! PARK ELSEWHERE!

5567.   Knowing is not enough we must apply. Willing is not enough we must do. -Bruce Lee

5568.   The first duty of love is to listen. -Tillich

5569.   Yesterday is not ours to recover, but tomorrow is ours to win or to lose. -Lyndon B. Johnson

5570.   If you haven't much education, you must use your brain.

5571.   I awoke with devout thanksgiving for my friends. -Ralph Waldo Emerson

5572.   Backward ran sentences until reeled the mind. -Wolcott Gibbs

5573.   I can get more out of God by believing Him for one minute than by shouting at Him all night. -Smith Wigglesworth

5574.   Talkers are no good doers. -Mary Bertone

5575.   Our friends show us what we can do; our enemies teach us what we must do. -Johann Wolfgang von Goethe

5576.   No bird soars too high if he soars with his own wings. -William Blake

5577.   Never love anything that can't love you back. -Bruce Williams

5578.   The lion and the calf shall lie down together, but the calf won't get much sleep. -Woody Allen

5579.   Too bad the only people who know how to run the country are busy driving cabs and cutting hair. -George Burns

5580.   There are two kinds of people: those who finish what they start and so on. -Robert Byrne

5581.   If life deals you a lemon, make lemonade.

5582.   The movies are the only business where you can go out front and applaud yourself. -Will Rogers

5583.   The man who can smile when things go wrong has thought of someone else he can blame it on. -Robert Albert Bloch

5584.   An open mind does not always require an open mouth.

5585. The season of failure is the best time for sowing the seeds of success. -Paramahansa Yogananda

5586. The brave man carves out his fortune and every man is the son of his own works. -Miguel de Cervantes

5587. Time will explain it all. He is a talker and needs no questioning before he speaks. -Euripides

5588. Silence is as full of potential wisdom and wit as the unhewn marble of a great sculpture. - Tom Lehrer

5589. Hard work spotlights the character of people; some turn up their sleeves, some turn up their noses, and some don't turn up at all!

5590. The superior man...does not set his mind either for anything or against anything what is right he will follow. -Confucius

5591. You cannot make a revolution with silk gloves. - Joseph Stalin

5592. He has achieved success who has lived well, laughed often, and loved much. -Bessie A. Stanley

5593. Education is not filling a bucket but lighting a fire. -William Butler Yeats

5594. Anger makes you smaller while forgiveness forces you to grow beyond what you were. -Cherie Carter-Scott

5595. Procrastination is the art of keeping up with yesterday. -Donald Robert Perry Marquis

5596. Come, for the House of Hope is built on sand: bring wine, for the fabric of life is as weak as the wind.—Hafiz

5597. We Americans have no commission from God to police the world. -Benjamin Harrison

5598. The mere process of growing old together will make the slightest acquaintance seem a bosom friend. -Logan Pearsall Smith

5599. Persistent work triumphs. -Virgil

5600. Pride would be a lot easier to swallow if it didn't taste so bad. - Brad Moore

5601. There are only two lasting bequests we can hope to give our children. One is roots; the other wings. -Hodding Carter

5602. To get profit without risk, experience without danger, and reward without work is as impossible as it is to live without being born.

5603. Every time we say Let there be in any form, something happens. -Stella Terrill Mann.

5604. Time, as he grows old, teaches all things. -Aeschylus

5605. You will find it a very good practice always to verify your references, sir.-Martin Routh

5606. True is it that we have seen better days. -William Shakespeare

5607. Last Monday a string of amendments were presented to the lower House these altogether respect personal liberty... -Senator William Grayson

5608. There is a kind of pleasure which comes from sacrilege or the profanation of the objects offered us for worship. -Marquis de Sade

5609. Kill no more pigeons than you can eat. -Benjamin Franklin

5610. Life must be lived as play. -Plato

5611. People never improve unless they look to some standard or example higher or better than themselves. - Tryon Edwards

5612. Nothing endures but change. -Heraclitus

5613. Women love us for our defects. If we have enough of them, they will forgive us everything, even our intellects. -Oscar Wilde

5614. There are no passengers on spaceship earth. We are all crew. - Marshall McLuhan

5615. Young men hear an old man to whom old men hearkened when he was young.-Caesar Augustus

5616. No man is happy without a delusion of some kind. Delusions are as necessary to our happiness as realities -Christian Nestell Bovee.

5617. None climbs so high as he who knows not whither he is going. -Oliver Cromwell

5618. Love the moment and the energy of that moment will spread beyond all boundaries. -Corita Kent

5619. There is no king who has not had a slave among his ancestors, and no slave who has not had a king among his. -Helen Keller

5620. We know what happens to people who stay in the middle of the road. They get run over.-Ambrose Gwinett Bierce

5621. I would never have amounted to anything were it not for adversity. I was forced to come up the hard way. -J. C. Penney

5622. No man can be a pure specialist without being, in the strict sense, an idiot. -George Bernard Shaw

5623. The right man is the one who seizes the moment. -Johann Wolfgang von Goethe

5624. Nothing tastes as good as slim feels.

5625. Sometimes the fool who rushes in gets the job done. -Al Bernstein

5626. Sometimes the answer to prayer is not that it changes life, but that it changes you. -James Dillet Freeman

5627. The true mystery of the world is the visible, not the invisible. -Oscar Wilde

5628. The privilege of absurdity to which no living creature is subject but man only. -Thomas Hobbes

5629. Marriage happens as with cages; the birds without despair to get in and those within despair to getting out. -D. A. Battista

5630. Focus on remedies, not faults. -Jack Nicklaus

5631. Thou wilt find rest from vain fancies if thou doest every act in life as though it were thy last. -Marcus Aurelius

5632. If you don't have the time to read, you don't have the time or the tools to write. -Stephen King

5633. Under capitalism, man exploits man. Under socialism, it's just the opposite. -Anon.

5634. Example is the school of mankind and they will learn at no other. -Kurt Herbert Alder

5635. Make new friends but keep the old; one is silver and the other's gold. -Unknown Author

5636. To him who is determined it remains only to act. -Italian Proverb

5637. Two-thirds of the earth is covered by water. The other third is covered by Garry Maddox. -Ralph Kiner

5638.	Sometimes you gotta create what you want to be a part of. - Geri Weitzman

5639.	I take it as a man's duty to restrain himself. -Lois McMaster Bujold

5640.	We must be willing to let go of the life we have planned so as to have the life that is waiting for us. -E. M. Forster

5641.	Whatever you want too much you can't have, so when you really want something, try to want it a little less. -Joel Rosenberg

5642.	Service... Giving what you don't have to give. Giving when you don't need to give. Giving because you want to give. -Damien Hess

5643.	Marriage. It's like a cultural hand-rail. It links folks to the past and guides them to the future. -Andrew Schneider

5644.	The worst-tempered people I've ever met were the people who knew they were wrong. -Wilson Mizner

5645.	You must be still in the midst of activity and be vibrantly alive in repose. -Indira Gandhi

5646.	God cannot alter the past, but historians can. -Samuel Butler

5647.	Nearly all men can stand adversity, but if you want to test a man's character, give him power. -Abraham Lincoln

5648.	If I chance to talk a little wild, forgive me. -William Shakespeare

5649.	Patriotism is the last refuge of a scoundrel. -Samuel Johnson

5650.	The noun of self becomes a verb. This flashpoint of creation in the present moment is where work and play merge. -Stephen Nachmanovitch

5651.	Mistakes show us what we need to learn. -Peter McWilliams

5652.	If pro is the opposite of con, is progress the opposite of congress? -Richard Lederer

5653.	We live in the present, we dream of the future, but we learn eternal truths from the past. -May-lin Soong Chiang

5654.	Of all the liars in the world, sometimes the worst are your own fears. -Rudyard Kipling

5655.	We relish news of our heroes forgetting that we are extraordinary to somebody too. -Helen Hayes

5656.   God is a comic playing to an audience that's afraid to laugh. -Francois Marie Arouet Voltaire

5657.   If you just set people in motion, they'll heal themselves. -Roth Gabrielle

5658.   No evil propensity of the human heart is so powerful that it may not be subdued by discipline.-Seneca

5659.   The dullard's envy of brilliant men is always assuaged by the suspicion that they will come to a bad end. -Sir Max Beerbohm

5660.   The worst moment for the atheist is when he is really thankful and has nobody to thank. -Gabriel Rossetti Dante

5661.   When you get a thing the way you want it leave it alone. -Sir Winston Leonard Spenser Churchill

5662.   If you chase two rabbits, both will escape. -Anonymous

5663.   Christmas is a season for kindling the fire for hospitality in the hall, the genial flame of charity in the heart. -Washington Irving

5664.   Mediocrity can talk, but it is for genius to observe. -Benjamin Disraeli

5665.   Would those of you in the cheaper seats clap your hands? And the rest of you, if you'll just rattle your jewelry. -John Lennon

5666.   Teachers open the door but you must enter by yourself. -Chinese Proverb

5667.   Do your bit to save humanity from lapsing back into barbarity by reading all the novels you can. -Richard Hughes

5668.   You must welcome change as the rule but not as your ruler. -Denis Waitley

5669.   Trees are the earth's endless effort to speak to the listening heaven. -Rabindranath Tagore

5670.   Middle age starts when you have been warned to slow down, not by a motorcycle cop, but by your doctor.

5671.   Happiness is not in having or being; it is in doing. -Lillian Eichler Watson

5672.   The trees reflected in the river - they are unconscious of a spiritual world so near to them. So are we. -Nathaniel Hawthorne

5673.   Our job is not to straighten each other out but to help each other up. -Neva Cole

5674.   Art attracts us only by what it reveals of our most secret self. -Jean-Luc Godard

5675.   I believe that one of life's greatest risks is never daring to risk. -Oprah Winfrey

5676.   I am always doing that which I cannot do in order that I may learn how to do it. -Pablo Picasso

5677.   Yesterday ended last night. Every day is a new beginning. Learn the skill of forgetting. And move on. -Norman Vincent Peale

5678.   Worry does not empty tomorrow of its sorrow; it empties today of its strength. -Corrie Ten Boom

5679.   Spiritual force is stronger than material force thoughts rule the world. -Ralph Waldo Emerson

5680.   The great and glorious masterpiece of man is how to live with purpose. -Michel Eyquem

5681.   Anything that can be changed will be changed until there is no time left to change anything.

5682.   Education and intelligence aren't the same thing!

5683.   Great is the art of beginning but greater is the art of ending. -Henry Wadsworth Longfellow

5684.   I'd rather be lucky than good. -Lefty Gomez

5685.   I can't forgive my friends for dying I don't find these vanishing acts of theirs at all amusing. -George Bernard Shaw

5686.   Happiness makes up in height for what it lacks in length. -Robert Frost

5687.   What really interests me is whether God had any choice in the creation of the world. -Albert Einstein

5688.   Sarcasm is just one more service I offer.

5689.   Find out what your hero or heroine wants and when he or she wakes up in the morning; just follow him or her all day. -Ray Douglas Bradbury

5690. Peak performance begins with your taking complete responsibility for your life and everything that happens to you. -Brian Tracy

5691. Character may be manifested in the great moments, but it is made in the small ones. -Les Brown

5692. You feel a little older in the morning. By noon I feel about 55. -Robert Joseph Bob Dole

5693. Challenges are what make life interesting; overcoming them is what makes life meaningful. -Joshua J. Marine

5694. There must be more to life than having everything. -Maurice Sendak

5695. Unable are the Loved to die for Love is Immortality. -Jean Pierre Claris De Florian

5696. Only a brave person is willing to honestly admit and fearlessly to face what a sincere and logical mind discovers. -Rodan of Alexandria

5697. There are few nudities so objectionable as the naked truth. -Agnes Repplier

5698. Lets have faith that right makes might and in that faith let us to the end dare to do our duty as we understand it. -Abraham Lincoln

5699. The generation of random numbers is too important to be left to chance. -Robert R. Coveyou

5700. The spirit of a person's life is ever shedding some power, just as a flower is steadily bestowing fragrance upon the air. -T. Starr King

5701. Life is a succession of moments, to live each one is to succeed. -Coretta Scott King

5702. The course of true anything does not run smooth. -Samuel Butler

5703. Four hostile newspapers are more to be feared than a thousand bayonets. -Napoleon

5704. It is not often that someone comes along who is a true friend and a good writer. -E. B. White

5705. Doubt is not a pleasant state of mind but certainty is absurd. -Francois Marie Arouet Voltaire

5706. You don't just stumble into the future. You create your own future. -Roger Smith

5707. You're not the only one who's made mistakes, but they're the only things that you can truly call your own. -Billy Joel

5708. When we lose one we love, our bitterest tears are called forth by the memory of hours when we loved not enough. -Maurice Maeterlinck

5709. Reality is nothing but a collective hunch. -Lily Tomlin

5710. Money talks...but all mine ever says is goodbye. -Anon.

5711. Advice is seldom welcome; and those who want it the most always like it the least. - Lord Chesterfield

5712. I had a monumental idea this morning but I didn't like it. - Samuel Goldwyn

5713. Astronomy compels the soul to look upwards and leads us from this world to another. -Plato

5714. Always treat your employees exactly as you want them to treat your best customers. -Stephen R. Covey

5715. Character is like a tree and reputation like a shadow. The shadow is what we think of it; the tree is the real thing. -Abraham Lincoln

5716. Only that which makes you feel bad after doing is immoral. - Ernest Hemingway

5717. If there is something to pardon in everything there is also something to condemn. -Friedrich Nietzsche

5718. Reagan won because he ran against Jimmy Carter. Had he run unopposed he would have lost. -Mort Sahl

5719. Charity sees the need not the cause. -German proverb

5720. The tendency of democracies is in all things to mediocrity. - James Fenimore Cooper

5721. One important key to success is self-confidence. An important key to self-confidence is preparation. -Arthur Ashe

5722. Nowadays men lead lives of noisy desperation. -James Thurber

5723. There is great force hidden in a gentle command. -George Herbert

5724. Genius makes its observations in short-hand; talent writes them out at length. -Christian Nestell Bovee

5725. If I would be happy, I would be a bad ballplayer. With me, when I get mad, it puts energy in my body. -Roberto Clemente

5726. Do not despise the bottom rungs in the ascent to greatness. -Publilius Syrus

5727. We all grew up in spite of our parents. I trust our children will do likewise. -Sandy Farquhar

5728. Doubt is a pain too lonely to know that faith is his twin brother. -Kahlil Gibran

5729. Anger makes dull men witty but it keeps them poor. -Queen Elizabeth I

5730. Trust in the Lord with all you do and you will be prosperous. -Christian Proverb

5731. The more perfect the artist, the more completely separate in him will be the man who suffers and the mind which creates. -T. S. Eliot

5732. Not everything that can be counted counts and not everything that counts can be counted. -Albert Einstein

5733. How would you like to spend eternity: Smoking or Non-Smoking?

5734. That government is best which governs the least because its people discipline themselves. -Thomas Jefferson

5735. Freedom is actually a bigger game than power. Power is about what you can control. Freedom is about what you can unleash. -Harriet Rubin

5736. Now join your hands and with your hands your hearts. -William Shakespeare

5737. The secret of my success is that at an early age I discovered I was not God. -Sri da Avabhas

5738. There are no secrets better kept than the secrets that everybody guesses. -George Bernard Shaw

5739. Some people go to priests, others to poetry, I to my friends. -Oscar Wilde

5740. The doors of wisdom are never shut. -Benjamin Franklin

5741. My words fly up my thoughts remain below Words without thoughts never to heaven go. -William Shakespeare

5742. The flower that follows the sun does so even on cloudy days. -Robert Leighton

5743. Though it sounds absurd, it is true to say I felt younger at sixty than I felt at twenty. -Ellen Glasgow

5744. Wherever I have gone in this country, I have found Americans. -Alf Landon

5745. Dream no small dreams, for they have no power to move the hearts of men. -Johann von Goethe

5746. All things come alike to all there is one event to the righteous and to the wicked. -Ecclesiastes Bible

5747. The pursuit of truth will set you free; even if you never catch up with it. - Clarence Darrow

5748. You can determine how confident people are by listening to what they don't say about themselves. -Brian G. Jett

5749. The price of greatness is responsibility. -Winston Churchill

5750. Be on the alert to recognize your prime at whatever time of your life it may occur. -Muriel Spark

5751. Light tomorrow with today. -Elizabeth Barrett Browning

5752. Ideologies separate us. Dreams and anguish bring us together. -Eugene Ionesco

5753. An idea, to be suggestive, must come to the individual with the force of revelation. -William James

5754. Eat and drink with your relatives; do business with strangers. -Greek Proverb

5755. Hope like faith is nothing if it is not courageous it is nothing if it is not ridiculous. -Thornton

5756. As far as we can discern the sole purpose of human existence is to kindle a light in the darkness of mere being. -Carl Jung

5757. An honest politician is one who when he is bought will stay bought. -Simon Cameron

5758. It's a scientific fact that if you stay in California, you lose one point of your IQ every year. -Truman Capote

5759. In the fight between you and the world, back the world. -Frank Zappa

5760. Our test of truth is a reference to either a present or imagined future majority in favor of our view. -Oliver Wendell Holmes

5761. Change is not merely necessary to life - it is life. -Alvin Toffler

5762. This time, like all times, is a very good one if we but know what to do with it. -Ralph Waldo Emerson

5763. Ye shall know the truth and the truth shall make you free. -The Bible

5764. Biography lends to death a new terror. -Oscar Wilde

5765. That's one small step for man, one giant leap for mankind. -Neil Armstrong

5766. Education is what survives when what has been learned has been forgotten. -B. F. Skinner

5767. We shrink from change; yet is there anything that can come into being without it? -Marcus Aurelius

5768. The fellow who is fired with enthusiasm for his work is seldom fired by his boss.

5769. It is men who wait to be selected, and not those who seek from whom we may expect the most efficient service. -Ulysses S. Grant

5770. To die will be an awfully big adventure. -James Barrie

5771. The difference between ordinary and extraordinary is that little extra.

5772. The government is us; we are the government, you and I. -Theodore Roosevelt

5773. The first duty of a revolutionary is to get away with it. -Abbie Hoffman

5774. The only substitute for good manners is fast reflexes.

5775. As a well-spent day brings happy sleep, so life well used brings happy death. -Leonardo da Vinci

5776. We can pay our debt to the past by putting the future in debt to ourselves. -John Buchan

5777. Good thoughts bear good fruit; bad thoughts bear bad fruit. - James Allen

5778. Acceptance of what has happened is the first step to overcoming the consequences of any misfortune. -William James

5779. Which dreams indeed are ambition, for the very substance of the ambitious is merely the shadow of a dream. -William Shakespeare, Hamlet

5780. Marriage is punishment for shoplifting in some countries. - Wayne's World, Wayne Garth

5781. Don't dig your grave with your own knife and fork. -English Proverb

5782. Affirmations are like prescriptions for certain aspects of yourself you want to change. -Jerry Frankhauser

5783. Never judge someone till you've walked a mile in their shoes, cause then you're a mile away and you've got their shoes. -Unknown

5784. Joy is a net of love by which you can catch souls. A joyful heart is the inevitable result of a heart burning with love. -Mother Teresa

5785. I never forget a face, but in your case I'll be glad to make an exception. -Groucho Marx

5786. It is of no consequence of what parents a man is born, as long as he be a man of merit. -Horace

5787. A man, as a general rule, owes very little to what he is born with - a man is what he makes of himself. -Alexander Graham Bell

5788. The day I see a leaf is a marvel of a day. -Kenneth Patton

5789. An intellectual snob is someone who can listen to the William Tell Overture and not think of The Lone Ranger. -Dan Rather

5790. There are no passengers on spaceship Earth- we are all the crew.

5791. The truth. It is a beautiful and terrible thing and should therefore be treated with great caution. -J. K. Rowling

5792. The place where optimism most flourishes is the lunatic asylum. -Havelock Ellis

5793. We are what we repeatedly do. Excellence then, is not an act, but a habit. -Aristotle

5794.   Books are not made to be believed, but to be subjected to inquiry. -Umberto Eco

5795.   Friendship is a strong and habitual inclination in two persons to promote the good and happiness of one another. -Eustace Budgell

5796.   Anatomy is destiny. -Sigmund Freud

5797.   When you want something it's not that easy. You have to know what you want and keep going for it. -Taylor Hanson

5798.   Live as if you were to die tomorrow. Learn as if you were to live forever. - Mahatma Gandhi

5799.   When you are in any contest you should work as if there were - to the very last minute - a chance to lose it. -Dwight D. Eisenhower

5800.   Don't be afraid your life will end; be afraid that it will never begin. -Grace Hansen

5801.   Thinking is like loving and dying. Each of us must do it for himself. -Josiah Royce

5802.   If a man can see both sides of a problem, you know that none of his money is tied up in it. -Verda Ross

5803.   Beliefs are what divide people. Doubt unites them. -Peter Ustinov

5804.   Your bottom line starts with your front line. -John Villere

5805.   You begin saving the world by saving one person at a time all else is grandiose romanticism or politics. -Charles Bukowski

5806.   I think the presidency is an institution over which you have temporary custody. -Ronald Reagan

5807.   Knowing your destination is half the journey. -Unknown Author

5808.   He conquers who endures. -Persius

5809.   Emotions are your worst enemy in the stock market. -Don Hays

5810.   In war there is no substitute for victory. -Douglas MacArthur

5811.   Here we are the perfect pair... Beauty and the Beast. Mind you, if anybody calls you beast, I'll rip their lungs out. -Batman The Joker

5812.   Imagination gallops; judgment merely walks. -Proverb

5813. I just never let anything bother me man. I know myself really well. Nobody's opinion of me can shake my opinion of myself. - Ruben Studdard

5814. The lusts and greeds of the body scandalize the Soul but it has to come to heel. -Logan Pearsall Smith

5815. Not where I breathe but where I love I live Not where I love but where I am, I die. -Robert Southey

5816. You shouldn't say it is not good. You should say you do not like it and then you know you're perfectly safe. -James Abbott McNeill Whistler

5817. Hating people is like burning down your house to get rid of a rat. -Harry Emerson Fosdick

5818. Poetry the best words in the best order. -Samuel Taylor Coleridge

5819. Life is too complicated not to be orderly. -Martha Stewart

5820. A good man can be stupid and still be good. But a bad man must have brains. -Maxim Gorky

5821. Thy words, I grant, are bigger, for I wear not my dagger in my mouth. -William Shakespeare

5822. Though no one can go back and make a brand new start, anyone can start from now and make a brand new ending. -Carl Bard

5823. Anger is as a stone cast into a wasp's nest. - Unknown

5824. Rumor is not always wrong. - Publius Cornelius Tacitus, from Life of Agricola

5825. I concede. -Richard Milhous Nixon

5826. It is not failure itself that holds you back; it is the fear of failure that paralyzes you. -Brian Tracy

5827. He who stops being better stops being good. -Oliver Cromwell

5828. It takes guts to get out of the ruts. -Robert Schuller

5829. Something we were withholding made us weak until we found out it was ourselves. -Robert Frost

5830. Seeking to forget makes exile all the longer; the secret of redemption lies in remembrance. -Richard von Weizscker

5831.   Many a man thinks he is buying pleasure, when he is really selling himself to it. -Benjamin Franklin

5832.   We must be the change we wish to see in the world. -Gandhi

5833.   Take care of the sense and the sounds will take care of themselves. -Lewis Carroll

5834.   Deep Thoughts: If God dwells inside us, like some people say, I sure hope He likes enchiladas, because that's what he's getting. -Jack Handey

5835.   A very small degree of hope is sufficient to cause the birth of love. -Stendhal

5836.   No one is entitled to the truth. -E. Howard Hunt

5837.   ...Happiness gives us the energy which is the basis of health. -Henri Frederic Amiel

5838.   Creativity is allowing yourself to make mistakes. Art is knowing which ones to keep. -Scott Adams

5839.   Defining and analyzing humor is a pastime of humorless people. -Robert Benchley

5840.   It's easier to go down a hill than up it but the view is much better at the top. -Arnold Bennett

5841.   Some folks, as they grow older, grow wise, but most folks simply grow stubborner. -Josh Billings

5842.   To belittle is to be little.

5843.   Put yourself on view. This brings your talents to light. -Baltasar Gracian

5844.   If you've never been hated by your child, you've never been a parent. -Bette Davis

5845.   It is not the man who has too little, but the man who craves more that is poor. -Seneca

5846.   Dieu me pardonnera cest son metier. (God will pardon me, that's his job.) -Heinrich Heine

5847.   Life is the flower for which love is the honey. - Zora Neale Hurston

5848.   People seem to enjoy things more when they know a lot of other people have been left out of the pleasure. -Russell Baker

5849. Trust yourself. Think for yourself. Act for yourself. Speak for yourself. Be yourself. Imitation is suicide. -Marva Collins

5850. Luxury is more deadly than any foe. -Juvenal

5851. A man is a worker. If he is not that he is nothing. -Joseph Conrad

5852. When a man tells you that he got rich through hard work, ask him "Whose?" -Don Marquis

5853. Without God, I cannot. Without me, God will not.

5854. It is better to be envied than pitied. -Herodotus

5855. Thinking is heavily endorsed. -Mal Pancoast

5856. Character is higher than intellect. A great soul will be strong to live as well to think. -Ralph Waldo Emerson

5857. No man is wise enough by himself. -Titus Maccius Plautus

5858. A lie told often enough becomes truth. - Lenin (Vladimir Ulyanov)

5859. Baseball is 50% percent mental. The other half is physical. - Lawrence Peter Berra

5860. That fellow seems to possess but one idea and that is the wrong one. -Samuel Johnson

5861. Take care your worship those things over there are not giants but windmills. -Miguel Cervantes

5862. The nice thing about teamwork is that you always have others on your side. -Margaret Carty

5863. Wisdom is knowing when to speak your mind and when to mind your speech. - Evangel

5864. Such power there is in clear-eyed self-restraint. -James Russell Lowell

5865. I'm going to memorize your name and throw my head away. - Oscar Levant

5866. The scientific name for an animal that doesn't either run from or fight its enemies is lunch. -Michael Friedman

5867. Whatever you can do or dream you can begin it. Boldness has genius power and magic in it. -Johann von Goethe

5868. Big egos have little ears. -Robert Schuller

5869. Falsehood is easy; truth so difficult. -George Eliot

5870. The position of the artist is humble. He is essentially a channel. -Piet Mondrian

5871. Never become so much of an expert that you stop gaining expertise. View life as a continuous learning experience. -Denis Waitley

5872. Debate is the death of conversation. - Emil Ludwig

5873. If the only tool you have is a hammer, you tend to see every problem as a nail. -Abraham Maslow

5874. Seize today and put as little trust as you can in tomorrow. - Horace

5875. It isn't always necessary to achieve great things. Sometimes just surviving is a great achievement. -Unknown

5876. Remember what is unbecoming to do is also unbecoming to speak of. -Socrates

5877. Every choice you make has an end result. -Zig Ziglar

5878. Mistake not. Those pleasures are not pleasures that trouble the quiet and tranquility of thy life. -Jeremy Taylor

5879. A little experience often upsets a lot of theory. - Cadman

5880. There comes a time in the affairs of man when he must take the bull by the tail and face the situation. -W. C. Fields

5881. The only good luck many great men ever had was being born with the ability to overcome bad luck. -Channing Pollock

5882. The fear of death is more to be dreaded than death itself. - Publilius Syrus

5883. The enemy of my enemy is my friend. -Arab Proverb

5884. Be beautiful if you can, wise if you want to...But be respected, that is essential. -Anna Gould

5885. Wealth is the product of man's capacity to think. -Ayn Rand

5886. In three words I can sum up everything I've learned about life; it goes on.-Anonymous

About the author

Devin Metzger is a new media and social media junkie. He spends most of his time reading and writing about new media and social media. He also enjoys a good cup of coffee.

Other books by Devin Metzger

Highly Quotable: 4000+ Quotes to Motivate and Inspire You

www.ingramcontent.com/pod-product-compliance
Lightning Source LLC
Chambersburg PA
CBHW070104290526
45789CB00005B/1916